Shakunetsu

Chronicles of the creation of shintaido, a Japanese martial art

Pierre QUETTIER
Coordination, writing and analysis

Mieko HIRANO
Consolidation of biographies and translation

Peter FURTADO
Preface of English edition

Pascal LARDELLIER
Foreword

Jean-François DÉGREMONT
Afterword

Cover calligraphy:
«Incandescence»
By Masashi Minagawa

Design:
Pierre Quettier -Sarah Baker

A publication of Shintaido of America
ISBN: 979-8-218-21148-6
July 2023
info@shintaido.org

Original publication by Shakunetsu Editors
Legal deposit at the Bibliothèque Nationale de France
N° DLE-20220112-2173 on Jan 12th, 2022
ISBN: 9782958072902
© Richesses du Japon - 2021

References and follow-up:
www.shakunetsu.net

Contents

Preface to the English edition

Peter Furtado
Journalist and historian
British Shintaido Senior Instructor

"Shakunetsu" literally means scorching heat, the heat of a furnace that turns steel white-hot before it is beaten and folded to create a precious, potent, beautiful *katana*, the heat that Hiroyuki Aoki alluded to in his visionary manifesto for a new martial art beyond karate, a manifesto he entitled, 'Life, Burn.' Here it refers to the intense experience of the group of a few dozen Japanese men and women just out of teenage years, that came together in the mid-1960s, under the inspiration and leadership of Hiroyuki Aoki, in an extraordinary attempt to explore and transcend the known limits of karate, *budo*, spirituality and the arts – and ultimately, to reach previously unknown realms of human potential. This group was the Rakutenkai or "group of optimists," and the fruit of their efforts was shintaido, the New Body Way.

This unique book is complex in its ambition and structure. At its heart is the raw material of history – it brings together the oral testimony of 19 Rakutenkai members who describe in their own words how they came to join, what they were seeking and what they found. But this is supported, and given meaning, by the more academic commentary of sociologist and shintaido instructor Pierre Quettier, who carefully places their testimony in the contexts of the Japanese martial and other arts, and of the youth culture – in Japan and around the world - of the time, which had many similarly grand ambitions to change the world, though taking a different path up the mountain. He also offers a personal, honest, and sometimes painful account of the process of meeting the contributors and assembling the texts. As a social scientist who takes the name of that discipline seriously, he sticks closely to the evidence he has collected, declining to conjecture or judge, and refusing to repeat myths unless they can be grounded in fact. In the introduction, he explains the physically and emotionally arduous – and extended – process of preparing this work.

Creating an oral history of this kind is fraught with difficulties. How the testimonies are collected: whether questions are offered to the participant in advance, or flow from a conversation with an interlocutor; how the interlocutor may unintentionally affect what is said and what is heard; how silences or evasions are recorded, and how they are interpreted; how misunderstandings are minimized (especially important in a cross-cultural exercise like this one); and how the participant feels when they read back their comments at a later date – all these are genuine methodological issues with any project of this kind. They are exacerbated when the subject is a truly emotive one concerning a genuinely extraordinary period in the participants' lives, a period that now lies half a century in the past.

The result here is in some ways rough-hewn, complex and inevitably somewhat uneven, describing a remarkable experiment in living and being, from both "inside" and out simultaneously. It will be of intense interest to all those who practice shintaido, the martial art that derived from the experiments of the Rakutenkai group; but it will also provide important insights to those who wish to understand more about the counterculture of the 1960s (especially but by no means only in Japan), and its legacy for our day.

The voices here are unmediated, direct, and the passions of more than six decades often shine through. Many members eagerly talk about a heightened and exceptional period in their young lives, one that transformed them forever; others describe leaving the Rakutenkai apparently without looking back, then moving on with their lives and careers. This is, perhaps, what you would expect from the recollections of any such group of young people then in their 20s, and now seen from the perspective of later middle age.

Where he can, Quettier offers careful contextualizations and explications to help the reader understand the choices these men and women made. However, no work of history can prove the whole truth about the past, and this book is no different: it cannot explain everything about the group and how it worked. Some Rakutenkai members had already died before their contributions could be recorded. Some chose not to be involved in the project at all, while others initially took part but later changed their minds; we cannot say why. Some of those who did contribute were voluble and unrestrained, but others were more formal and guarded in their comments. As a scholar Quettier is unwilling to speculate beyond the evidence available to him, and this may lead to inevitable frustrations for the reader. One may concern Hiroyuki Aoki himself, charismatic founder and leader of the Rakutenkai group. His presence looms over almost every page of the book, but his voice is not directly heard. As Quettier explains, Aoki supported the project throughout the collection of the members' interviews; but had little interest in exploring his own past in this manner. As a result, information about him and his actions is second-hand, derived from his own writings and other published material. The interviewees naturally have much to say about him, in comments that are often vivid, but inevitably personal and subjective (and sometimes still raw). They are no substitute for a rounded portrait of an exceptional man and a visionary artist at a key moment of his creative life.

The events described here took place many decades ago, and the interviewees come from a culture that puts a high value on politeness, one where silence can be as expressive as words. Today we live in a different age and in a different culture, and should take care to avoid drawing mistaken conclusions from what we read here. In this, Quettier's professional experience of the "life-story" method, combined with his own experience of studying shintaido in Japan in the 1970s and since, plus the practical support and guidance he received from H.F. Ito, provide an excellent grounding and guide in what we can and cannot understand about the Rakutenkai and its members.

For those who practice shintaido in the 21st century, without the presence of Aoki and, at some point in the future, without the last direct active links with the Rakutenkai, H.F. Ito, M. Minagawa and M. Okada, this book forces us to consider our relationship with the past, with the moment of genesis of the mysterious, beautiful "*do*" (way) that we follow. The Rakutenkai practice, with its emphasis (vividly recalled by many interviewees) on going beyond, on softening through exhaustion, on endless jumping through the cold night, is now the stuff of legend, not of contemporary daily practice. The ambition, the dedication, the seriousness, the idealism – these are equally challenging. They should surely also be inspiring, and can be so again now that Pierre Quettier has provided the opportunity to see the depth, complexity and importance of this precious, evanescent moment and the fruits that came from it.

This volume ends with the dissolution of the Rakutenkai and merely hints at the creation of shintaido as a coherent discipline, with a rich curriculum of its own, that could be offered to the general public. The history of that discipline, as it developed in Japan and then spread around the world, the development of new forms of practice, its modification in the face of very different cultures in Europe and America, the maturation (and aging) of its leaders and many practitioners, and the personality and institutional conflicts that led some (including eventually Aoki himself) to move away – all this could be the subject of yet another project, though that is likely to be just as laborious to assemble as the present book has been.

Anthropologist Margaret Mead is famously supposed to have said, sometime in the 1960s, "Never doubt that a small group of thoughtful, committed citizens can change the world; indeed, it's the only thing that ever has." I cannot say whether she had ever met or even heard of the Rakutenkai, but its couple of dozen members undoubtedly formed just such a small group of thoughtful and exceptionally committed citizens of Japan and the entire world. Their legacy hasn't quite changed the world yet, but never doubt that one day, and with the help of this book, it will.

Foreword
From life stories to the story of a life

Pascal Lardellier,
Professor (Burgundy University, Dijon) and author

During his thesis defense in 1961, Michel Foucault had a famous formula: "I did not want to write the history of this language, rather the archeology of this silence."

Pierre Quettier takes a path parallel to that of Foucauldian dazzling, in the precious work that he offers to his readers. It is not really a question of silences to be exhumed, since things are partly said here; but neither is it a matter of instituted discourses. Because there are myths, "legends," free interpretations of lived realities, but above all shared, incorporated by the Rakutenkai community ethnographed in these pages.

On this crest between discourse and representations, between practice and reflexivity, between reality and myth, between history and ethnography, Pierre Quettier invites us to journey with him. The perspectives are wide, there is both height and depth in what he offers us to consider as an expert.

Back to Foucault ... Pierre Quettier is a valuable "social archaeologist" as well as a radiologist of cultures. He is both a linchpin and a mastermind, knowing to perfection the art of tracing the paths of memory and the paths of life, of following the genealogies, taking us from a community to the other, "from esotericism to exotericism," as in the golden age of the schools of Greek philosophy. For he has the compass, and he has the keys. Above all, Pierre Quettier takes on the guise of a formidable insider, in turn actor and narrator, scriptwriter and stage director of an art, which originally martial, is much more than that. He knows it from the inside, having been initiated, in body and soul, in flesh and senses, to the techniques he collects and describes. And in his words, we feel the empirical, sensitive, phenomenological anchoring, and the spiritual depth of ways that are first interior.

In this labyrinth of schools, techniques and traditions, Pierre Quettier orients, brings meaning and order. All of this is done through patient scholarly, genealogical, and recursive work. This work is above all a theoretical-practical sum with autobiographical aims in its subject and epistemological in its ambition. And it is nothing less than contributing to the history of countercultures and the sociology of Japanese martial arts.

This "life-work" offered by Pierre Quettier is based on an anthropological and of course ethnomethodological foundation, as is recalled from the book's epigraph: "in this extraordinary moment of the 1960s, a group of young idealists embarked on a quest for authenticity typical of the time and a very martial requirement; a modern epic that aimed to revolutionize the venerable *budo*. In doing so, they forged myths that became original for their successors. From an anthropological point of view, this study offers new access to these myths." [Introduction, page 18]

Like the rites (which they truly are, I will come back to this), the martial arts "recycle" practices, values, symbols in order to show the full importance of the common culture, of belonging. "Culture is everything you need to know to belong," said Ward Goodnough. Entering the apprenticeship and then the technical mastery of a martial art is "entering the form," to make it one's own, and by doing so, to reproduce gestures but above all to tell stories, to perform a culture and an identity.

More broadly, Pierre Quettier proposes, behind the patient modesty of this ethnography of the Rakutenkai community, an ambitious economy of symbolic forms. Because social life is made up of forms, which, architectural and mental, discursive, and social, create being, appearing, belonging, receiving, and transmitting. These symbolic forms, before making us "be in the world," make us "be with," because they are crucibles and bridges. Greetings and exchanges of gifts, ceremonies of all kinds and invitations, meals shared and tributes paid, everything is a "*sym-bol*"[1], therefore a link to others, made aware by the incorporated and transmitted form. *Kata* means "form" in Japanese; and to perform a *kata* is to "enter into form," then find your way there, to meet there, to find the soul of tradition, while reinventing the *kata*, living source, vital energy. We know the gradation of *shu, ha, ri*. However, the Rakutenkai, which is hyper-ritualized, is a chemically pure symbolic form, archetype and even quintessence for the ethnologist, the historian, the ethnomethodologist.

Hyper-ritualized, the Rakutenkai makes its posture coincide with the radical hypothesis of Maurice Hocart in *Social Origins* (1954). Because ultimately, the watermark of Pierre Quettier's words reminds us that everything is ritual, because everything is symbolic. The gesture is identity, tradition, belonging. Similarly, the rite is an instance containing violence, putting it on stage and at a distance at the same time, via a symbolic and theatrical mediation giving shape to the agonistic nature of social relations, to produce (martial) art, consensus, and belonging.

Above all, the *kata* is a mystique: it does not exhaust itself in its physical performance, but embraces the features of a life project, which links the intimate to the infinite. In this sense, it is also a

---

[1] From the Greek *syn* (with/together) and *ballein* (to throw/to put), for "putting together". [Ed. note].

cosmogony: performing a *kata* connects with other dimensions, powerful and harmonious, whose energy comes from elsewhere, and from above. The *mana* and the *numen*[1], primordial anthropological powers, come together in a perfect *kata*, and commune in the body-crucible of the master in action. The *ki* surfaces, the intensity is perceptible, palpable. It is an authentic dramaturgy that is brought into the light of day and given life.

It therefore goes without saying that karate is indeed an art and a way, it is a powerful vector of individual and collective transformation.

The desire to create, out of a traditional base, a martial counterculture by giving birth to new myths that will be taken for original by the practitioners of the future, is another tale, carefully related in these pages by Pierre Quettier, between tradition and innovation.

"Practices of the self," the school of life, the path towards one's deep and authentic self, the ultimate and intimate encounter with an "inner infinity" reached by effort, stubborn repetition and by asceticism, the Rakutenkai is powerfully "psychagogic," which means, in Greek, nothing less than "training the soul." The soul of the individual, the soul of the community. This is what Pierre Quettier proves to us and reminds us of, at the end of these pages. In this sense, he is a searcher in the noblest sense of the term: a scout, a bearer of light. He inherited the torch, carried it with conscience and responsibility. Today, he fulfills its transmission. But the flame remains in him. May thanks be given to him for the gift of memory and history that he gives us.

---

[1] *Numen* is the Latin equivalent of the Polynesian notion of *mana*, characterizing the "acting power" of a God [Ed. note].

Introduction

This book reports on the formation, activity, and dissolution of the Rakutenkai, a group of Japanese artists brought together during the 1960s with the idea of creating a radically modern martial art.

As such, the book is initially memorial: to reconstruct the story of an adventure in collective living. The book is also-an enterprise of "recognition" of the experience of those whose life stories it collects, in the sense given by Jean-Louis Le Grand when he writes that "one of the essential functions of a history of collective life... is the need for recognition"[1]. It offers "self-recognition, obviously so for the members of the Rakutenkai themselves, but also for modern practitioners of shintaido, the discipline that came from their action-research.

In this extraordinary moment of the 1960s, this group of young idealists embarked on a quest for authenticity which was typical of the time and a very martial requirement; a modern epic that aimed to revolutionize the ancient world of *budo*. In doing so, they forged myths that have become foundational for their successors.

---

[1] Le Grand J.L. (2000), « Repères théoriques et éthiques en histoires de vie collectives » in. *Histoires de vie collective et éducation populaire*, dir. Marie-Jo Coulon and Jean-Louis Le Grand, L'Harmattan ed., p. 150.

From an anthropological point of view, this study offers a new access to these myths, in their original cultural context.

Finally, this book aims to contribute both to the history of counterculture and to the sociology of Japanese martial arts. This sociological intention guarantees the scientific content of the project as a whole; it seeks a truth that is, as far as possible, neither subjective not conjecture, and the information within it derives from known sources. Additionally, it endeavored not to hurt anyone's feelings, and the choices made have been done with doubt and care, to take responsibility for the impact it may produce on readers.

Conduct of research

If a researcher is an existing member of a community that he or she then makes a field of study, this has been called "complete participating observation by opportunity" (in the words of French psychosociologist Georges Lapassade[1]). As an ethnomethodologist and researcher in Information and Communication Sciences myself[2], I had also been a long-time member of the shintaido collective when this survey began in 2004. This dual aspect guarantees both the relevance and the validity of the data produced here:

- Relevance, through the intimate knowledge I had of the field and through my personal relationships with most of the

---

[1] According to Adler & Adler (1987), themselves using the categories of Gold and Junker: Lapassade G. (2002), "Observation participante", in *Vocabulaire de psychosociologie*, dir. Jacqueline Barus-Michel, ERES, p. 379.

[2] Assistant Professor for the University of Paris 8 in 2000 and member of the Laboratory of Applied Ethnomethodology (attached to the Paragraphe laboratory EA 349).

interviewees, thereby providing "materials for developing a complex holistic perspective of society and culture."[1]

- Validity, by controlling the interpretative biases that I carried out as they occurred at various stages of the study. See below a biography of the research.

Method

To conduct a historical study of a collective that had dispersed long ago, it was important, both for practical and epistemological reasons, to collect life stories in the subjects' own words. In practice, what could be more natural, or perceived as such, than asking, "Please tell me your story?" On the epistemological level, this approach avoided several interpretative biases that could potentially be induced on both sides by more specific questioning.

THE PARTS OF THE BOOK

The heart of the book is made up of the autobiographical accounts of the Rakutenkai members, which are presented in the order of their joining the group.

My initial intention was not to go beyond these testimonies, and to save any analysis for later publications. However, the reluctance of some of my informants to see themselves put forward in this way, and the opinion of Makoto Suemoto, then a professor at the University of Kobe and a recognized Japanese specialist in the method of life stories, convinced me to introduce this presentation with a commented chronology of events, and to follow it with a historical analysis. In both cases, I understand that I have only touched the surface. Readers already familiar with the main lines of the Rakutenkai period will probably prefer to start by reading the testimonies of the members.

---

[1] Breton H. & Gonzalez-Monteagudo J. (2019), « Engagement versus objectivité : 'Histoires de vie en formation' et recherche biographique en sociologie », in *Histoire de vie et recherche biographique : perspectives sociohistoriques*, dir. A. Slowik, H. Breton & G. Pineau, L'Harmattan, p. 88.

A glossary of Japanese terms is placed at the end of the book.

MY BACKGROUND IN THE FIELD

I myself practiced shintaido in Japan for five years between 1976 and 1981. When I started, the practices were led by Masatake Egami [p. 213]. Hiroyuki Aoki made occasional appearances at them. I later learned that at that time he was only a shadow of what he had been a short time before. I couldn't help finding him quite odd[1]. I really liked my instructor, Masatake Egami, and his alter-ego, Masashi Minagawa [p. 227], but I was left bewildered by the sudden note-taking frenzies that everyone, including them, went into as soon as Master Aoki opened his mouth to speak. They all told me that he was the founder of shintaido, that it was appropriate to call him Aoki-sensei and that he was an extraordinary character. I wanted to believe them, even if I couldn't help feeling a certain unease.

With the assistance of the bodily practices, I entered the heart of the study and I was soon engaged with the questioning and new perspectives that opened up for me: about myself, the nature of practices and martial arts, my relationship to effort, commitment, concentration, memorizing forms, and the powerful changes that all this had on my daily life. I practiced every day with my two instructors and I met the members of the legendary Rakutenkai during practices on Friday evening and Sunday afternoon. I also took advantage of their presence during major training courses or thematic workshops (karate, bojutsu, etc.) and thus engaged in my own learning relationship with them.

After a few years, I became aware of activities specific to this alumni group on the fringes of our practices. It might be pre-

---

[1] I shared this impression with him in 2003 during one of our interviews as part of the biographical project. While seeming to enjoy it, he recognized that he had experienced burnout, an unknown phenomenon at the time, which had suddenly drained him of all energy. He seemed to think that was the price he had to pay after years of hard work during the creative period.

courses reserved for them and at the end of which some members seemed somewhat pensive, even closed. It might also be the evocation by Master Aoki of the role of one or the other, or even allusions to certain "difficulties" or even "resistance," which seemed to annoy him without him ever specifying what they were or who they might have come from.

In 1978, Master Aoki suddenly left for what would today be called a sabbatical, which lasted a little over a year – a trip to Europe, the United States, and South America. The only notable difference for me was that the members of the Rakutenkai made themselves more available, supporting our two "young" instructors.

And then, as suddenly as he was gone, Master Aoki was back, now full of great energy, truly radiant, and of brand-new practice ideas. Shortly after this, the resignation of the Egami/Minagawa pairing was announced. I was surprised and, to be honest, sorry. They spoke of their need for rest, they were publicly thanked for the immense work accomplished, and they gave way to Yoshitaka Ito [p. 353] and Shigeko Toshima [p. 352], assisted for certain courses or internships by senior practitioners such as Kazuo Hokari [p. 136], Hideko Hokari [p. 277], Chieko Kato [p. 354], Tomonori Kato [p. 92], Mitsuru Okada [p. 357] or Takeo Handa [p. 205]. Gan Okada [p. 254], whom I had known when I started out, had disappeared.

Then began for me a period of deep engagement in the practice. I remain deeply indebted to the action led jointly by Yoshitaka Ito and Kazuo Hokari to bring the practice and its social context within reach of the group of foreigners of various nationalities who were then practicing at the *honbu-dojo* in Tokyo. Both had the professional experience of working with foreigners and they understood that it was difficult for us to cross the cultural gap to access the in-depth study of a Japanese *"do,"* partly through lack of a shared cultural reference but also because of the apparent "Western" modernity of the discipline. Shintaido certainly wanted to be modern, but it nevertheless remained an Asian path full of enigmas. We needed someone to explain to us, at least a little, certain differences between things, spaces, and people, but also to be taken by the hand to make us taste the softness and the power inherent with a strong commitment. This was done and, thus committed, we began to progress rapidly and were able to learn-how-to-learn. Thereafter things became much easier for me.

For his part, Master Aoki was often asked by Y. Ito to share the new practices brought back from his sabbatical leave. This leave had really got him back in shape and he was very creative again. Looking back at the charisma and creativity he radiated in those days, I can get a sense of the Rakutenkai practices at the time of the creation of the fundamental forms Tenshingoso and Eiko. I then came to consider him as *sensei*.

It was in 1980 that Y. Ito and S. Toshima were ousted. This happened on their return from the first international *gasshuku* which had taken place in San Francisco and, without knowing the details, I clearly understood that the operation was not without pain. Sometime later, Y. Ito, S. Toshima, M. Egami and T. Handa all disappeared definitively. We were told that the practice would henceforth be ensured by "a collective of members of the Rakutenkai." K. Hokari coordinated it. T. Kato, C. Kato, H. Hokari, M. Okada and M. Minagawa were present in the background but, now absorbed in their professional or family lives, they rarely intervened. I also met some of them personally. T. Kato, who became an acupuncturist, helped me to recover the proper use of a knee, which had been weakened by an inconsiderate practice of various jumps.

In 1981, now promoted to instructor and after making a detour to California to meet H.F. Ito there, I returned to France and began to teach shintaido. I lost contact with the daily life of the Japanese group and only had a relationship with those members of the Rakutenkai who were playing a role in the international organization (H.F. Ito, K. Hokari and M. Okada).

In a few years of intensive practice "in the footsteps of Ra-kutenkai," the French organization in which I actively partici-pated took an unexpected turn. These years had been intense and allowed me to immerse myself deeply in the technical culture of shintaido, karate, bojutsu and kenjutsu, under the expert direc-tion of Robert Bréant, technical director of the French federation, within the general framework established by the international shintaido organization. They also made me realize that the com-bination of the social model of Japanese martial arts, a certain Jac-obin spirit and the extremism of the Rakutenkai practice had combined to formidable effect: we had created a "shintaido cult." It was almost immediately dismantled and did not do too much damage but the adventure still left me perplexed and charged with an experience that I kept questioning in the light of the hu-manities and social sciences.

Then in 1988, K. Hokari suddenly announced his decision to leave his responsibilities within both the international organiza-tion and the Japanese organization. Others, like H. Hokari, T. Kato and C. Kato, also quietly slipped away. In the end, from the initial forty members, only H.F. Ito, M. Minagawa and M. Okada re-mained active. For my own part, I began a period of study and university research that was to last more than 20 years.

THE AUTOBIOGRAPHIC APPROACH

In 1988, I began training in adult educational design at INFAC, a popular-education training institute located in Nogent-sur-Marne. During the first seminar, the trainer, Luc Blondel, urged us to take all the time necessary for a detailed presentation of our reasoned life history. This was my first encounter with the use of life stories in training. A few years later, I concluded this training by writing a dissertation, which allowed me to step back a little from the various shintaido collectives, and offered me an official diploma from the Ministry of Labour.

With this diploma, I began, on the initiative of Jean-François Dégremont, studies of ethnomethodology in the Master-DESS Ethnomethodology and Computer Science of the Paris 8 University. There I again encountered the use of life stories, partly as a vector of training but also as an epistemological injunction – each research dissertation had to be introduced by a reasoned presentation of the student's own journey. We were also introduced to them as qualitative methods for collecting field data.

From that moment, each of my academic productions has been, in one way or another, impregnated with a certain "biographical turn."

PREMISES OF THE SOCIOHISTORICAL PROJECT

At the end of the 1980s, my friend Bernard Ducrest told me of his project to tell the story of the Rakutenkai in an epic way, like a modern saga, based on a series of interviews with original members. He thought of involving his friends Léon Mercadet and Patrice Van Aersel, journalists at the monthly revue Actuel, occasional writers and practitioners of shintaido, in the adventure. Before that, Bernard left to travel to India but died there, under the combined effect of untreated hepatitis and malaria, thus putting an end to any project.

In the very early 2000s, I became aware that H.F. Ito and M. Minagawa could in turn find themselves estranged from Aoki and perhaps pushed out of the organization. If they departed, we would lose two of the last three witnesses of the seminal shintaido group. It had become high time to act. Having studied ethnology in the meantime, now holding a teaching-research position at the Paris 8 University and well versed in biographical methods in the social sciences, I decided to take up Bernard Ducrest's historical project as my own and to initiate a process of collecting life stories of the Rakutenkai members. H.F. Ito was enthusiastic about it and in 2002 I obtained a small budget from the head of my service at the University; with these funds, H.F. Ito and I traveled all over Japan to interview the members one by one.

COLLECTION AND PROCESSING OF THE RAKUTENKAI LIFE STORIES

Some members, rather committed to the religious side of the Rakutenkai, immediately declined or avoided our request for an interview, but most accepted with good grace.

H.F. Ito acted as a research assistant and his help was invaluable to me: he compiled the list of Rakutenkai members, looked up their contact details, arranged meetings, accompanied me to appointments, made introductions (of the researcher, of the project and the work process), initiated conversations, ensured follow-ups, and translated when necessary. Obviously, his closeness to the informants and his personal interest in their history, even their common history, sometimes led him to forget his role somewhat and enter direct interaction ("By the way, do you remember...?") in a somewhat excessive way at times, but never truly counterproductive. Nothing in any case that cannot then be exploited or corrected by attentive listening to the recordings by my other research assistant, my wife Mieko Hirano[1]. I also met some of the members by myself, especially those I knew personally and who had a good command of English, such as M. Egami, T. Handa, K. Hokari, Y. Ito, M. Minagawa, S. Toshima and M. Suzuki.

On each of my trips, I spoke with H. Aoki in order to keep him informed of the project and to supplement the biographical elements which I already had for him in the work of K. Hokari (1990). Because he had always been "the" public face of the community, I could not engage with him in a narrative interaction like that which I had with the other members. His biographical elements had very early on been made public, repeated, and possibly embellished until they became mythical. Engaging in a biographical

---

[1] Without their combined assistance, this study would have had no chance of being published. I could never thank them both enough.

interview with him would therefore have meant something else, necessarily more substantial, than a simple narration of a life story: a full biography? A biopic? Whatever it might have been, it was not in my plans.

It was also clear that he was not personally interested in the past, in the sense of "what happened" or, more simply, in his own past. His speeches, his texts, his public acts and even his works, the *kata* of shintaido, all carry the same message: "Does the past encumber you? Cut it and go forward!" He was, though, keen on history, in the form of knowledge that nourishes present thought, and as such he approved of my project of collecting testimonies from "grassroots actors," "for History;" a bit like, he said, the NHK documentary series "Project X"[1] that deals with great Japanese achievements in fields as diverse as science, technology, sports or social affairs, and which was then very fashionable in Japan. I saw no inconvenience, and he seemed to regard my restraint as a mark of respect due to his position as founder[2].

This is how he shared some of his memories, made comments on the study in progress, mentioned (without naming them) people who had contacted him for advice on participating[3], offered us a financial contribution – refused – and took care of us as a master should; giving us his latest ideas on the practice – with documents to take away – or telling us about his artistic projects, calligraphy and kenjutsu. I am grateful to him for having taken the trouble and I have ensured that any element of interest for the study was duly integrated into the historical and analytical parts of this work.

---

[1] https://library.osu.edu/wiki/index.php?title =NHK_program:_Project_X)

[2] He explicitly affirmed that position, alluding to the creator of aikido, M. Ueshiba, and to the founder of butoh, T. Hijikata, both of whom, towards the end of their lives, identified to their art by declaring "I am aikido" for one and "I am butoh" for the other.

[3] Opinion implicitly favorable, but I was duly informed in doing so that he kept a certain remote control over the project.

Throughout the period of collecting field data, I had maintained the posture of a "member": disciple for Master Aoki or *kohai* for H.F. Ito and the members of the Rakutenkai. H.F. Ito understood this well and sometimes encouraged his interlocutors to consider me "unimportant," rather as one does with juveniles authorized to attend debates between adults for their edification[1]. This posture is required by ethnomethodologists and so posed no problem for me. On the other hand, it was to prove problematic to varying degrees later.

Once all the available testimonies had been collected, the recordings were transcribed in 2004-05[2]; but things stopped there. The vagaries of university life, the lack of time and resources forced us to put work on hold for 14 years. My wife and I had tried to take advantage of certain periods of leave to move it forward, but the magnitude of the task persuaded us to wait until our respective retirements to devote ourselves to it. I had an additional reason not to speed up the process. Being an involved member of the shintaido collectives, I felt that each passing year increased my capacity for "indifference"[3] regarding the memorial issues of the original group.

CONSOLIDATION OF TEXTS AND COLLECTION OF CONSENT FOR PUBLICATION

In 2018, my wife and I retired. We immediately restarted the work of translating and consolidating the biographical accounts. When they were ready, we made two trips to Japan, in the spring

---

[1] I have clear memories of such an interaction between him and M. Okada: when the latter hesitated to express himself in my presence, he put him at ease by "denying" me with a wave of his hand, thereby reinforcing the man-to-man character of their discussion.

[2] Thanks to the help of Japanese members of shintaido.

[3] I use this term in the sense of "not making a difference" given to it by ethnomethodologists in their practice of "ethnomethodological indifference." See the development of the concept on pages 150-152 of Quettier P., (2007), *Les dispositifs d'Ingénierie Socio-Cognitive*, mémoire d'Habilitation à Diriger les Recherches, Burgundy University.

and autumn of 2019, to meet each member, present them their text in Japanese, make any corrections, and obtain their consent.

When I asked Makoto Suemoto, Japanese specialist in life stories[1], what would be the best way to proceed in order to collaborate with our informants, he recommended that I present all the elements as required prior to the first interview and then have the text reread during a second interview, at the end of which I had to get the person's verbal approval. He went so far as to gratify me with a demonstration of such "Japanese-style" agreement: gesture of handing over a document, intonations, and exchange of glances. I realized the full force of his advice at the time of the text validations.

During the first interviews, the various presentations had been duly made either by H.F. Ito or by myself. I started the second interviews with a simple formal introduction of the work to be completed. Certain reactions of embarrassment or requests for clarification quickly made me realize that something was wrong.

I immediately saw two reasons for this issue. The first was quite simply that in 15 years my informants must have forgotten the exact terms of the initial presentation concerning the purpose, the conditions, and the progress of the work of study, and could no longer know very well why they received us. A second reason, more insidious perhaps, could be that the very extent of the delay had created a doubt as to the seriousness of the study: for what obscure reason had we let 15 years pass before giving any sign of life?

Working on the texts had also shown me that corrections carried out outside the interactive framework of an interview (by sending the text beforehand and correction by the informant in

---

[1] I knew Makoto Suemoto through my colleague Jean-Louis Le Grand. Suemoto, who was then a professor at Kobe University, was one of the first Japanese researchers to take an interest in the life history method. He translated into Japanese *Produire sa vie – autoformation et autobiographie* by Gaston Pineau and Marie Michelle (1983), one of the reference books in the field.

private) tended to result in the texts being smoothed and thereby impoverished, but sometimes meant that argumentative or didactic parts were added which, however interesting, drastically reduced the vivacity of the text. I therefore chose not to send the text to the interested parties beforehand.

Finally, and perhaps more radically, during the initial interview I had mostly left H.F. Ito make the introductions and lead the interview, thus myself taking a secondary posture, more "natural" as I was, in the martial world, the *kohai* of both. Though this facilitated communication between them and therefore enhanced the informational richness of the first interviews, it nevertheless left the impression of H.F. Ito as the project leader. His absence therefore created a void and a prerequisite for the second interview should imperatively restore the reality of the research, of its academic context and of myself, its manager.

For these reasons, M. Hirano and I agreed that from now on we would introduce each interview with a time of (re)presentation between the informant and me, during which I would speak directly in French. M. Hirano would translate back and forth, leaving plenty of time for each of us to reflect and weigh the other's words. We would take all the time necessary to go to the end of the questions or comments specific to the situation and reach this moment of tacit approval where the work planned on the text would arrive as the "quite natural" continuation of the exchange.

This prerequisite served its purpose perfectly and the work on the texts now went off without a hitch.

PUBLICATION

Anonymity

The question of the anonymity of informants concerned me, as this anonymity seemed so difficult to maintain, until I read the passage devoted to it by J.L. Le Grand:

> In some social science research, names of people or places have sometimes

been changed to preserve anonymity; in communities it is quite different. Indeed, when it comes to villages, companies, associations, it is often difficult to modify data without detracting too much from the relevance of the subject... In the case of collective life stories, when the name of the collective is announced, it becomes difficult to ignore the names of the people because they can be easily recognizable.[1]

It cannot be any clearer. We therefore kept the names of the persons.

Secret

A few enmities were also revealed in certain interviews and I must admit that I had a hard time wondering what to do with them so as not to hurt anyone. In this case, Le Grand recommends the greatest caution. So, I did my best to follow his advice. The only one who sometimes still bears the brunt of some resentment remains Master Aoki. The reader may refer to the "Community" chapter [p. 67]) for contextual information. However, some criticism seems inevitable to me when it comes to a character as charismatic and public as he; the contrary would even have been suspicious. And as the content of the remarks may also contribute to the understanding of the world of martial arts – especially magical thinking and "feudal" relationship to the *sensei* – I kept them.

Withdrawals

Between the initial interviews in 2004 and the text validations in 2019, the situation had changed. H. Aoki had distanced himself from the international organization of shintaido and I had had to "choose sides" against him. I thus found myself in trouble with those members of the Rakutenkai who remained close to him. Others had lost interest in the project for various reasons. In the end, Mrs. Aoki, E. Ho, Y. Ito, K. Ishide, M. Okada, S. Toshima-Ito, and C. Tsuchiya-Kato asked for their autobiographies to be withdrawn. Others, like T. Ishide, H. Ishide and T. Kato, had died in the

---

[1] J.L. Le Grand article "Theoretical and ethical landmarks in collective life stories": (2000), p. 153

meantime and we addressed our request to their heirs. Only the text of T. Kato was authorized for publication.

To maintain the general coherence of the story and using the elements at my disposal, I wrote a short biographical file for each of these people – mentioned in the autobiographies of their companions at the time – and have brought them together in Appendix 3. Considering her own founding role, Mrs. Aoki's presentation is made in the same way but within the historical chapter rather than the Appendix.

REVIEW AND PROSPECTS

From the point of view of Information and Communication Sciences and that of Education Sciences, I have presented, seen from the inside, an original learning system in its three dimensions – individual, social, and cultural. In doing so, I have highlighted the "founding myths" of the learning community in their emerging context. From a socio-historical point of view, I have shown what was remarkable about this inculturation of Western modernity of the 1960s within the conservative milieu of Japanese martial arts. As an ethnomethodologist and actor in the field, I remain forever indebted to the members of the Rakutenkai, for the paths they have traced in the field of human ethnosciences; paths that I will never tire of exploring.

CAUTION

Although multiple cross-checks and checks have been made, it is possible that some approximations or errors remain in the autobiographical texts. If this is the case, the responsibility falls entirely on me.

ACKNOWLEDGMENTS

Like its purpose, this book is the result of the work of a community. My most sincere thanks go first to the members of the

Rakutenkai who agreed to tell and then publish the story of their young years. Their availability and friendliness during each of our visits have been of great support to us. I remain deeply grateful to Haruyoshi Fugaku Ito who allowed me to meet them and talk to them. Thanks also to each of the transcribers cited in the credits of the biographies. They made it much easier for us to get started. Special thanks to Masashi Minagawa and Kazuo Hokari as well as H.F. Ito for their transcriptions but also for their availability whenever clarification was needed later in the process. I am immensely indebted to my wife, Mieko Hirano, present at all stages of this adventure, precise, demanding and without whom this work would really have had no chance of reaching publication. Thanks to my colleagues in education sciences, Jean-Louis Le Grand, Makoto Suemoto and Hervé Breton for their valuable advice. Thank you to the reviewers cited in the credits of the biographies for their patient work in improving the text. Thanks to Philippe Amiel, fellow ethnomethodologist, for his help with the layout and his advice. Thanks to Pascal Lardellier for his "heartfelt" preface to the French edition, and his expert analysis of *kata* as "forms of communication." Thanks to my mentor and friend Jean-François Dégremont for his insightful afterword and his precious help during proofreading.

The English publication owes its existence to the relentless efforts and coordination of Ito Fugaku and Connie Borden, on behalf of Shintaido of America. May they all be warmly thanked. Thank you to the reviewer/rewriters cited in credits of the life-stories. The cumbersome task of tracking mistranslations was made much lighter, and quicker, by their number. A special mention for Lee Ordeman, whose vigilance, attention to detail and pugnacity allowed us to make the text better understood by English-speaking readers.

Special thanks to Peter Furtado for his delicate preface to the English version and for his proofreading/rewriting of the texts presenting and analyzing the Rakutenkai phenomenon. His skills as a historian and professional editor were of decisive help. Thanks to Nancy Billias for her proofreading of these texts and her valuable academic advice. Thanks to Lee Seaman, in collaboration with Fugaku Ito, for rewriting the glossary and for her overall proofreading of the book. Heartfelt thanks to Stephen Billias for the precise, implacable and at the same time delicate way in which he tracked down the many small inconsistencies that translation and multiple proofreading inevitably create.

Finaly, thanks to Geneviève Planton who took care of the cover design, to Masashi Minagawa for his powerful *shakunetsu* cover calligraphy and to Sarah Baker for formatting the digital version for Amazon publication.

Origins and community

We begin with the key characters in the founding of the Rakutenkai (the "community of optimists") and continue with a historical account of the artistic and spiritual adventure of this community during the 1960s.

SHIGERU EGAMI

Many of the first members of the Rakutenkai entered the practice of martial arts in one of several *dojos* led by Shigeru Egami. He was also present, even if from afar, at all stages of Rakutenkai's development. The following biographical sketch has been compiled from his book *The Heart of Karate-do*[1], from the Shotokai Karate Encyclopedia[2], and from the biographies of certain members of the Rakutenkai.

Shigeru Egami (1912-81) was president and chief instructor (*shuseki*) of the Shotokan Dojo of Japanese Shotokai Karate-do. Born in the prefecture of Fukuoka in the island of Kyushu, on December 7th, 1912, he began in 1932 to study karate at Waseda University, where he helped to found the Club.

---

[1] Egami S. (1975), *The heart of Karate-do*, Kodansha International.
[2] https://shotokai.com/shigeru-egami/.

He then continued to study under Gichin Funakoshi, the founder of modern karate[1], and became a member of Karate-Kenkyukai and, in 1935, of the Shotokai association which brought together Funakoshi's students. In 1937, Funakoshi appointed him to the evaluation commission.

During the Second World War, he was hired as an instructor in the Nakano Gakko, the Japanese army's elite spy school[2], where his mission was to teach the lethal techniques of karate. In contact with other instructors and students, themselves often experts in various esoteric or martial disciplines, he became familiar with the techniques of human development, physical and psychological, from different esoteric traditions.

Once demobilized in 1945, Japan's defeat and the loss of so many young people he had helped to train, affected him deeply. For a time, he stayed away from any *dojo* (the martial arts had been banned by the American occupying power) and tried to go into business [M. Egami, p. 213]; but this endeavor was not successful, and he returned to teaching karate. At this time, and in his constant search for the improvement of karate, he met Inoue Hoken[3], nephew of the founder of Aikido and teacher of an art then called shinwa-taido. Under Inoue's direction, he integrated the heritage of the Japanese martial tradition. This influence was

---

[1] Traditional karate originated in Okinawa. Among the different "ways" (*te* 手 or "hands") of martial practices of the village militias, karate was the one that came from China (唐 *kara*). Having studied this "Chinese Hand" as well as others practiced on the island, Funakoshi synthesized what he had learned, enriched it with elementary pedagogical practices, the *kihon*, and structured everything into a new art, which he named "Empty Hand" (*kara* 空 meaning "empty"), in reference to the Heart Sutra of Buddhism, of which he was a devout practitioner. Ambitious to disseminate this new karate more widely, he did not hesitate to exile himself to Tokyo in 1922.

[2] Mercado, S.C. (2002), The Shadow Warriors of Nakano – A History of the Imperial Japanese Army's Elite Intelligence School, Potomac Book Inc.

[3] Master Inoue adapted his name in accordance with the periods of his life: Kitamatsumaru (1902), Yoichiro (1909), Yoshiharu (1920), Seisho (1940), Hoken (1948), Teruyoshi (1971), Noriaki (1973), according to Pranin A. S. (1991) *The Aiki News Encyclopedia of Aikido*, Aiki News.

to prove very powerful and modified his practice to the point that Egami's karate was classified by Tokitsu Kenji[1] as one of the two forms of karate to be influenced by Japanese *budo*.

In September, 1955, Egami was named *shihan* of the Gakushuin University club. After the death of Master Gichin Funakoshi, on April 26th, 1957, the Tokyu Karate Dojo opened, of which Egami was officially named *shihan*, on September 1st, 1957. A month later he was named *shihan* of the clubs of the universities of Toho and Chuo. In Chuo a particularly gifted student appeared: Hiroyuki Aoki.

HIROYUKI AOKI

The Rakutenkai was intimately linked to Aoki, both through the original practices he devised and directed, and through the ways in which the members identified with his person.

The elements of this biographical notice are taken from the work of K. Hokari[2], from Aoki's own book *Shintaido - The body is a message of the universe*[3], from the author's own thesis[4], and from H.F. Ito's book *Ito Gaiden – Stories from the Shintaido Heritage*[5].

Hiroyuki Aoki was born in 1936 in Yokohama. During the war, he was sheltered in his father's native region. When he returned, his mother, one of his sisters and his brother had perished in the fire-bombings of Tokyo[6]. He was permanently affected[7]. Hokari

---

[1] Tokitsu K. (1995), *Histoire du karaté-do*, Editions S.E.M., p. 130. One may also read with profit his presentation of S. Egami's biography, pp. 137-154.

[2] Hokari K. (1989), *Origins : a history of shintaido*, Shintaido of America.

[3] Aoki H. (1992), Shintaido : The body is a message of the universe, Shintaido of America.

[4] Quettier P. (2000), Communication des messages complexes par des séquences gestuelles : les kata dans les arts martiaux japonais : école shintaido, ARNT ed..

[5] Ito H.F (2016), Ito Gaiden – Stories from the shintaido heritage, Ed Amazon,.

[6] https://en.wikipedia.org/wiki/Air_raids_on_Japan.

[7] These wartime deaths, together with those of pre-war illness, reduced the number of children in the family from nine to three.

describes him as a child of great artistic sensitivity, rather solitary and affected by a strong feeling of inferiority. From these predispositions, it seems that he drew a powerful aspiration towards art and spirituality – both as an ideal and as a power of the mind – as well as a great thirst for knowledge.

He was curious about everything, read a lot, and built up a solid artistic and scientific culture over the years. In 1951, at the age of fifteen, he read the Bible, found reasons for hope in it, and converted to Christianity. Entering Chuo University, he studied law but rather planned to dedicate his life to art and to the theater which he explored in the university drama club. To strengthen himself physically, he joined the karate club. He found little interest in it as the practices were so brutal[1], until the moment when Egami became the referent instructor.

By 1958, Aoki had overcome his initial reluctance and had become the captain of the club, therefore a teacher. One can imagine that this charming young man, cultured and so determined in his quest for knowledge, appealed to his new instructor.

Moreover, Egami had learned a lot from his contact with the participants of the Nakano Gakko and from his study of Inoue's shinwa-taido. His conception of karate was radically transformed and he was full of new ideas, both for the development of practices and for the training of the new Japanese elite. The expectations of the master thus met those of the disciple. After Aoki graduated, Egami convinced him to continue teaching karate for a while longer.

REFOUNDATION OF KARATE

The intangible heritage of karate kata, a critical review

There is a corpus of around 30 karate *kata*. Their forms are varied and their sequences complex. The meaning of the

---

[1] Hokari K. (*ibid.* p. 3-3) explains that, advised by his spiritual director, he stayed there only out of evangelism and a sense of challenge.

movements or sequences of movements is most often obvious (attacks, receptions) but can take a surprising turn, with meditation postures or martially improbable movements. Moreover, each movement has infinite variations – speed, height, direction of gaze, small differences in the posture of various parts of the body, correlation with breath, etc. – and contextual interpretations, such as reception of different attacks or sequences of attacks by one or more people. All the *kata* thus constitute a "survival know-how" manual, underpinned by a "social know-how" manual, both "coded" in a gestural language, hermetic by nature.

This is why, like the myths and legends of oral traditions, the gestural tradition of *kata* has been perpetuated from master to disciple by demonstration and imitation, from century to century, down to us. Whether obvious or hidden, the meaning of the movements had to be rediscovered again and again by the disciples. In the end, many were called but few, perhaps very few, were chosen! A master might teach his entire life without having a sufficiently determined and gifted disciple present himself to assimilate, and therefore reconstruct, under his guidance the entire heritage of the *kata*. Some of the many gestures that comprise the *kata* could thus have been transmitted without "intelligence." Nevertheless, if the gestures had been transmitted faithfully, from time to time a practitioner might appear who was sufficiently gifted to understand the original meaning, possibly with the help of written documents left by earlier practitioners. Otherwise, certain enigmatic parts of the *kata* might have been minimized or, conversely, hypertrophied, reinvested with a simpler meaning, or distorted in one way or another.

As one of Funakoshi's successors, Egami knew the entire corpus of *kata*. Taking a quasi-scientific approach, he had questioned the true effectiveness of *tsuki*, the cardinal technique of karate[1],

---

[1] See on this subject Tokitsu K., 1975, pp. 143-147. See also Egami S., 1976, pp. 66-67, as well as the testimony of his son Masatake Egami.

and this had led him, through a period of doubt and a period of learning from Inoue, to develop a much more fluid and ample form of *tsuki* and then, by rebound, to greatly fluidify and amplify his karate. Having done this, he regretted that an important part of the gestural heritage of *kata* was still largely misunderstood. Once Aoki became his student, he seized this rare opportunity of having for some time a sufficiently gifted disciple on the physical level, voluntary, intelligent, and creative. He aspired to examine the understanding of the *kata*, criticizing and decoding their heritage to remove elements that proved useless and to rediscover aspects lost over time.

He also had available the action-research workshops of karate clubs, mostly at universities, attended by hundreds of enthusiastic young Japanese, eager to become stronger and to understand ancient Japan in order to build their own lives and to build the new Japan, on the international scene of the immediate post-war period.

The initial places: dojo and karate clubs

Readers interested in understanding the functioning of university karate clubs, can consult Appendix 1 [p. 341], which is dedicated to their structure and make-up.

The biographical summary of Shigeru Egami mentions the universities of Gakushuin, Toho, and Chuo. These, along with the universities of Niigata, Hosei, and Tokyo Joshi Taiiku, crop up in autobiographies of several members of the Rakutenkai. No member of the Rakutenkai came from the Toho club, so we will not speak of it further. We will also introduce the company club Tokyu Karate Dojo, opened to non-student practitioners, whose operation was modeled on that of university clubs and which played a major role in the coming together of the Rakutenkai.

What follows is a brief description of each of the clubs that existed when Rakutenkai began. A later presentation will be made for the clubs that were founded by members of Rakutenkai: that of Hosei University, Giwakai, and that of Tokyo Joshi Taiiku Daigaku, the Women's Gymnastics University of Tokyo.

Chuo University Karate Club: Suzuki [p. 184] calls it the "Mecca of Shotokai". In 1957, Egami became its leader, while Aoki, in his third year of university, was club captain. Several of those who later joined the Rakutenkai also belonged to this club, including Haruyoshi F. Ito [p. 112] in 1960, Yoshitake Matsuhashi [p. 129] in 1961 and Toshikatsu Nishiyama [p. 356], also in 1961. The life and practice of the Chuo club is described in their accounts. They practiced every day, and held occasional *gasshuku*, at which they met practitioners from other university clubs.

Gakushuin Karate Club: We have little information about this club. The Gakushuin educational institution had been imperial, intended for the peers of the empire, then, having become private, it started again from scratch after the war. The Gakushuin group provided, and still provides, all training courses from primary to higher education. At the time, boys and girls only studied together when they arrived at university. The after-school association, the Hojin-kai, offered many sporting activities and Egami was named *shihan* of the karate club in 1955. Of the Rakutenkai, only Chieko Tsuchiya [p. 354] came from the Gakushuin group. She practiced there from college to university. In higher education, some evening classes were given by Aoki, for advanced practitioners. He brought some of his most assiduous students there, such as Y. Ito [p. 353] and Matsuhashi [p. 129]. In return, they invited Tsuchiya to participate in the practices of other universities and those of the Tokyu Dojo.

Karate practice at Gakushuin University, Tokyo (1964)

The Tokyu Dojo: This was opened in 1957 on the initiative of Sutejiro Kobayashi, employee of the Tokyu railway company and a former student at Chuo University. The opening was scheduled for April, 1957, but the death of Master Funakoshi forced a postponement until September, with Egami as its *shihan*. The Tokyu company underwrote the provision of the place, the advertising via posters in its railway stations, and the remuneration of the instructors. The management of the Tokyu Dojo was carried out by one of the assistant masters [*shihan-dai*], under the supervision of Kobayashi. The *dojo* was opened daily from 12 a.m. to 9 p.m. and the testimonies mention several practices, during the day and in the evening. The Tokyu Dojo quickly counted hundreds of regular practitioners. Around 1959, Aoki became the assistant master in charge of practice. Among the members of the future Rakutenkai, Tomonori Kato [p. 92] and Katsuhiro Ito [p. 100] were among the very first practitioners at the Tokyu Dojo, which Mitsuru Okada [p. 357] soon joined, along with Yoshitaka Ito [p. 353], Eiichi Ho [p. 347] and Shigeko Toshima [p. 352].

Niigata University Karate Club: The city of Niigata, in the prefecture of the same name, is located about 350 km north of Tokyo. Separated by the mountain range that spans the entire length of Japan, it faces northern China and eastern Siberia. Winters are very harsh there. Niigata University is a national university. We do not know its rating in the 50s and 60s. We note, however, that Tetsuo Hanaki [p. 159] mentions having passed the entrance exams for the universities of Chuo, in Tokyo, and Niigata; both were very far from his city of residence Toyama, and he chose to go to Niigata.

Various testimonies mention Tokyo as the only place to study karate properly. The Niigata University karate club was founded in 1948 by a group of about twenty students, but began without a teacher until Toshihiko Igarashi, a graduate of Chuo University, who had studied with Funakoshi during the war and now worked outside the University, agreed to take over the management in 1950; this was the official date of creation of the group. Although chronically lagging behind the evolution of Tokyo practices, the club regularly sent its best students to study during university courses in Tokyo, those of Chuo in particular. As no-one had real authority and each adopted what his comrades reported, several conceptions of the practice coexisted in relative harmony. The use of *makiwara* was typical: some used it assiduously while others had banned it, and one practitioner even reinstalled one outside the *dojo* when its practice had been abandoned inside [Koyama p. 191].

Niigata University had two separate campuses, 90 minutes apart by train: one based in Niigata for Human and Social Sciences (economy, law, languages, etc.) and the other in Nagaoka for Higher Technologies (chemistry, mechanics, architecture, etc.). Each had its own karate *dojo*, but the members met to practice together during *gasshuku* or to go together to Tokyo.

The Niigata club was undoubtedly the club most in harmony with the Rakutenkai and this is due to K. Hokari [p. 136]. Having entered in 1962 at the faculty of chemistry in Nagaoka, he went regularly to Chuo *gasshuku*. Impressed by what he saw and felt there, he invited other Niigata members to accompany him: Hanaki [1964, p. 159], T. Ito [1964, p. 172], Suzuki [1965, p. 184],

Koyama [1965, p. 191] and his younger brother T. Hokari [Handa, 1967, p. 205]. Once he entered employment, he did not hesitate to offer the club his financial support.

Egami/Aoki action-research collaboration

In 1952, and again in 1953, Egami had part of his stomach removed; he then suffered a serious heart attack in 1956[1]. As a result, his physical condition no longer allowed him to assume the direction of the daily practices in the various clubs, and especially those, several times a day, of the Tokyu Dojo. As *shihan-dai*, Aoki would therefore provide all the teaching directions, while Egami regularly joined him in each *dojo*. The two men worked together: Aoki focused on the action and interactions; Egami on observation, comments, and suggestions.

H.F. Ito describes this as "the golden age of Egami/Aoki collaboration."[2] Some oral testimonies report that at certain points in the practices, the participants had the right to attack their teacher as soon as they perceived an opening. It is easy to imagine that this simple fact could have created a situation of intense stress for the teacher, very similar to that encountered on the battlefield, with potential "death" coming from anywhere and at any time.

Many accounts of critical situations (wars, but also fires or accidents endangering the death of oneself or a loved one, children, etc.) relate that ordinary people suddenly transcend their physical or mental condition and accomplish extraordinary feats that are difficult to rationalize after the fact (racing at inconceivable speeds, moving loads totally exceeding human capacity, *a priori* impossible evacuation of cumbersome furniture through the impassable exits of a dwelling, running in total darkness as in broad daylight, etc.). In the warrior arts, certain *kata* are reputed to have been discovered in such desperate situations, the mind entering an altered state of consciousness and the body "taking over" to

[1] Egami S., 1975, p.17.
[2] Ito H.F., 2016, p.15.

put together a series of actions leading, against all expectations, to survival. If such transformations can affect virtually anyone, it is nonetheless true that, for samurai steeped in martial culture and daily undergoing the pressure of survival, these "irruptions into the extraordinary" suddenly offered them a real competitive advantage. To that end, they still had to exploit the event, to record the slightest gestural or cognitive details, the states of being, and to create simulations allowing them to cultivate that experience until they acquired an easy mastery of it; the ability then becomes "second nature." This is how *kata* were created whose paradoxical parts or aspects, often meditative, contained some of these original teachings, discovered in the heat of battle.

One can suppose that the experimental practices orchestrated by Egami, with the support and active participation of Aoki, could let Aoki aim to reach and maintain himself as close as possible to these situations lived on the battle-fields of bygone eras of martial culture. When one or more practitioners suddenly attacked the instructor, unexpected and varied handling combinations occurred by which Aoki's highly trained and kata-kneaded body went straight to the most efficient, original, or already documented solution in one of the *kata*; his consciousness allowed him to access the sensitivity, vigilance, and distance useful for such actions.

We know nothing of the bond that united Egami, as the observer, and his disciple, Aoki, in action in these circumstances, but we can imagine that it was of great density and that the results of the experimentation were most productive. H.F. Ito testifies to the changes in behavior that this activity provoked:

> "Egami-sensei and Aoki-sensei were visiting the *keiko* every Monday. The other days of the week, it was my job to take care of the practices.[1] It had been very common in university karate clubs that when most of the members reached the fourth year of university only the captain or sub-captain, or even the manager sometimes, would take care of the practice.

---

[1] "...to take care of the practices", meaning to give *gorei*, to teach.

The rest of the fourth years hardly ever practiced. But starting with my generation, this completely changed. Even after graduation, the fourth years loved the practice so much that they kept practicing. For our *sempai*, this was an amazing development. I think that this was because Egami-sensei's teaching started blossoming." [p.114].

Aoki's own action-research

In addition to this commitment to teaching and research with Egami, Aoki also pursued his explorations in the artistic, spiritual, and religious fields.

As K. Hokari indicates[1], Aoki's primary motivation was art. It was for the theater that he had started practicing karate, and he also had a regular practice of painting, even if he had never been satisfied with his production to the point of exhibiting it. He maintained an ongoing relationship with Ono Kazuo, the butoh dancer, he read a lot and, if he did not play music, he listened to a lot of it and of all kinds.[2]

On the spiritual level, he had obtained from Egami initiation into the esoteric practices of Mikkyo Buddhism[3]. As bodily techniques that lead to the extraordinary states of being that are described above, these practices were part of the martial curriculum, integrated within some of the *kata* or in specific meditations. K. Hokari tells us[4] that Aoki was especially interested in such practices, and that he pursued a personal search that led him to travel to certain places in Japan to practice specific forms of

---

[1] 1989, p. 3-5.

[2] Several visitors of the time testified to their surprise to find, in his otherwise rather dilapidated house, a high-end audio system and an impressive collection of music albums [H.F. Ito, interviews from August 2020, and T. Handa p. 208].

[3] A synthesis operated in the 9th Century by the monk Kokai between esoteric Buddhism coming from India and Tibet mainly through China and traditional shamanic practices. The Mikkyo consists of various forms of meditation, whose effects on the development of the neural system are beginning to be known, thanks in particular to the work of Francisco Varella, the neurobiologist who worked with the Dalai Lama, and to the Buddhist monk Matthieu Ricard.

[4] 1990, p. 5-3.

meditation assiduously and to experiment with them in his practices of receiving the attacks of his young disciples [H.F. Ito
p. 120].

On the religious level, he took part in the activities of his parish
and put as much as possible "his footsteps in those of Christ." But
here, too, he was conducting personal research aimed, like the
great Western artists who had brought Christianity to life in their
works – Romain Rolland, Van Gogh, Dostoyevsky, Beethoven, etc.
– to match the essence and the expression of the bodily movements of attack and defense of the martial arts with the ideals to
which his readings of the Bible made him aspire. The beauty but
also the efficiency of the movements had to stem from and testify
to the power of feelings and the purity of intentions. We will hear
the echoes of this quest in the testimonies of his disciples.

Aoki conducted this research within the framework of the
Shotokai *dojo* under the authority of Egami. He could not share
them all openly, however, and in particular the Christian dimension, which Egami might not have approved of, and certainly not
the Shotokai senior practitioners. For anything that went, or
promised to go, beyond classical karate, he had to have his own
dojo. The *dojo* is to the martial artist what the studio is to the
painter. The *dojo* (道場) is a "place" in which the cultural phenomenon of the practice "stands" or "takes place"[1]. In his case, it was
mainly the public spaces of a park located next to his home as well
as certain rooms of his house.

This house was also the "place" of his family. To make it a *dojo*
in which to welcome his disciples, he needed not only the agreement of his wife, Etsuko Aoki, but also her active participation.
Etsuko Aoki was in fact the second pillar of the Rakutenkai. This

---

[1] The notion of "place," marked by the character jo or ba 場, is found in the term *dojo*
道場 and obviously designates a physical, material, but also and above all cultural,
spiritual space. "Something" happens between spirits, including the spirit of the place
itself, in the place. According to this conception, nothing happens without a place, and
there is no place where nothing happens.

was so because she opened her house wide to her husband's students, but also because she contributed directly to their training, as a Christian and as a tea ceremony teacher.

ETSUKO AOKI – THE TEA CEREMONY

Born in Tokyo in 1937, Etsuko Ishide was raised in a family of entrepreneurs who were both very active and very devout in the Buddhist faith. Her grandfather, with whom she had spent the wartime in Chigasaki and who greatly influenced her, was a colorful character, at the same time president of the local fishermen's union, member of the municipal council, Buddhist monk, and healer.

With her father's business destroyed, Etsuko grew up in a post-war Tokyo dominated by American occupying forces, at a time when her ideals of justice, personal and social, found little space to flourish. Arriving at university, she describes herself as "desperate for a humanity that seemed doomed to the failure of its expectations and its hopes"[1].

There she met Hiroyuki Aoki and, through him, Christianity. By entering the Christian faith, she says she finally saw meaning in what she was feeling and found a solid foundation on which to base her existence. Young Aoki was burning with a faith that could topple mountains and asked her to join their lives together to help build the new Japan. She gave up her ambition to become a missionary evangelist and enthusiastically accepted.

After graduating from university in 1960, she found a job as a trainer in the Kyogoin Center for the education of young delinquents or pre-delinquents. She worked there until the birth of her first child, in 1964. She then devoted herself to teaching the tea ceremony and the art of flower arrangement, learned very early from her mother and a friend of hers. This is how she taught the tea ceremony to the first visitors to Nogeyama.

---

[1] Interview of August 31st, 2005.

The tea ceremony, known to the West as the esthetic and ethical ritual way the Japanese share a bowl of tea, can only be understood if viewed more broadly from its cultural perspective, regarding the position it occupies in the Japanese folk arts and its social utility, as a mode of lifelong-training in a certain way of "being together": a traditional "art of living."

As a moment of shared privilege, the tea ceremony occupies a pivotal position between different Japanese arts. Upstream of the ceremony, we find architecture, the art of gardens, cooking, clothing, arts and crafts (wood, pottery, ceramics, lacquer) for utensils, interior decoration (painting, calligraphy, flower arranging). At the heart of the ceremony, we find the art of initiating, maintaining, or closing a relationship, of maintaining one's posture, both external and internal, and one's role in a collective performance (posture, attitude, conversation, poetry, etc.); both esthetic and ethical practices, stripped of artifice and directly inherited from Buddhism[1]. And downstream from the tea ceremony, all the arts of action are *expressed*, whether formalized, like the martial arts, or not, like the daily quest of each person to elevate their behavior daily towards excellence[2]: arts "in the world" for which the tea ceremony constitutes a time "out of the world," distinct and complementary.

There is also a deep though little-known relationship between the tea ceremony and Christianity. As Benoît Jacquet mentions[3]: "Rikyu [founder of the discipline in Japan] himself, although a

---

[1] See the article by Pascal Bouchez (2014): " Le chanoyu, cérémonie japonaise traditionnelle du thé, comme exemple d'éducation à la présence ", in : *Voix Plurielles / Iconicité et imaginaires collectifs*, Vol 11 N°1, 2014, pp. 31-38. https://doi.org/10.26522/vp.v11i1.915 .
See also the article by Marin Wagda (2002): " La longue histoire de la cérémonie du thé au Japon ", in *Hommes & Migrations / Flux et reflux*, n°1235, January-February 2002, pp. 126-129, https://doi.org/10.3406/homig.2002.3798.

[2] As an illustration of what "a life of tea" can be, see the biography of Kenji Sato.

[3] Jacquet B. (2011), " Dans les secrets du pavillon de thé, d'hier et d'aujourd'hui ", in *Siglia / Architectures secrètes*, n°28, 2011/2, Ed. Gris-France, https://doi.org/10.3917/sigila.028.0091, p. 96.

recognized practitioner of Zen Buddhism, was close to Christianity and most of his disciples were converted by the Jesuits. Certain objects dating from this period – bowls (*chawan*), censers (*koro*), kettles (*kama*) – bear the mark of the Christian cross and remind us that the ritual of the tea ceremony is not without relation to that of the mass[1]." Rikyu was active during the reign of Hideyoshi Toyotomi (1537-98); at this time, and even more so during the two centuries of the Tokugawa shogunate that followed, Christianity was banned and then very harshly persecuted, forcing the faithful into strict secrecy; the *shogun* had extremely keen hearing and very heavy hands, not hesitating to exterminate families and entire villages. Christian practice nevertheless persisted, always secret and sometimes sublimated, as in the values and practices of simplicity and conviviality of the tea ceremony, to the point that the trace of it has evaporated.

Etsuko Aoki was the perfect companion, idealistic and pragmatic at the same time, to accompany her husband's projects. Dynamic and enterprising, she embodied a model of Christianity but also of modernity. Thus, their house in Nogeyama became the center of Rakutenkai, the atypical community that formed there at the same time as their family grew.

Located on the heights of Yokohama, the Aoki family home consisted of two twin buildings, separated by a narrow passage leading to a backyard. The house belonged to Hiroyuki Aoki and his sister Takeko. It seems that originally one of the two wings of the house was reserved for Takeko-san and the other for her brother's family. As time passed, however, the testimonies indicate that one of the two wings was reserved for the private

---

[1] François Lachaud, "Matteo Ricci et les excentriques", *Empires éloignés. L'Europe et le Japon (XVIe-XIXe siècle)*, Dejanirah Couto et François Lachaud (eds.) Paris, EFEO, 2010, p.87.
Also see the thesis by Pytlick, Damian *Chanoyu and Christianity in 16th Century Japan*, University of Adam Mickiewicz, Faculty of Neophilology – Department of Japanistics, Album   N° 352807,   Poznan,   2014,   https://tealife.audio/wp-content/uploads/2015/10/Christianitea.pdf.

domain of the Aoki family, brother and sister, and that the other was devoted to public activities: the art of tea, the art of flower arranging, meditation, discussions, meals, dormitory, meetings, or evangelistic activities.

On a hill a few minutes from the house, the park of Nogeyama offered open spaces at night, distant from dwellings, for dynamic practices, and wooded areas conducive to meditation practices.

Both the house and the practice spaces came to life as the Aoki husband and wife invited their students to come and share their activities.

MASTERS AND DISCIPLES

The practitioners of the clubs affiliated with the Shotokai were all disciples of Egami. For them to become Aoki's disciples specifically, they had to choose in his favor. This choice could only be made very gradually.

Japanese masters possess to the highest degree the art of keeping hidden the most advanced dimensions of their discipline and revealing them only when certain conditions are met. Conversely, Japanese learners know that public education is, of course, a necessary but never sufficient condition for learning. To obtain the "codes" and access higher levels of understanding of forms, it is strongly recommended to get closer to the master, in a more private, less formal space, and to behave there in such a way as to establish the climate of trust conducive to the transmission of more essential knowledge[1].

The teachings of the *dojo* were therefore supplemented by talks during the courses or, for the most committed, at Egami's own home. Wednesday evening was reserved for first-years, who

---

[1] In Japan, knowledge is considered as a quasi-organic phenomenon, which requires the establishment of an appropriate context for its expression. It is not a question of anyone's "good" or "bad" will. Simply put, knowledge is information-in-context; out of the context appropriate to it, no meaning, and therefore no knowledge, is possible.

could come, after the meal, to sit in the common room of the master's house to hear him tell the epic tales of martial arts, karate and Shotokai. This knowledge, transmitted orally, is always an integral part of the corpus of a school. It is through them that the meaning of certain, more hermetic practices can be understood or that the meaning of "obvious" practices – what could be more obvious than a *tsuki*? – can be reconsidered and understood on another level of meaning. It is only by approaching a teacher in more ordinary circumstances – by becoming even an *uchi-deshi*, "house disciple" – that one can access it.

H.F. Ito testifies [p. 115] that there was a certain "price to pay" for these Wednesday evening lectures, an incentive for emancipation. Egami indeed spoke in an intense and continuous manner impossible to interrupt and, although renowned for his great sensitivity, he never seemed to notice the exchange of glances between the listeners as the speaker approached, then passed the fateful hour of the last train. It was then necessary either to return by foot – no one had the means to pay for a taxi – or find improvised accommodation with a friend or relative.

For those practitioners who had learned to appreciate Aoki's teachings, this investment, classic with Egami, was soon doubled by a second, more modern but also more engaging, which was to lead them to venture much further off the beaten track. One of the first may have been H.F. Ito. Here is what he says about it:

> "Then, around fall of 1962, I started to visit Aoki-sensei's place as well. Onozato-san, a senior practitioner from the Chuo club who was mentoring me, was already a familiar of Nogeyama and suggested the possibility. These visits took place on weekends, whereas visits at Egami-sensei's were on Wednesday, so that there couldn't be a schedule conflict.
>
> I was attracted by Aoki-sensei's understanding of western philosophy, music and art. Aoki-sensei's world was very different. Egami-sensei was also very intelligent, but his philosophy was based exclusively on Asian culture. In his generation, most Japanese got a very patriotic education. So even if he knew creators like Beethoven or other western artists, he couldn't really appreciate or understand such things. Aoki-sensei was very

different. He was completely free. Great things were great. So, every time I went to meet him, we didn't talk about karate; he talked about his impression of reading Dostoevsky or other things like that. There weren't any other *sempai* or *sensei*, instructors of Shotokai, to talk with about such things. Altogether it was a strong culture shock to me, and at the same time, it was like opening a new world.

Another difference was that with Egami-sensei, we kept listening, while with Aoki-sensei we had interactions. More friendly, more open. We could ask questions. So gradually, my passion started to shift from Egami-sensei to Aoki-sensei. I am sure that Egami-sensei was conscious of it, but as the relationship between the two *sensei* was good, it didn't create a problem." [p. 115].

For others, like K. Ito, things seem to have been a natural extension of their practices:

"So, I took my university classes in the morning, I had lunch in the canteen and then I walked to Chuo, which was only a train station away. Then, I often went with Aoki-san to practice at the Tokyu Dojo, where I met my friends Okada-san and Kato-san. When the Tokyu Dojo closed, I would take the train home in conversation with Aoki-san, who lived further along the same line. After a while, I no longer got off at my station but continued to Sakuragicho, to Aoki san's home. We talked, we discussed... and in the end we went outside to practice in the night." [p. 104].

Post-war Japan was developing at a rapid pace and turning towards the West. The undeniable martial skill of their instructor, directly measured in the daily life of the *dojo*, correlated with his ability to reinterpret their practices in the broader perspective of artistic and spiritual traditions around the world, thus attracted all those who were in search of new meaning for their practices and for their lives. Joyfully crossing and filling the gap ranging from the *tsuki* attack to the painting of Van Gogh, the music of Beethoven or luminous interpretations of the Bible, Aoki thus involved the avid consciences and the sharpened sensibilities of his *keikonin* in a quest for innovation and achievement that deeply satisfied their aspirations for a more open, more just, more beautiful, more generous or, quite simply and radically, more "modern" world.

THE FIRST GENERATION

From Sunday, at the very beginning, meetings moved on to whole weekends, to which evenings were soon added, and from simple conversations, the group moved on to practical exercises on the heights of Nogeyama Park. Aoki could give the full measure of his creativity there. For this, faithful to Egami's method of "endangering," he had set himself the principle of never repeating himself. This is how he gave substance to the idea that *gorei*, group leadership, already highly valued by Egami, could become a real artistic performance, like that of a conductor.

He was, as we have seen, an undeniable expert in martial arts and he often encouraged his students, seasoned practitioners, to attack him as best they could. He was particularly fond of these exchanges, seeing in them ways of bringing the interaction to the highest possible level of artistic performance. Pushed to their limit, these students would enter states of exhaustion and trance such that their expressions and movement became, as they strove again and again to attack, very much like that of butoh dancers. He thus made them follow very regularly, through the grace of techniques, the path of transformation leading from the most offensive martial expression to a quest for beauty, accomplishment, and pure enjoyment of the moment.

Breaking with tradition, he considered no practice as secret, integrating into it all the aspects of his great culture and measuring them by the yardstick of the martial efficiency, alpha and omega of his students. He gradually led the group in the exploration of forms of bodily expression that were both constantly renewed, and constantly more hybridized.

Christianity

Without openly proselytizing, Aoki made no secret of his Christian faith. As H.F. Ito relates,

"He would always carry some heavy bag, and whenever he would have some time, he would be reading this big book. At first, I thought that this probably was some kind of text on fighting strategy or something like that. Then on Sundays, before the meal, his wife Etsuko would do some prayer. I thought, "What an interesting couple!" Anyway, I respected them and what they were doing, so I started to read the Bible. Doing so, I realized that it was interesting, and I kept reading it on my own behalf." [p. 117].

Everything suggests that Aoki was not so attached to the religious practice of faith as to the appreciation of its effects in daily life, in ideas, and, above all, in the arts. According to the testimony of his wife, he had created, for the first parts of the evening, a reading group of the works of a dozen authors likely to inspire young minds, both by their works and by their very lives: Dostoyevsky, Rolland, du Gard, Van Gogh, etc. Through these readings and the exchanges they generated, he shared his ideas and the relationships he saw with the practice of martial arts. These exchanges, and their lived example, led some to share the faith of the Aoki couple.

Emulation

The activity of the group soon took on a regular, almost daily rhythm. There were no rules, no registration, no schedule. Those who wanted came, after the day's practices, after a university course or a small food job. They talked among themselves, with the master or mistress of the house, then, when they felt it, when the conversation led to it or, more often, at the signal of the *sensei*, they changed to go and practice "a certain time" under his direction, often until well after midnight. Practice, consisting largely of jumps[1], was extreme, beyond the ordinary limits of the human

---

[1] At that time, the *usagi-tobi* (rabbit jump) had been broken down by Aoki into two different jumps: the first, named *kaikyaku-zenshin* consisted of jumping, squatting with your knees wide open, pushing the pelvis powerfully forward and the second, called *renzoku-soritobi*, consisted, still from the squatting position, in "diving" straight ahead and as high as possible then in arching arms and legs backwards before squatting down to start again. They also practiced karate jumping, called *moro-geri*, consisting of jumping as high as possible from a squatting position then coming

organism, and, according to the testimonies, always fantastic; giving life to extraordinary states of consciousness and sensitivity. Then, all returned to the Aoki house and shared a potluck meal prepared by the mistress of the house and a few helpers, commenting on the practice in a relaxed atmosphere Some then went directly to their daily tasks and others slept for a few hours in the same room where, in the Japanese way, they had previously conversed, eaten and sometimes practiced.

If, for one reason or another, someone hadn't come one day, they would then hear about the extraordinary practice that they had missed and, if the reasons for not coming had not been so "good" as that, then they felt deeply sorry. *Ichi-go Ichi-e*, one-life-one-chance, a cardinal principle of the tea ceremony, became their leitmotif. One should not miss anything because, with the work of reflection and experimentation advancing rapidly, there was a real risk of finding oneself distanced at the slightest break. No need for stimulation, their taste for competition was doing its job.

> "At the time, we wanted to do as much *keiko* as possible. Missing even once was a tragedy. We didn't want to feel something like 'I wish I was there'. From each *keiko* we wanted to come out saying 'I did not do things by half', 'I did my best,' or 'I gave everything.'" [K. Ito, p. 104].

The quality of the practices and its benefits were obvious, both in terms of effectiveness measured in the *kumite* and recognition of the group for the progress of each one. And to that, the *sensei* devoted all his energy and all the means at his disposal.

---

together and whipping a double kick, either forward, in *mae-moro-geri*, or to the sides, in *yoko-moro-geri*, then to gather the legs together while falling to bounce, again and again. The biographies testify that a good half, and sometimes more, of each practice was devoted to this conditioning. Practitioners of Shotokai karate thus developed great strength and flexibility in the hips and lower limbs, resulting in powerful movements. The corollary of this power was the search for the most absolute possible relaxation of the movements accomplished with the upper body.

He thus obtained in the space of a few years a close-knit group of young enthusiasts strongly aware of contributing to the creation of a formidable art which would undoubtedly transcend, while encompassing them, the borders of the martial arts which all loved and respected to the highest degree.

FOUNDATION OF AN ASSOCIATION OPEN TO ALL, WITH A FEW RULES

At the end of the summer of 1965, an official ceremony was held to found a pioneering research group under the leadership of Aoki.

Matsuhashi was the master of ceremonies and about thirty people were invited, in the first row of which sat S. Egami. We have no further record of this event, but from that moment the group identified itself under the name of Rakutenkai. K. Hokari[1] translates the term *rakuten* as expressing the ideas of "perfect freedom," the ultimate stage of development in the martial arts, of "optimism," in reference to the beginner's mind which animated them, and of "enjoyment of Heaven," in reference to the Christian ideal.

On November 28th of the same year, this ceremony was followed by an internship, also called "founding", on the beaches of Iwai and for which we have a photo, on which we note that no one wears a black belt.

---

[1] K. Hokari (1990), p. 4-2.

No prerequisites were necessary to be part of the group. It was enough to participate in at least two practices in the year and to adopt the following regulations:

1. Do not go beyond your own moral principles
2. Do not forget your original spirit
3. Do not judge others
4. Love your neighbor as yourself
5. ...

The fifth rule, which remained empty, could be filled in according to one's choice.

They set themselves the following missions:

"To seek the truth in everyday life
To acquire perfect freedom
To live in the light of freedom
And become the light of the world."

During the years that followed, the group numbered about thirty people of all origins – not only martial – of all physical conditions and of all ages.

EMERGENCE OF PRACTICE FUNDAMENTALS: THE APOGEE

Thus formalized, the group entered a phase of the most intense experimentation. Among the members of the Rakutenkai, a more specific "research group," composed of the most assiduous participants in the practices of Nogeyama, devoted itself to the advanced development of the practices. To do this, they intensified their practices to the extreme, coupling them with periods of prolonged fasting. Some of them carried the "regulation," duly supplemented by their own fifth rule, inscribed on a piece of paper inside their *keikogi* during practices. It is also said that, as a sign of their determination, they did not leave their room until they had tidied up their belongings and left their last wishes there.

Tenshingoso

Aoki's research into Mikkyo meditation practices and their direct application in the martial field were beginning to bear fruit. He had finally isolated about ten essential expressions present in different attack or reception movements of the *waza* and *kata* of the martial arts but proving equally effective in other areas such as health or psychological development. He had practiced these movements solo as well as in *kumite*, and began to draw from them "active principles" which he formulated in teachable contents within the framework of experimental practices. H.F. Ito testifies to having seen him on many occasions link these different expressions, passing from one to the other without apparent order, until in April, 1965[1] he presented his students with a coherent set of movements, a *kata*. This coherence was not so much due to a logic of martial sequence as to a more universal vision,

---

[1] According to K. Hokari (1989, pp. 5-2 à 5-4) and Aoki (1992, pp. 44-46).

inscribing this new *kata* as an expression of principles common to different life cycles, from birth to death.

Although the remarkable movements of this cycle number about ten[1], the name he gave it, Tenshingoso "Five Expressions of Universal Truth," designates five as the main ones, each reinforced with the expression of the breath sounding one of the five vowels – AH, EH, EE, OH, UN – vowels which will identify them in later developments and applications of the *kata*.

Eiko

Aoki's method, true to his training, was to place himself and the group in conditions so extreme – some would say so real – that, having reached breaking point, their bodies reacted instinctively and new forms emerged from the physical and psychological chaos that had been so systematically established.

Thus, during the cold night of December 1st, 1966, a group of eight people[2] engaged in intense *bokuto* assaults under Aoki's relentless rule, simultaneously entered an unprecedented trance. Each seeking uncompromisingly the opening in the posture of the other and each attacking intention of one being instantly perceived and countered by the other, the swords remained raised and their reciprocal intentions were gradually and irresistibly drawn upward, to the point of forgetting any fighting spirit and no longer being able or willing anything but to melt into this powerful vertical attraction. These people, at one moment engaged in an uncompromising "struggle for life," found themselves the next moment in a posture of absolute contemplation and universal adoration.

A participant [desiring to remain anonymous] gives a testimony full of freshness of this moment, in essence:

We started with *kumite*, cutting with the fist, then we moved on to *bokken*.

---

[1] K. Hokari suggests 14 (*ibid.* p. 5-4).
[2] H.F. Ito, K. Ito, Y. Ito, T. Kato, M. Okada, T. Onozato, Y. Matsuhashi, T. Nishiyama.

We ran for about ten meters, which seemed very long to me, before cutting each other; and again and again. After a while we couldn't take it anymore and we calmed down a bit, but Aoki-sensei became very tough: "Cut!" And then things suddenly got more comfortable. I felt really comfortable, to the point that I had forgotten the existence of my partner. But, looking for him, I saw that he too seemed very comfortable[1]. It was interesting, we had completely forgotten each other and our bodies were stretched to the sky. The *dojo* was covered with stone cobblestones and surrounded by a fence. At the beginning, we were very careful not to hurt ourselves on this fence, but from that moment we forgot everything. Nothing mattered anymore, not even the *sensei*. With a little worry, I looked around and saw that everyone was in the same condition. We were completely free and enthusiastic.[2]

Aoki, who witnessed the scene, realized that he was witnessing the very incarnation of the Japanese martial ideal, as he had been taught: peace and war expressed in one and the same form. While it was true that a remarkable person might unquestionably achieve this ideal, there was no established form, no *kata*, that expressed it. But that form was now there before him: a union of opposites, squaring the circle, embodied in these bodies oscillating gently under the brightness of the stars. He understood its full significance, both mystical and martial, and saw its various practical applications. He returned home, put on his best clothes, and he and his wife returned "as spectators" to give thanks to the phenomenon which had not ceased in the meantime.

When it was over, they all went home. He shared with them Psalm 19:14 from the Jerusalem Bible[3] and everything that came to mind at the *dojo*. Most testify to this practice and these exchanges as an extraordinary moment, a turning point in their lives. Oddly enough, according to H.F. Ito, Takashige Onozato [p. 358], who was a longtime student of Aoki, walked away shortly after that day.

---

[1] In today's language, the expression would rather be "to get our thrill" or "to dig it."
[2] Interview of September 2004.
[3] Aoki H., 1992, p. 47.

THE HEIHO KENKYUKAI

If one pointed the sword towards one's partner and the world with the same intentionality as one had pointed it towards the sky during this memorable practice, one then entered a state of presence sensitive to the other and to the world that truly abolished any notional barrier between war and peace. Instilling in the "state of peace" the capacities of attention, sensitivity, and consciousness specific to the "state of war," such was the true goal of Japanese martial arts. Thus testified Inoue and Egami by insisting on defining their arts as much as "methods of war" (兵法, pronounced *heiho*) as "methods of peace" (平 法, also pronounced *heiho*)[1]. Although sharing these ideals, Aoki found that the forms in which they were expressed were not the sign of them:

> "I was the leader of a karate group and I found myself confronted with a persistent problem, common to all karate clubs: the aggressiveness, the belligerent spirit of the practitioners. [...] Whenever, as a result of this attitude, a violent incident took place, it was always the people involved who were criticized without ever questioning the nature of the practice itself. [...]. I am convinced that each technique must safeguard our mental and spiritual faculties and that in return, these must support our technique. [...] If at the base of the movement studied, we find *tsuki* or *nage*, it is very normal that the problem of violence arises. [...] The ancient martial arts texts present many great ideas. But often the forms themselves do not correspond to these sublime ideals. I could not convince myself, I must say with regret, that what they were saying was entirely without sophistry. [...] I wanted the form to convey exactly its meaning" [2007, p. 53].

Now, with the discovery of this new form, his aspirations and criteria were fully satisfied. Certain that he had thus materialized

---

[1] As an example of the traditional use of the concept, consult the Heiho Kadensho, work of the 16th-century sword master Yagyu Munenori, *The life-giving sword: secret teachings from the house of the Shogun*, trans. William Scott Wilson (2012), Shambala Publishers.

the dream of earlier practitioners[1] and in reference to Psalm 19:14, he named the *kata* Eiko-no-ken, "sword of glory," then simply Eiko, "glory."

H.F. Ito remembers [p. 120] that from the moment when Eiko became the reference of the practice, Tenshingoso too was transformed. Its initial impulse, the movement associated with the vowel "AH" integrated the very form of Eiko, and the following movements flowed from it.

The work of the group was now to develop basic practices and applications renewing the technical offer of karate. For this the group took the name of Heiho Kenkyukai, Peace Research Group, in explicit reference to the martial ideals transmitted by Egami and Inoue.

THE NOGEYAMA CHURCH

Following these events, many of the members who came to Rakutenkai through the martial arts converted to Christianity, began Bible studies, and were baptized. The common room became a place of worship and on Sunday mornings a time for Sunday celebrations.

Conversely, for people who frequented Nogeyama for the tea ceremony or evangelical activities, Eiko and Tenshingoso represented spiritual practices that could lead them to take an interest in the martial dimensions of movements (development of perceptions, attention, concentration, etc.). By a fair return, the teaching of the tea ceremony intensified with the establishment of specific sessions for members of the Rakutenkai, led by the disciples of Etsuko Aoki, and hybrid practices emerged.

---

[1] It is not certain that they, Inoue or Egami, thought so but Egami did not dissuade him from continuing. We even find in the writings of the latter an explicit reference to the practice of the first two movements of Tenshingoso, stretching arms raised towards the sky, under the title of Aun no gyo, conjunction of Yang [a] and Yin [a] (Egami, ibid. pp. 122-123). It is interesting to note that this indication is placed in an appendix, at the very end of the book.

Of course, there were visitors to Nogeyama who were only slightly, if at all, sensitive to some aspect of the place. This did not seem to be a problem and, with rare exceptions (cf. T. Ito, p. 177), there is no report of any direct pressure one way or the other. However, people like T. Onozato [p. 358], suddenly left the group, and one suspects that some may have felt uncomfortable with the sudden rise in Christianity that followed the arrival of Eiko.

INFLUENCE ON KARATE PRACTICES

According to a classical approach to the teaching of martial arts, techniques such as Tenshingoso and Eiko would have been kept secret or revealed only in an enigmatic form, as "cherries on the cake," leaving practitioners free to pass by without seeing them. But Aoki came from the world of arts and was in tune with the liberation movement of the time, which sought to break down class lines and provide free access to knowledge of the greatest value for all. He therefore gave everything, immediately and understood who could.

We know from the testimonies available on the life of Egami, that the transformations he himself had made in karate had not been to the taste of his peer instructors. Before him, Funakoshi had also had great difficulties with the instructors of Okinawa and, later, within his own *dojo*, to make the evolutions which seemed to him necessary. It is possible that the traditional martial arts milieu, "studying the ancient" has a certain tendency to conservatism. Be that as it may, it is easy to imagine that changes such as those proposed by Aoki, that distanced the practice so radically from the canons of martial arts, had very little chance of being appreciated or understood.

After several years of existence, university karate clubs came to be headed by an alumnus group, some of whom took an active part in supervising the club. Thus, the clubs of Chuo, Toho, or Gakushuin had less need of Aoki than younger clubs. At most he visited them from time to time, accompanied by a few devotees like

Matsuhashi and Y. Ito. His influence was therefore quite weak and the drastic changes he made in the karate practices were rejected unceremoniously. On the other hand, in younger clubs such as Tokyu Dojo, Hosei University's Giwakai, and Niigata University, in which he had taught directly for several years, he had left a much deeper imprint in the minds of practitioners. Debates of conscience and conflicts of allegiance were therefore harsher there.

After practice at a joint university karate workshop near Tokyo (1966)

We find in the testimonies of practitioners of these clubs like Mr. Iwase [Hosei, p. 248], A. Koyama [Niigata, p. 191] and K. Ito [Tokyu Dojo, p. 100] traces of the perplexity caused by the practices of Tenshingoso and Eiko on the students most attached to the martial logic of karate. This is more so since the new practices were introduced there without explanation, according to a typically Japanese approach based on implicit trust in the knowledge of the teacher and on the idea that one could understand something only after having personally experienced it.

By reading the testimonies of the members of these "young clubs," one understands the debates which agitated the *dojo*. The

Niigata University club, located on the fringes of the Shotokai
world, was only slightly affected. Several of its members even became assiduous practitioners of Rakutenkai, and its *dojo* served
as a place of continuous experimentation until its disappearance
in the 1990s [Koyama p. 191]. Hosei University's Giwakai put up
more resistance and, in 1972 under the direction of Daisaku Mat-
suo, finally returned to the Shotokai fold, through Matsuhashi
[p. 129]. The Tokyu Dojo was undoubtedly the club that suffered
the most. It experienced two distinct flights of practitioners: first,
those who left because they did not approve of the new practices
and second, those who approved them but found it easier to seek
them directly at the source:

> "Ka-chan[1] used to say, 'There's no need to keep practicing at Tokyu Dojo,
> I'm going to Nogeyama,' He was a member of the Tokyu Dojo, but already
> well involved in Nogeyama. It was the same for Kuni-kun and Tashiro. They
> knew that the Tokyu Dojo would go bankrupt and so preferred to go
> directly to Nogeyama" [Kato, p. 97].

The few veterans of the club, loyal to Shotokai, resisted bravely
but could not prevent its definitive closure in 1967 by the Tokyu
Corporation. Reading Kato's testimony [p. 92] one understands
that the loss of this *dojo* was heavy in more ways than one for
S. Egami.

CONSOLIDATION AND DEVELOPMENT OF NEW PRACTICES

The young people, for their part, "[let themselves] be carried
away by the situation and what was happening [seemed] natural
to them in view of the evolution of Japanese martial arts"[2]. Aoki
was implementing the visions he had had of the different ways to
combine Eiko. The intensive practices were numerous and varied
in the different *dojo* of Yokohama: the park on the hill of Nogeyama of course, but also the park located on the edge of the

[1] Katsuhiro Ito.
[2] Kato, Ibid.

docks, very long and deserted at night, perfectly adapted to long practices of the running form of Eiko or even the gymnasium of a primary school rented at the weekend for specific practices, more meditative or in connection with the tea ceremony. Aoki gave full measure of his creativity combining the new with the old and developing the different parts of an original teaching curriculum.

The first generation of Rakutenkai, who called themselves the "seven samurai"[1] and had been at the heart of the action until then, were now joined by those of the next age group. This is how Hanaki [p. 159], Suzuki [p. 184], T. Ito [p. 172], H. Ishide [p. 348], E. Ho [p. 347], Toshima [p. 352] and Tsuchiya [p. 354] came to swell the ranks of assiduous practitioners to participate in the consolidation of new types of practice and the development of applications. The teaching was very open:

> "In the general *gasshuku*, Aoki-san taught. In ordinary *gasshuku*, other people, like me, could teach. At the time of Rakutenkai, there were no instructors, only senior practitioners.
>
> For our practices, we decided by ourselves... for example "OK, let's do Eiko" and we would go on for two hours... [laughs]. No one to say "stop" either; we were simply going to the end of our energy: "Should I stop? Ah, this person continues, well, let's go! " [laugh]. No real *gorei*.
>
> I remember that at a *kangeiko*, some people stopped after two hours and others were still there four hours later! Some people could do Eiko while others jumped in *usagi-tobi*. A person like Kato-san could stand still like a rock "damahhhhhh!" while another like Okada-san went "Ah!" ah! ah! " ... [mimicry and laughter] or Fugaku-san was going " hey! hey! hey! [laugh]"[2].

THE FIRST GENERATION ENTERS ACTIVE LIFE

Once the university years were over, with a year of extension for some, the question of entering working life arose.

As early as 1964, H.F. Ito had found a job as a cook in Yokohama, in a Chinese restaurant, Eian-ro, whose owner, Mr. Cho,

---

[1] K. Hokari, K. Ito, Y. Ito, H.F. Ito, Kato, Matsuhashi, Nishiyama, T. Okada.
[2] From a contributor willing to remain anonymous (09/2004).

was a former member of the Chuo club. The name of this restaurant is very often mentioned in the testimonies because Mr. Cho was over the years a real support for the members of the Rakutenkai, employing them, feeding them, lending them rooms, or making his restaurant available for celebrations. H.F. Ito had chosen to work there as a sort of practical internship in management but above all because of the geographical proximity to Nogeyama, which allowed him to join common practices after his hours of service. His weekends, on the other hand, were no longer available and he says he felt a real anxiety to see himself distanced by his comrades. Etsuko Aoki believes that from the moment he took this job, H.F. Ito became more exclusively focused on the practice, neglecting to participate in domestic tasks. In 1967, he left this job to become a bodyguard and driver, then a real estate agent, in the service of Mr. Fujio Saito, friend of the Aoki family and owner of a small construction company, Fuji Sangyo [Ito, p. 124]. He was then, moreover, married to Harue Ishide, the sister of E. Aoki, having thus become a brother-in-law of the Aoki couple, and lived in Nogeyama.

Others typically entered jobs at their skill level, in universities for Suzuki, in the family business for Hanaki and in large corporations for Y. Ito and K. Hokari.

Some who found a little respite from parental and social pressure, took convenient jobs with arranged hours (taxi driver for Mr. Okada or door-to-door sales for Matsuhashi) or unskilled (cleaning, delivery, handling, etc. for the others), which they could leave when the pressure of practices was too strong and they became obviously unable to carry out their tasks properly. Y. Matsuhashi reports that even Aoki once offered to work as a warehouseman with him, after the closing of the Tokyu Dojo caused him to lose his regular salary [p. 133].

ARRIVAL OF THE SECOND GENERATION

The university karate clubs constituted an environment with marked generations. Indeed, intensive daily practices, boosting the natural transformations of young people of this age, powerfully increased their physical presence (muscle mass, flexibility, speed, etc.). The difference between generations from one year to the next was extremely marked: for a first-year, the second-years seemed like veritable colossi, the third-years extraordinary beings and the senior practitioners (fourth-years and *sensei*) powerful demigods.

Those who entered the Rakutenkai after the creation of Eiko and Tenshingoso in 1966 thus formed the "new generation." The effect of differentiation was further accentuated by the fact that the latter were, unlike their elders, not so much attracted by the martial dimension of the practices as by its spiritual and artistic aspects. They came from the Niigata University club, the Tokyo Women's Gymnastics University club, from Hosei University's Giwakai, from the tea ceremony, or through their personal relationship with one of the existing members of the Rakutenkai. By their new expectations, these new members destabilized the more senior members but also reinforced them in their conviction of being on the right track. So, they took great care of them.

Members of the Niigata University Club

Those of K. Hokari's generation had made the effort to go regularly to the courses of the Tokyo clubs (Chuo, Tokyu, etc.) and had brought back new practices, those of "classic" Shotokai karate at first, then those resulting from the research of Egami and Aoki. In 1966, after this generation had left the management of the club to their cadets, standards fell. To remedy this, K. Hokari ensured that Aoki became the club's *shihan*[1], which then became one of his

---

[1] Out of respect for the club's founder, Aoki in fact asked not to be named as such, but that is the role he played.

privileged martial experimentation grounds. Subsequently, M. Suzuki and T. Hanaki made several trips to Nogeyama and, despite the distance, became active members of Rakutenkai. Takeo Hokari, encouraged by his brother, spent six months in Nogeyama during an unexpected break in his studies [p. 205], then, his diploma in hand, allowed himself a time of immersion in Rakutenkai. T. Ito, who was of the same generation as Hanaki but had lost some time initially, went to live in Tokyo, where he became part of the second generation. Finally, A. Koyama practiced with Rakutenkai during *gasshuku* and, more rarely, in Nogeyama. Engaged in taking over the family business, he remained in Niigata where he took over the management of the university club. He says he highly valued Aoki's practice, while enjoying being at a respectable distance from it [p. 198].

The Tokyo Women's Gymnastics University Club (Tokyo Joshi Taiiku Daigaku)

Shigeko Toshima had started at the Tokyu Dojo in 1964 when she was only 16 years old.

Very invested, she had soon been invited to join the practices of Nogeyama. In 1967, when the Tokyu Dojo was closing its doors, she began studying physical education and sports at the Tokyo Joshi Taiiku Daigaku. At the end of a year, committed and enthusiastic, she mobilized some classmates, Kayo Hirata and Hideko Handa in particular, and together they founded a sogo-budo club[1] which some first-years joined, such as Michie Hashimoto.

> "We did the same kind of practice as in the male groups: jumps, Eiko, bojutsu, pretty much the same. Toshima-san taught about three times a week but, as captain, Kayo Hirata gave *gorei* every day. We were organized

---

[1] From sogo 総合 complete, integral, synthetic, holistic and *budo* 武道 martial art. This is the very first "official" occurrence of the term for a group. We imagine that the members of Rakutenkai may have at first used the term among themselves to qualify what was no longer quite karate without being something else yet.

like a university sogo-budo club, with a leader, Toshima-san, in charge of the orientation of the practices, a captain, Kayo Hirata, in charge of the organization (practice program, reservation of *dojo*, meetings, etc.) and members, Hideko-san, Michie-chan, Yamaguchi-san, Mami-chan, Yamashita-san"[1].

A demonstration by club members at
Women's Gymnastics Universityof Tokyo (1969)

She soon introduced them to Rakutenkai and together they went to participate in the practices of Nogeyama, apparently attracted at least as much by Christianity as by *budo*.

---

[1] A contributor willing to remain anonymous (09/2004).

Some of them mischievously suggest that they weren't entirely indifferent to these handsome boys, who were both serious and full of vitality.

Members of Giwakai at Hosei University

The Hosei University club was an offshoot of the Tokyu Dojo, founded by Toshio Ishikawa around 1965 as the Giwakai[1]. Under the direction of Ishikawa and Chinen, it first practiced Shotokai karate in the style of Tokyu Dojo. For want of anything better, the group trained outside, on the roof of one of the university buildings. In 1968, Masatoshi Iwase [p 248] and Masashi Minagawa [p. 227] entered the club. In 1969, Matsuhashi became its referent and, in 1970, Iwase and Minagawa became captain and second-in-command respectively.

The Giwakai was one of those karate clubs whose youth and geographic proximity to the Rakutenkai exposed them very early on to the dynamics of change. Minagawa became a devotee of Rakutenkai, and Iwase participated in Giwakai until he entered professional life.

Connections of Rakutenkai members

These were mostly due to Etsuko Aoki. In 1964, she left her job at the Kyogoin school center for young delinquents in order to devote herself to teaching flower arrangement and tea ceremony. Later, she opened an arts and crafts shop near Yokohama Station and, being too busy, handed over the management of Nogeyama's tea ceremonies to one of her very first disciples, Yasuko Saito [p. 152], also a member of the group.

---

[1] According to H.F. Ito (August 2020 interview), T. Ishikawa was not in favor of the Westernization of Asian culture. This was evidenced by the name of Giwakai (義和会), from the Chinese 義和拳 (Yihequan) for "Fists of justice and harmony" that he chose for his group, referring to the Chinese rebels, nicknamed the Boxers, who rose against Western power between 1889 and 1901, in the name of a very martial attachment to traditional Chinese values and fierce anti-Christianity.

Another of his disciples, Kayoko Shimma [p. 349], from a Christian family and a co-worker at Katei Gakuen[1], was very active in the Rakutenkai though almost never participating in the practice. Eventually, she replaced Y. Saito as tea master, officiating during workshops and during weekly practices at his home.

Mrs. Aoki's sister, Harue Ishide [p. 348], who lived in Nogeyama, also took an interest in the practices of the group, and soon became a member.

Sato Kenji [p. 291], a disciple of Saito, joined the group and actively participated in the practices.

Etsuko Aoki had also asked her husband to "take under his wing" her younger brother, Tadashi Ishide [p. 350], who led a somewhat carefree life at the time. Out of admiration for his brother-in-law, T. Ishide agreed, without much enthusiasm, to participate in the harsh practices of the Tokyu Dojo. Then in 1966, living with his sister in Nogeyama, he was "invited" to participate in the practices of the Rakutenkai and, as his life transformed little by little, he became a full member of the group.

The aspirations and physical condition of these "non-initially martial" people being obviously very different from those of karate students, they undoubtedly had a decisive influence on the way the practices hybridized.

In 1967 Gan Okada [p. 254] was invited to join the group by his brother Mitsuru Okada [p. 357].

Finally, in 1968 Masatake Egami [p. 213], the youngest of the Egami sons, then an advanced practitioner of aikido, was invited to lead an aikido course for the Heiho Kenkyukai, following which he began to engage in the practices of Rakutenkai. As a certain distance gradually grew between Aoki and S. Egami, certain testimonies show that over time not only the Egami family but also the

---

[1] Or "Family School" [Ambaras, 2006, p. 50], that E. Aoki [interview 08/31/2005] names Kyogoin (Child Autonomy Support Center), where she worked as a tea ceremony teacher and K. Shimma as a boarding school mistress.

Shotokai community were moved to see the son of the "house" disappear in this way, in what appeared to them more and more like a cult. The testimony of Tomoji Miyamoto, then a very young karate practitioner, describes the turmoil of the Shotokai community after Masatake returned slightly injured from a sogo-budo course, giving a measure of the attention he received[1].

Those of the new generation began by integrating themselves into the practices of the senior practitioners, showing their taste for effort or, at the very least, their will not to be defeated by getting, however one could, to the end of practices that were always very long and intense.

OTA'S APPARTEMENT

In 1967, the boss of Fuji Sangyo, a friend of the Aoki family and recently employer of H.F. Ito, offered to rebuild the Nogeyama house inexpensively[2]. This came at a time when the senior practitioners were becoming aware of the considerable burden that the Rakutenkai activities placed on the Aoki family, and especially on the hostess. The entire Aoki family, as well as the Ito couple, therefore temporarily moved to the Fuji Sangyo employee dormitories in Sagamihara, and the former[3] arranged to rent an apartment in the town of Ota. They were thus near the Tama River, on the banks of which there were many sports areas always open to the public. They organized practices there, of which Kato took the direction and at the end of which Aoki came. Even when work on the Nogeyama house was complete, this Rakutenkai household remained in Ota until the neighbors, tired of the noisy comings and goings at all hours of the day or night, made them leave.

---

[1] The event is related by T. Ito [p 178] and by T. Miyamoto, student in Shotokai karate at the time, future 1st disciple of S. Egami and whose testimony was collected during an interview in September 2004.

[2] Traditional Japanese buildings, flexible and made of fragile materials (wood, cob, paper, etc.), require regular reconstruction, approximately every 50 or 60 years.

[3] Specifically, M. Okada, Matsuhashi and Nishiyama.

Thereafter, they continued to use the banks of the Tama River from time to time for some of their practices.

The Aoki family returned to Nogeyama's new house. H.F. Ito, employee of Fuji Sangyo, continued to stay in the Sagamihara dorm and walked back and forth to Nogeyama. It seems that this new house had enough rooms that several members of the Rakutenkai rented them: K. Hokari – finally becoming a full member of the Rakutenkai after two years post-graduate study in Niigata – and many members of the new generation, who crammed into a single room. The common room was used as a dormitory for those passing through in the evening and more particularly on weekends.

THREE AREAS OF DEVELOPMENT: RELIGION, ART AND *BUDO*

The senior practitioners made sure to maintain their connection with this new community at Nogeyama by participating as much as possible in weekend activities, religious celebrations, or Heiho Kenkyukai *gasshuku* on the beaches of Chiba. Each worked out for oneself what one's life would be, depending on practical possibilities, on family or social pressure, but also on the place he or she intended to give to the practice in their life and therefore what their role in the community might be. The visions of the role of some did not always correspond with those of others, nor with those of Aoki; tensions began to arise, and with them emerged a new dimension in the group life: politics.

One day (the exact date is unclear), Aoki presented the future organization as coming under three domains: religion, art and *budo*. It was agreed that Mr. Okada would take charge of the religious side, that H.F. Ito and Matsuhashi would take charge of the *budo*, and that Kato and H. Ishide would take charge of the artistic.

The religious domain - Shukyo

Mitsuru Okada was recognized by all as the one who would become the pastor of the new church in Nogeyama. Most of the senior practitioners had taken a catechism in Bible study, under the direction of Pastor Shelhorn of the Kawasaki church, and had been baptized[1]. Okada continued with serious theological studies and was ordained a pastor three years later. In the meantime, he began to structure the Sunday service of what was to become the church of Nogeyama, and in 1968 he organized for those of the inter-generation[2] a specific baptism ceremony, officiated by the Reverend Shelhorn, on the beaches of Kenzaki, on the Miura peninsula.

With the foundation of a church requiring funds, some senior practitioners like Matsuhashi, Mr. Okada and Nishiyama [p. 356], who played a structuring role for the community at that time[3], were actively seeking financial means. They had already attempted to create a "cleaning business for schools, businesses, or other such facilities" [T. Handa p. 206], the outcome of which we do not know. Later, an acquaintance of the Ishide family offered to act as an intermediary for the establishment of a business of fresh flowers and it seemed like a good idea. K. Ito, who had experience of wholesale purchases in his family's grocery store, joined the team. They mobilized a back room of the Eian-ro restaurant for the storage of flowers and hired some of the boys of the new generation who had nothing better to do. The harsh reality of commerce nevertheless caught up with them: flowers wither when you are too busy practicing to go and sell them, a child passing by finds it very funny to cut off the heads, and so on. The final blow was given by the sudden disappearance of funds that had been paid but never reached the wholesaler. The event created tensions and even suspicions that deeply damaged the relationship between some members. Following this, and perhaps for

---

[1] H.F. Ito, Y. Ito, Kato, M. Okada, H. Ishide, and K. Ito. The last four were baptized on March 22nd, 1967, in Kawasaki and the Ito brothers (H.F. and Y.) were baptized in their hometown of Kure, in their mother's church (to which they themselves had converted).

[2] "[himself], H. Kishida [...] as well as two or three others" [T. Ito, p. 177].

[3] M. Okada, interview of 10/11/2019.

other reasons as well, Matsuhashi distanced himself from the group. Many of the "young people" who appreciated him very much testify to the shock it caused them.

T. Nishiyama[1] had a brief stint in the electronics industry before undertaking theological studies and being ordained a pastor. Breaking away from Aoki's Christianity as being too syncretic[2], he moved away from the Rakutenkai to exercise his ministry on behalf of the religious community of Kawasaki, though he himself was later excluded from it for his ideas which were considered too "liberal." He now continues his evangelistic ministry independently in the Kyoto region[3].

Once the ambitions of a material church were abandoned, M. Okada remained the living beacon of the Christian dimension of the group. To earn a living, he became a taxi driver, a job that allowed him to remain in control of his work schedules.

Tenso practice in preparation for the celebration of baptisms
by Mitsuru Okada on the beach at Kenzaki, Miura Peninsula (1973).

Ultimately, Minagawa recounts [p. 241] that in 1973, during a seminar bringing old and young together and whose theme was "going out into the world", there was a last celebration and

---

[1] Since T. Nishiyama declined participation in this study, we have no information on how he made his transition to pastoral ministry.
[2] Nishiyama was a very close friend of Matsuhashi.
[3] Interviews by T. Ishide [03/2004] and E. Aoki [10/11/2019].

practices during which Aoki invited them to "make their practice a celebration." The *keiko* itself had become their cult.

The artistic domain - Geijutsu-teki hyogen

The artistic field was the original field of Aoki. Just as Eiko symbolized the spiritual dimension and Tenshingoso the martial dimension, Hikari-to-tawamureru, a practice of free movements, which appeared when Aoki received the continuous attack of his students[1], symbolized the artistic dimension. Like Eiko, Hikari had "appeared" in the interaction between Aoki and his followers.

Kato not being really attracted by the artistic field, H. Ishide remained alone. She held her position bravely and interacted with many "free" artists of the time, theater, jazz, performance, etc. Later, she was assisted by one of the members of the new generation, G. Okada [p. 254] and together they organized an avant-garde festival on the beaches of Kujukuri, the Ningen to Uchu no Matsuri (Festival of Humanity and the Universe), with many other artists. She then radically changed direction, in favor of the religious dimension, at the Kawasaki church and, like Nishiyama, dissociated herself from the too-syncretic approach of Aoki.

The holistic martial art – Sogo-budo

Several of the Rakutenkai senior members remained strongly anchored in the martial dimension. They could have moved away from it to go towards the spiritual dimension, the search for purity, truth and love, or the artistic dimension, the search for freedom and beauty, which H. Aoki taught them. But he also taught them that a free movement proceeding from the purest love was not only beautiful and gentle but also effective. Egami had taught them that for their movements to be effective, they should not

---

[1] After the attacker had exhausted all energy, he or she was encouraged to maintain, by an effect of pure will, active contact with his or her "target." Then emerged, within the attacker or receiver median space, a phenomenon of great freedom, later called "playing with light," Hikari-to-tawamureru. It was eventually fixed in a formal process to be taught to all in the ordinary circumstances of *keiko*.

actively strive for efficiency: rather, relaxation and letting go were key. Aoki had offered them to fill this letting go with love and beauty and it had proven to be highly effective. Martial art – as a way to develop a complete and universal range of capacities for action – therefore remained a structuring dimension of the practice and of the group.

H.F. Ito, having acquired business skills from his two bosses, aimed to make himself useful by using these skills and his knowledge of law in the community affairs. The opportunity soon arose: a project dear to the heart of S. Egami, the publication of a photographic compilation, in book form, of karate *kata* according to his approach. Unable to carry out the demonstrations himself, Egami asked his most capable disciple to assist him. This project, long evoked among Shotokai practitioners, especially those of Heiho Kenkyukai, therefore became a Rakutenkai project, with Aoki as the main actor, H.F. Ito as project manager[1], and any available members of Rakutenkai helping with the shooting of the photos during many *gasshuku* of the Heiho Kenkyukai on the beaches of Kujukuri, and with the production work[2]. The financing of the operation was ensured by preselling copies to future readers: members or relations of Shotokai and Rakutenkai for the most part. The book, published under the aegis of Sogo-budo Renmei, appeared in November, 1970 as *Karate-do Kata for Professionals* and all royalties[3] were paid to Egami.

A little before that, in May and June, 1969 on the beaches of the island of Oshima, images of the practice had been shot by a French team led by Philippe Ferrand and Michel Martin. Coming with the support of the French Ministry of Culture to make a documentary

---

[1] Under an arrangement with the boss of Fuji Sangyo, H.F. Ito was able, while working on the book, to maintain his remuneration while maintaining a completely free schedule.

[2] In an interview of September, 2004, a contributor willing to remain anonymous evokes entire nights spent in a small improvised laboratory on the first floor of the Nogeyama house, printing photos of each weekend.

[3] ¥300,000 at the time, equivalent to around €9,000 in current value.

on Japanese martial arts, they had been so impressed by the power and beauty of Rakutenkai practices that they had changed their filming program in order to devote a specific film to them. The images were then effectively edited into an avant-garde film showing various sequences of practices, some of them very impressive, such as a vigorous *kumitachi* thigh-deep in the waves, between Matsuhashi, Suzuki, and Y. Ito, while a voice-over declaimed verses by Henri Michaux.

Practice of Eiko free cutting during the making of the film,
"Prologue pour un movement", by Philippe Ferrand and Michel Martin
on the beaches of the island of Oshima (1969)

At this point K. Ito went his own way. When the Tokyu Dojo closed, he had started a small karate teaching club, the Heiho Tenshinkai, on the first floor of his family's grocery store. Just as his family had sold vegetables to people in the neighborhood, he intended to make a living as a local martial arts instructor. He had nevertheless remained present in the practices and celebrations of the Rakutenkai [p. 108], even hiring one of his *kohai* from the Tokyu Dojo to replace him at his *dojo* on these occasions. Shortly after the controversy that followed the fiasco of the flower business, and precisely at the time of the filming event on the island of Oshima, he accepted an engagement to teach karate to a yoga group gathered for a three-week course on the Izu peninsula. Having taken this first step back, he prolonged it by walking quietly back to Tokyo, thinking and writing down his ideas, as Aoki had taught him to do. In the end, he decided to devote himself only to his club, a branch of Shotokai, and never returned to Rakutenkai. Today, this *dojo* has become a small family business that has replaced the grocery store and educates, through martial arts, generations of young people of this part of Tokyo.

After college Kato had started working as an accountant. He remained in office for six months, enough time to understand that the profession would not suit him, then determined to live in the way of the *keiko*, even if that made him live in poverty [p. 95]. Until the closing of the Tokyu Dojo in 1967, the Tokyu corporation had provided him with a regular, if minimal, salary. He also owned a family home, which he had equipped with a small *dojo* in which he gave a few lessons.

During 1971, the martial branch of the Rakutenkai, structured by the dynamics of publication and filming, absorbed the other two. The organization Sogo-budo Renmei (Federation for a Holistic Martial Art) was formalized, and its office was set up by H.F. Ito in the 2nd district of Shinjuku. He was assisted there by G. Okada and then by M. Minagawa, who contributed to making sogo-budo known through various promotional activities. A *dojo*, with regular practice and monthly dues, was instituted in the Tokyo gymnasium, near Sendagaya station, where the direction of the teaching was entrusted to Kato. During that year, a public demonstration was given to officially celebrate the institution of Sogo-budo Renmei. S. Egami, who had been invited, complimented them on their remarkable accomplishments. Before leaving, he wished to contribute to the success of the organization and handed over an envelope containing exactly the amount he had received as royalties for *Karate-do Kata for Professionals*. This was their last official contact.

From the fall of 1971, two annual *gasshuku*, called Daienshu[1], were established on the slopes of the Asama volcano.

INTERNATIONAL OPENINGS

Foreign karatekas now came to Japan to practice with Rakutenkai. Ken Waight of Great Britain and Marc Bassis of France, both black belts, had practiced under Mitsusuke Harada. They were sent by their respective clubs to study directly with S. Egami. Arriving in Japan, they met Aoki and expressed a desire to practice with Rakutenkai. To do this, however, they were first asked to return to Europe and only come back on their own financial means; which they did, thereby breaking away from European Shotokai. Harada was understandably more than bitter[2]. This was a sign of the tensions that were emerging between Shotokai and the Sogo-budo Renmei. Other non-Japanese participants in Rakutenkai were the South American Carlos Greibben and an Israeli man nicknamed Bennie.

Aoki's openness to foreign cultures should have led him to travel long before. We can assume that he was prevented from doing so by the rapid sequence of actions in which he had been involved and by the lack of means. A first opportunity arose around 1967 with the invitation of the manager of Eian-ro, the providential Mister Cho, to accompany him on a trip to Asia. He traveled to Malaysia, Thailand, and India. In 1971, he responded to Marc Bassis's invitation to lead a major sogo-budo *gasshuku* (about 70 participants) at Saintes-Maries-de-la-Mer, which filled him with enthusiasm.

---

[1] Literally meaning "big maneuvers."
[2] Anonymous, interview of May 2005.

He was accompanied by K. Hokari and there met Y. Ito who was working in Germany as well as E. Ho [p. 347] who was traveling. Finally, in 1973, he traveled to the United States, accompanied by H.F. Ito, T. Kato, M. Suzuki, M. Minagawa and G. Okada. There he visited personalities from the counterculture, in particular psychologists whom he had met at a conference in Japan, as well as some New Age communities.

THE NIHON JUKU

Whatever disagreements arose among the senior practitioners, they made sure to keep them to themselves and offer the second generation the best of their original experience, as evidenced by the biographies of M. Egami, T. Hokari-Handa, M. Hashimoto, K. Hirata, H. Handa-Hokari, M. Iwase, M. Minagawa and G. Okada:

M. Egami

"My life was trouble-free. Just before my graduation from university, Mister A. came to my house, and before leaving he asked, "Would you please come and teach us aikido?" It might have been manipulative on his part, but it made me proud, and I led an aikido *gasshuku* for them. Later, I went to a *daienshu* in Asama, after which I started to practice. I did it very seriously. What I was especially interested in was what happened outside *keiko*, in daily life." [p. 217].

T. Hokari-Handa:

"Senior members like Matsuhashi-san, Okada-san, or Nishiyama-san were trying to start some sort of cleaning business for schools and other such facilities. I worked with them. I also cooked because Matsuhashi-san told me that "cooking is a very good practice." This is how I understand things, and so I cooked for them and practiced with them in the evening. It was a crazy time but so interesting." [p. 206]

"During *keiko*, while in motion, I got to the point of not feeling tired anymore, even if, for example, I was running in Eiko for a very long time. Regardless of the distance covered, I never had the urge to stop because of my fatigue or because I had difficulty breathing. I remember such a practice of infinite round trips of Eiko with my *bo* at night in a park along the port of Yokohama. It was as if I had lost the sensation of my body. Such experiences were truly joyful." [p. 208]

"One day, after I graduated from university, Aoki-sensei played music records for us at his house. Ma-chan[1], Toshima-san, and a few others were there. Aoki-sensei had a lot of music records. He started with modern jazz, then rock'n'roll, the Beatles, and others. I can't remember the precise order, but at one point he played traditional African music, concluding with a Bach violin concerto. The effect on me was absolutely extraordinary. Until my

---

[1] Affectionate abbreviation for Masatake Egami.

dying day, I will never stop thanking him and thanking shintaido for giving me the opportunity and the sensitivity to live such an experience. Every time the violin string sounded "gyunn!" it was like an arrow of light shooting into and through my body. I suddenly understood the value of art and of music to the highest degree.

It was not so much the technique of the musician as his or her understanding of the work being played, in a state of such high concentration that she became one with the very mind of the composer. This enormous shock of artistic emotion allowed me to understand how important music was for us humans. I had never had such a profound experience in *keiko*. We had heard this famous story of the "birth of Eiko," during which seven people had a very special experience. I had never experienced anything like it myself, but this musical experience was really something!" [p. 208].

M. Hashimoto:

"In Rakutenkai, I didn't do a lot of *keiko*. I was more drawn to the Bible or experiences like these dream stories. Among all the members of Rakutenkai, I am probably the one who has done the least amount of *keiko*. The *keiko* seemed very hard to me; I didn't understand it. Even when we were only discussing the *keiko*, I didn't understand anything about it. I preferred anything that had to do with the senses and sensibility, like dreams or the words of the Bible, and all that sort of thing.

Still, one day when I was running in Nogeyama Park, I remember being pulled upwards, like a feeling of being absorbed by the sky, and I was crying. I couldn't stop myself from crying; it was as if someone was inviting me and saying: "Come, those who carry a very heavy load!" [p. 288].

K. Hirata:

"I have incredible memories of training from that time. It was so fun and challenging at the same time! I would never have been able to change without these practices with the Rakutenkai people. I must say that I arrived at the right time. No need to be in the center, it was enough to take advantage of what had been prepared, to flow into the group. It is as if rails had been laid and by following the old ones, we were put on these rails, which we just had to follow. I have only benefited from the good sides of things, through the love of our *sempai*. I only have fond memories of those great times.

The teachers thought so much about what they had to do. And we just had to do what they had already done, focus on ourselves and do what we had to for ourselves. We did not have to think about the organization, but about ourselves, only about ourselves and our lives. I learned a lot from the teachers. They always talked about what to do in different situations, to make things work best: "If we are in such a place, it is necessary to do such a thing at such a time, etc." Or they would ask: "Rather than having a banal conversation, what place should we choose so that the conversation becomes more pleasant or more exciting? Should we move or do something else to make the meeting more productive?" etc. When I was with them, they always talked like that, and every day was like that. The *sensei* was constantly taking notes in his notebook and the *sempai* were studying diligently. It was all very fresh, very new to me, and I listened to their conversations eagerly. I probably didn't understand a tenth of what was being said, but I thought I understood, and I was like, "Yes, I can do it!" [p. 270].

H. Handa (Hokari)

"Shortly after the beginning of the practices at the university, Shigeko-san brought me to Rakutenkai and I met Aoki-sensei there, as well as other members of the group. Rather than the practice itself, I was strongly drawn to the ideals of Rakutenkai members, the atmosphere they created, and their tremendous energy. Toshima-san also took me to practice at the Tokyu Dojo with Matsuhashi-san, who I also thought was great. I was really impressed with these people.

[...] The most surprising thing I encountered in the Rakutenkai was Christianity. In my childhood, by tradition inherited from my grandparents, I had grown up in a Buddhist environment, close to the ancestors and the Buddha. I had had no contact with Christianity and I was greatly surprised to discover it within the framework of the Rakutenkai, at the same time as these people who took everything so seriously. These are probably the two reasons why I wanted to persevere. And of course, what Aoki-sensei said was always so new and attractive; I was excited about it." [p. 264]

M. Iwase

"In this way, and by deepening our understanding with Matsuhashi-san, shintaido gradually began to make sense in our practice of karate.

[...] I also remember taking part in a *gasshuku* at Kujukuri in 1971, towards the end of my last year of university. We learned to cut each other. We were many, but by cutting again and again we ended up forming a whole. I definitely felt that sense of unity. There were several dozen of us, but gradually we became one. It was completely unknown in the world of karate. I said to myself: "Ah, here is shintaido! ".

[...] I remember that the practice in Nogeyama Park lasted until two o'clock in the morning. We started at ten o'clock in the evening and after that we shared a potluck meal, each bringing something, then everyone slept side by side in Okada-sensei's prayer room. It was around 1970, before Kujukuri. Minagawa and Hando were also there. It was great. There was nothing like this idea of unification in karate. The idea was rather that everyone should assert themselves. For my part, I was very favorably impressed by this idea of unification.

I remember Ishide Tadashi, the younger brother of Aoki-sensei's wife, and how his personality changed dramatically over the practices. He was still a beginner when we first met in a *gasshuku*, and I had considerably more *keiko* experience than he did. But when I met him for the second time, his techniques and his personality were radically different. I felt like I was meeting a completely different person. His *waza*, and especially the cutting techniques, were extremely strong. His personality had also become very bright. It was the first time I had witnessed such a drastic change in someone. I imagine it was an effect of the techniques of shintaido, but I remain amazed at such a change in such a short time." [p. 250].

M. Minagawa

"During that time, university club captains would often visit Aoki-sensei in Nogeyama and participate in a special *keiko* based on Eiko and Tenshingoso, especially Eiko. I had heard about Eiko from my *sempai* at the club. It sounded like a strange thing. At Giwakai, we were still practicing a very low *kibadachi* for hours on end. So, when I did my first Eiko during this Heiho Kenkyukai gasshuku, I thought it was great. We were asked to get up in Tenso and stay there without ever giving up. It seemed that we were going to stay like that for 30 minutes or an hour, and we groaned together from the difficulty. And then I heard "Stop!" and we slowly lowered our arms. But when I reached Shoko, everything around had turned black, and I saw something like a candle burning in the distance. My body started to run naturally toward this light and ... I hit a wall, which sent me rolling. I got up and got caught up again in the race ... into another wall, and again, and again. Everyone laughed as they watched me, but I couldn't stop myself. In the end, I thought this Eiko *keiko* was really great.

Besides *keiko*, what Aoki-sensei told us was also interesting. We were so enthralled that no one wanted to go home, and we often missed the last train. He talked to us about many things and always in such simple and understandable ways." [p. 236].

G. Okada

"That's how I started hanging out with Rakutenkai, at Aoki-san's, where I met members like Matsuhashi-san and Jugoro-san, Fugaku-san's [H.F. Ito's] younger brother, and how I started to practice karate. I then went to live in Yokohama. At that time, Matsuhashi-san was someone important. I remember he took great care of me. He took me to Chinatown, here and there. He was a great support to me. Over time, different things happened between the main members of Rakutenkai, and one day Matsuhashi-san left. Apparently, he disagreed with the politics of the practice. Personally, I found the circumstances of his departure shocking.

[...] At that time, the center of our lives was practice, and practicing was more important to us than eating. As soon as an idea came to Aoki-san, we got together and practiced right away. This made any regular job impossible to hold. That's why we preferred a part-time job so we could work when we wanted to. But in the end, it wasn't very satisfying. I passed my taxi driving test, and I became a taxi driver." [p. 256].

Attempts at community living

Subsequently, most of the senior members having moved away to professional and family commitments, Aoki took the time to travel and devote himself to the new generation. A special "new generation" course was dedicated to them and, with a view to training them to promote shintaido, eloquence contests were organized. M. Egami was expected to lead the group, and Minagawa was to assist him. Thus, to "face the world," both were assigned to go to work for a company selling encyclopedias, in which, after a period of adaptation, they succeeded very well. All practiced almost daily, by themselves or together, and sometimes under the direction of a *sempai*.

The epoch was favorable to community life experiences and the most invested, strongly encouraged, considered trying the adventure. They visited several established communities, both in Japan and in the United States, where some accompanied Aoki and H.F. Ito. Their first intention, suggested by Aoki, was to settle in the countryside. Kanagawa, a mountainous region near Tokyo, was considered, but those who went there to explore returned unenthusiastically. They then thought of going much further, to Hokkaido where, again on Aoki's suggestion, it seemed possible to set up a business of breeding mink.

T. Ishide went there to explore with G. Okada. The latter came back unconvinced by the breeding plan but above all worried that it might be so involving that it would divert the community from the practice. T. Ishide remained in favor and K. Shimma as well. So, they left together, got married and worked in mink farming though without setting up their own business. As G. Okada had foreseen, the activity nevertheless left them no time to establish a branch of Rakutenkai. Even so, they stayed there for five years and then returned to Tokyo. T. Ishide underwent theological training, was ordained a pastor, and together they founded a parish affiliated with the Kawasaki church, which in many ways upheld the ideals of the Nogeyama church.

For his part, as soon as he returned from Hokkaido, G. Okada took the plunge and rented an apartment in the Yoyogi district. The group then gave itself the name of Nihon-Juku[1], set themselves some rules, and tried to lead a community life based on the values of Rakutenkai. After some time, however, each feeling called to other projects, they abandoned the experiment.

The end of Rakutenkai

T. Hokari got married[2], took a job in a large company and participated for a few more years in the practices of the Sogo-budo Renmei. K. Hirata, who had become a special educator for mentally handicapped children, emigrated for a time to Brazil, where she married, had children, and returned to Japan for their entry

---

[1] Juku are traditional private schools. Based on the name Nihon Juku, "the Japanese School," one can suppose that it was to serve as a model for other schools of the same kind which would be established abroad.
[2] Taking the name of his wife, he became T. Handa.

into university. Today, she is an educator recognized for her special talent for communicating with the most disturbed children. G. Okada, returned to his native region, where he started as a taxi driver and then became an educator of mentally handicapped children and finally director of care institutions for these same children. Subsequently, with the ageing of the Japanese population, he became one of the founders of retirement homes adapted to different audiences. Minagawa assisted H.F. Ito and Kato in their tasks of promoting and teaching Sogo-budo then, on their departure in 1975, took charge of the administration of the Sogo-budo Renmei while Egami took over the direction of the teachings.

With the departure of H.F. Ito in the United States in 1975 and of Kato to acupuncture school, the collective adventure of Rakutenkai came to an end.

Biographies of members

Order of presentations

To establish a general narrative of the biographies, we present them here in chronological order, based on when each individual began practice, whether in karate, at Nogeyama, or in the Sogo-budo organization.

Writing procedures and presentation conventions

Each interview was recorded on a dictaphone and then transcribed to obtain the first source text. The order of the story, subject to the vagaries of memory, was then reestablished in its biographical chronology. Minimal links were inserted as needed, but we did our best to preserve as much as possible that person's unique speech and expressions. The translations, although obviously "smoothing" the syntax, were also as respectful as possible of the original oral interviews.

We have prefaced each biography with a short editorial note providing context and have inserted some subtitles to facilitate reading.

In some biographies, non-verbal elements of conversation have been included in square brackets: some [gestures] and especially some [laughs], laughter being a Japanese way of marking or masking embarrassment.

Tomonori KATO

During the initial interview, in September, 2004, relations between T. Kato and H.F. Ito were marked both by great mutual respect and by an obvious formal distance. As an instructor and then as an acupuncturist, T. Kato had also played an important role in our own training, and we had maintained very cordial relations. Unfortunately, T. Kato passed away on July 2012, before we could present his life story to him to validate. Mrs. Kato, whom we met in May, 2019, did however, do us the favor of authorizing its publication.[1]

A wartime childhood

I was born in 1940 in Harpin, China, just at the start of the war. My father was an army officer, and I was his only son. He was injured and then fell ill. He was thus repatriated to the military hospital in Tokyo and my family returned to Japan in 1942. He died the following year. Subsequently, the air raids became increasingly intense. My mother and I survived, but the house burned down from the firebombs and we took refuge with relatives in Yokohama. In 1945, the air raids became more intense, to the point that Tokyo and its suburbs became a field of charred ruins. As a child in Yokohama, I witnessed the death of three people when their house burned. It all happened in front of my eyes, and there was nothing I could do to save them. I couldn't put out the fire; all I could do was to stand there, hearing their cries, dumbfounded. These terrible war experiences at such an early age worked their way into me, and I became painfully aware of how precarious and precious life and destiny are.

Beginnings in karate

There were a few bad boys in my high school who were causing trouble. I didn't suffer from it personally, but I couldn't bear it when my friends were victims. This is when I started thinking

---

[1] **Credits:** *Interview*: H.F. Ito, P. Quettier. *Transcription*: M. Hirano, M. Minagawa. *Editing*: M. Hirano, C. Kato. *Translation*: P. Quettier. *Proofreading*: Guy Bullen, L. Seaman.

about becoming stronger in order to protect my friends and myself.

During my first year of high school I lived in Meguro, and I regularly went past the train station on the way to high school. One day, I saw a big advertisement for the Tokyu Karate Dojo posted there. The announcement said that the master instructor of this *dojo* was Shigeru Egami. I did not know him, but his face inspired confidence. He gave off an impression of sincerity. That's how I went to my first lesson at Tokyu Karate Dojo. It was exactly how I had hoped it would be; I had found what I was looking for. Wonderful, isn't it?

Egami-sensei communicated better through his movements and attitudes than through his words. His personality was so dignified and noble that I don't believe he had an enemy. Egami-sensei didn't show us complex or difficult techniques, just *tsuki* or *keri*. I remember a lesson where we only did *keri*. However, through his *keiko* and *waza*, he transmitted to us what was essential, such as the importance of the soul, taking care of life, and helping people grow.

The Tokyu Karate Dojo

I consider meeting Egami-sensei to be a sign of my destiny. The instructor who taught us daily was also a good person, very close to Egami-sensei. His name was Fukuda-san and I learned with him during my three years at high school. Thereafter, I remained faithful to what had made me choose Tokyu Karate Dojo and when in 1958, I was admitted to Chuo University, I did not join the Shotokai club there but continued to practice at Tokyu Karate Dojo.

When I entered college, Fukuda-san stopped running the club to prepare for his law exams. And soon after, in the spring of 1958, Aoki-san, who had just graduated from college, came to teach as a second master, replacing Fukuda-san.

In 1962, I myself became second master of the Tokyu Karate Dojo, at the request of Egami-sensei. My *sempai*, Sugimoto-san, had asked to stop in order to prepare for his law exam. That's how I started teaching with Aoki-san.

I was planning to work as an accountant and I wanted to continue practicing karate at the same time. But in the end, after six months of accounting work, I realized that this job was not for me. Admittedly, it would be difficult for me to make a living with karate, but I always felt that my existence had to do with life itself and for that, karate was the direction I needed to take. That was how it was, even if I had to live in poverty. That's how I joined Rakutenkai.

From Tokyu Karate Dojo to Rakutenkai

Around 1964, the economic situation of the Tokyu Karate Dojo began to deteriorate. Sutejiro Kobayashi, who worked at the Tokyo Headquarters, did his best but failed to keep it afloat. It was he who, at the very beginning, had brought Egami-sensei as *shihan* of the *dojo*.

It was at this time that Rakutenkai began to form under the direction of Aoki-sensei. Master Egami therefore received a double shock: the *dojo* no longer functioned well, and many of his students left with Aoki-sensei. Disciples that he had carefully trained left him suddenly and without due regard. We were young, and I did not give this much thought. We let ourselves be carried away by the situation and what was happening seemed natural to us in view of the evolution of Japanese martial arts. I am aware today that we were the cause of great sadness for Master Egami.

Around 1965, one of my elders, Usami-san, took over the running of the club in a city *dojo* while keeping the name of Tokyu Karate Dojo. This is how the Tokyu Karate Dojo and Rakutenkai separated. Master Egami remained in charge of the Tokyu Karate

Dojo. It still exists [1], affiliated with Shotokai and located in Yukigaya in the Ota district of Tokyo. It is currently run by one of my younger colleagues, Akutsu-kun, and Shotokai is run by Jotaro Takagi.

One could also say that the practice resulting from research by the Rakutenkai group developed when the dynamics of the Tokyu Karate Dojo slowed down. Over time, the young practitioners were drawn to something new or stronger, while the older practitioners, who were also more conservative, wanted to maintain the old-fashioned practices. This created antagonism, which only grew worse in the three years before the Tokyu Karate Dojo closed.

Supervisors from the Tokyu Dojo were sent to the universities of Chuo, Gakushuin, Toho and Niigata. At the same time, those universities sent supervisors to learn these new practices. This is how university students quickly integrated them. I, for my part, participated in a few university *gasshuku* during those three years. *Sempai* such as Usami-san and Oguro-san, my classmate Ishihara-san, and many others, also came from time to time out of curiosity to learn about these new practices.

The Tokyu Karate Dojo closed definitively in 1967. I continued to teach there until it closed, while participating at the same time in Rakutenkai. Aoki-sensei also stayed until the end, although he didn't come often. I did a lot for the Tokyu Karate Dojo, for example, bringing the salary to Master Egami, giving *gorei*, etc. Aoki-san also did many things on his own, such as taking care of the practices at Rakutenkai, Sogo-budo Remmei and several universities, such as Chuo and Gakushuin, where he taught directly. He took care of the activities outside the club and I took care of those inside. When the Tokyu Dojo closed, I joined Rakutenkai once and for all.

---

[1] The interview took place in September 2004.

Kat-chan[1] said, "There's no need to continue practicing at To-kyu Dojo; I'm going to Nogeyama." He was a member of the Tokyu Dojo, but already well involved in Nogeyama. It was the same for Kuni-kun and Tashiro. They knew that the Tokyu Dojo would go bankrupt and so preferred to go straight to Nogeyama. Oguro-san, who was in active life, and other Tokyu Dojo alumnus continued to participate in the evening *keiko* until the Dojo went bankrupt. These senior practitioners were so brave and active! Their *tsuki* was very strong.

Rakutenkai

The reason why I was able to go to Rakutenkai without any hesitation was because it led to the world of the Bible. For me, the world of Christ and his teachings was more concrete. Egami-sensei's teaching was abstract, and I had to think about it in order to understand it. That of Rakutenkai was more specific and was clearly associated with the techniques that were taught, which made sense to me.

The Rakutenkai members practiced in different places. At first, it was at Aoki-sensei's house, but when that became too much of a burden on his family, we rented an apartment in Unoki [Ota] where Okada, Mat-chan[2] and others lived. But we had a lot of complaints from inhabitants of the building as we were very loud going up and down the stairs at all hours of the day and night. I vividly remember the Tenso *keiko* in the Nogeyama and Yama-shita parks. We also practiced Tenso with the sword, and I felt connected to heaven, as if it was open to me.

Much later, while giving *gorei*, during a workshop at Asama, I experienced a wave that formed and continued for a long time, as if for eternity. At the beginning there were several waves, but at the end of the *keiko*, eighty people joined hands, the whole thing finally forming a single big wave. Aoki-sensei was no longer there

---

[1] Katsuhiro Ito.
[2] Matsuhashi Yoshitake.

and the wave never ended. I wondered, "Is this a wave of life?" This kind of thing did not occur in other martial arts, but only in the practice of shintaido and Rakutenkai. I think people still remember doing this kind of movement all together.

We celebrated baptisms in Rakutenkai. At first, we asked the pastor of the Kawasaki church, Shelhorn-sensei, to perform them. Afterwards, since we wanted to do these celebrations on our own, Okada-san was sent to Kawasaki Bible School. Some others in our group also went there. Katsuhiro, Jugoro, Ito-san[1] and myself during the first year then, I believe, Harue-chan, Kato Etsuko, and a few others the second year.

This is how we organized baptisms by ourselves on two or three occasions. The first ceremony, with Shelhorn-sensei, took place in Kenzaki, in 1968, I think. The second was celebrated by Okada-san. There is a photo showing Minagawa being baptized by Okada-san on the Miura coast in 1973.

Chieko and I had started to get along well when we attended Bible study group and Rakutenkai together. Our wedding took place on January 1st, 1972 and our reception on January 25th, in a Chinese restaurant, Eian-ro, run by a friend. A hundred people were there, many of them from Rakutenkai. Our marriage also served to promote Sogo-budo Remmei. I had invited my students and the captains of the karate clubs there. Takeo-san played the master of ceremonies. This was shortly after the start of the Sogo-budo Remmei office in Shinjuku.

The first Sogo-budo Remmei *gasshuku* took place in the spring of 1971, in Kujukuri, and the second in the fall of the same year. From then on, two *gasshuku* were organized each year.

Acupuncture

I could have continued with Tokyu Karate Dojo, then Rakutenkai, then Sogo-budo Remmei, because they corresponded

---

[1] H.F. Ito

to what I had always sought and because my way of life agreed with these places. However, they were all finally discontinued.

Hokari-san and I acted as guarantors when Fugaku-san rented a place in Shinjuku to set up an office for Sogo-budo Remmei. I accepted this responsibility because relationships are important and life is precious. For me, everything in life is *keiko*, even after Rakutenkai.

While teaching for Sogo-budo Remmei, I began to study acupuncture and oriental medicine. It was, for me, a good way to face life as closely as possible. An acupuncture session is like a *kumite*. I have only one Way. In life, the only thing that matters is Life, whatever form it takes. Moreover, Egami[1], Minagawa, and other well-trained young practitioners were coming to the fore, and I no longer needed to be so involved with shintaido. Now was the right time. With acupuncture, I could earn a living while continuing to practice. I was bringing my life and my practice together.

I often had the intuition that such and such a practice could be dangerous or that there would be an injury if some people practiced together. After all, if you have a life, it is better to go to the end safe and sound, without illness or serious injury.

On the other hand, when I treat people, from time-to-time certain patients tell me that it is not necessary to give them so much care. But when I do an acupuncture session, when I think it would be a little better if I did a little more like this or like that, in the end I sometimes make the session last an hour and a half or even two hours. I have no sense of profit or loss, and I am comfortable with that approach.

When I stopped practicing shintaido, I left naturally. The atmosphere of the time made me feel that it was time to retire. The idea of staying to do a little more crossed my mind, but I didn't act on it.

---

[1] Masatake.

Katsuhiro ITO

For the first interview, organized in September, 2004, K. Ito received us in an adjoining room of his *dojo*; a room without any furniture. We sat directly on the linoleum floor in the purest martial tradition. The interview was conducted in Japanese through H.F. Ito, in a very friendly atmosphere. In May, 2019, when we visited him for the validation of the final text, the *dojo* had been considerably modernized and the interview took place in the *dojo* itself, in parallel with a karate session led by the son of K. Ito for neighborhood children.[1]

My childhood in Kawasaki

I was born on December 27th, 1941 in an area called Kizuki. My father was a fruit and vegetable merchant, but he was drafted in June, 1942 and never returned from the war. He died during the fighting on the island of Leyte in the Philippines. My older brother was born before he left, but I was born after. So, I did not know him nor, of course, did I have the pleasure of jumping on his lap. My mother took over the store, helped by her little brother, which she still does now with the help of my older brother and an employee.

In 1944, when the Battle of Leyte began, my father was sheltered because he worked for the Signal Corps, but he went into the jungle at the height of the bombardment and was never found. A survivor of his regiment told us that he had certainly died of starvation there. I got this story from my mother. She also has some photos of my father but they were very old, and extremely blurry and reddish. My mother showed them to me, telling me that he was my father, but I didn't feel anything.

During the war, to avoid the bombardments, my older brother and I went to live in the countryside with my mother's parents. I saw the bombers flying over the city in the distance. My mother and my grandmother, who had not wanted to leave, stayed here

---

[1] **Credits:** *Interview*: H.F. Ito, P. Quettier. *Transcription*: A. Nishida. *Editing*: M. Hirano. *Translation*: P. Quettier. *Proofreading*: Guy Bullen, L. Seaman.

and had a bomb shelter made in a nearby field. My mother then told me how terrible the shelling had been and how happy she was to know that we were safe. In March or April, 1945, Yoko-hama, Aoki-san's city, was bombed and Kato-san's house was burned down. I was between four and five years old at the time.

Afterwards, I went to my neighborhood elementary school in Kizuki, and then went on to middle school and high school at-tached to Nippon University, Hiyoshi. My mother preferred to send me to these schools because my brother had gone there and he had been successful. As I then entered Nippon University, I did all my schooling in the same academic system. This allowed me to enter high school directly and then university on a simple recom-mendation.

In my childhood, there was the large Rosai Hospital near here and in front of it a large park. This park had been requisitioned by the American army and all the gates were guarded. In the Shinto temple near the station, there was also a big black market where I saw Japanese women arm in arm with American soldiers in jeeps and saying, "Hi!". This black market lasted until my fourth or fifth year of primary school. It was very successful and was much used during the Korean War. Soldiers returning from war spent their money here, in Yokosuka, and elsewhere in Japan. This is how the country was able to benefit from good economic growth, and I grew up in this era. My mother was able to live com-fortably through her business that prospered, and that's how she was able to pay for our studies.

Karate: from hard to soft... to even softer

I started doing judo in the first year of middle school and then karate in the second year, in the high school club of Hosei Univer-sity, where students from Hosei University came to teach us. I practiced like this for three years, until my first year of high school. After that, as I was not a student of Hosei, I was able to continue to practice with them but was not allowed to take exams.

In fact, they accepted me to increase the number of participants in the club, which was quite low.

The Tokyu Dojo opened in September, 1957 and I started practicing the day after it opened. As Tokyu is a railway company, advertisements for its *dojo* had been displayed on trains and stations. They spoke of the qualities of the teacher, Egami-sensei, presented as one of the direct disciples of Funakoshi-sensei. As I was already learning Shotokan karate at the Hosei club, I immediately decided to enter this *dojo*.

Later I learned that the Tokyu Dojo should normally have opened earlier, but, due to the death of Funakoshi-sensei in April, 1957, the opening had been delayed until September. There was a memorial demonstration in 1958. This *dojo* was opened thanks to the efforts of Kobayashi-san, who was also an employee of the Tokyu company. Subsequently, Kobayashi-san and Minakami-san served as assistant masters. Funakoshi-sensei being the titular master, Egami-sensei had to come and teach as assistant master. But when Funakoshi-sensei passed away, Egami-sensei became titular master. At that time, Takagi-san also often came to practice.

So, it was in this *dojo* that I met Egami-sensei for the first time. I also met Kato-san there. I was in the first year of high school and he was in the second year at Suginami High School, attached to Chuo University. There was Tsuchiya-san, rice merchant and friend of Kato-san, Takakizaki-san, and Usami-san, who came almost at the same time as me while Oguro-san came a little later, in 1957-1958. The instructors then were Fukuda-san and Sugimoto-san. Then, when Sugimoto-san left that *dojo*, Aoki-san replaced him.

When I started in the Tokyu Dojo, before Aoki-san arrived, the *keiko* were very similar to traditional karate: high *koshi*, hard and strong movements, *makiwara*, and even a punching bag. Seeing them at the opening of the *dojo*, I understood that it was the karate that I knew and I immediately registered. Moreover, as I already had three years of practice, I had the satisfaction of being integrated into the most advanced group.

I once saw an old photo of Egami-sensei when he was training hard and tense karate, when he was a student of Waseda. How and why did his karate change? Why did he switch to soft karate? There was a turning point in his life as a karateka, which is said to have been due to Inoue-sensei. Egami-sensei started the Shinwa-taido *keiko* with Inoue-sensei when he was forty-four or forty-five years old [in 1956-57], and he found something different from the *keiko* he knew. Egami-sensei once told me that a *kohai* from Waseda University, named Okuyama, introduced him to Inoue-sensei by telling him about his *kumite* experience with Inoue: "Amazing! Faced with my attack, he didn't even have to move."

This is how Egami-sensei's *keiko* gradually changed. Egami-sensei was testing what he had learned from Inoue-sensei with his advanced students from Tokyu Dojo: Sugimoto-san, Fukuda-san, and brothers Takagi and Anoyugi-san from Waseda University. Among us, only Usami-san was allowed to participate. They practiced in the evening from nine o'clock. If we simple practitioners stayed there, they would tell us, "Go away! This *keiko* is reserved for advanced practitioners!" So, I went out, but I continued to observe them while hiding. But in the end, they were simply repeating the basic *kihon*, following Egami-sensei's *gorei*. This was just before Aoki-san arrived at the Tokyu Dojo, around 1958-59. As for me, I got the black belt after a year of practice, but no matter how hard I worked, I was not allowed to join this group working with Egami-sensei.

The Tokyu Dojo *keiko* then changed more and more rapidly. We removed the *makiwara* and the *tsuki* practices that went with it. When I went to Chuo University's Hakumon-sai party in 1957, I saw a *makiwara* there. The practice of *makiwara* was very popular, but in Tokyu Dojo, from 1959, we said "no more need for *makiwara*" and we practiced a more flexible *tsuki*. Later that year, when Sugimoto-san left the Tokyu Dojo, Aoki-san, who had finished college, arrived to succeed him. So, it was in my third year of high school, in 1959, that I first met Aoki-san at that same Chuo Hakumon-sai[1] celebration in Ochanomizu. He had been captain of the Chuo University karate club for two years. During the time Aoki-san taught us, the *keiko* changed even more than during Fukuda-san's time. When we were doing *kibadachi*, he would say to us "take your *koshi* lower, even lower!"

The Beginnings of Rakutenkai

In 1960, I entered Nihon University, which meant going to the Kanda area. Aoki-san then informed me of Chuo University's *keiko* days - Haruyoshi-san was the captain then - and I started participating. As a student, I could also practice in the courses of Gakushuin and Toho Universities. So, I took my university classes in the morning, I had lunch in the canteen and then I walked to Chuo, which was only a train station away. Then I often went with Aoki-san to practice at the Tokyu Dojo, where I met my friends Okada-san and Kato-san. When the Tokyu Dojo closed, I would take the train home in conversation with Aoki-san, who lived further along the same line. After a while, I no longer got off at my station but continued to Sakuragicho, to Aoki san's home. We talked, we discussed... and in the end we went outside to practice in the night. That's how things started with others like Matsuhashi-san, Nishiyama-san, or Haruyoshi-san, who had just started working at Cho. Everyone came to practice after work. I believe the year of the official beginning was 1965.

At the time, we wanted to do as much *keiko* as possible. Missing even once was a tragedy. We didn't want to feel something like "I wish I was there." From each *keiko* we wanted to come out saying "I did not do things by half," "I did my best," or "I gave everything." One day, I believe it was December 1, 1966 at Nogeyama Park, Aoki-sensei was moved to tears as he said to us, "You did a good

---

[1] Feast of the white door.

job!" So, everyone started crying and crying again! I believe there were seven people: Kato, Okada, Yoshitaka-kun from Tokyu Dojo, Nishiyama, Matsuhashi, Haruyoshi-san, and me. The students from Toho and Gakushuin were not there. They participated in *gasshuku* but not in these night *keiko*.

Other people who sometimes came to the Rakutenkai *keiko* were Hokari-san, Ito Toshio, Hanaki, and Suzuki. Hokari-san's practice was really impressive.

At the beginning, the style was "we go all out!" or "give it all!" What we practiced had no name, Aoki-sensei proposed: "We are going to do with our hands what we did with the sword," or even: "Well, what if we did with the *bo* what we did with the hands?" Then he gave names like Eiko-no-ken or Tenshingoso. Later, when we practiced during the day in the gymnasium of Ippon-matsu Elementary School, the content of the *keiko* became more detailed: how to use the sword, the trace of the cut, etc.

At the Mitsuzawa gymnasium, we also did practices to develop concentration: moving around while holding a plate filled with water, etc. Then we did more and more kneeling techniques. I remember races in *hanmi-handachi*. Outside, the *keiko* was mainly standing and inside often on our knees or seated in *seiza*.

Starting from the hard practice of Hosei, then more flexible at Tokyu Dojo and even more flexible with Aoki-san, my karate changed radically. When we started the *keiko* at night, I couldn't believe how well I was doing: "Ah, I'm getting there!" or "I didn't think I could do this!" That's how I was motivated to go there again and again without missing a single *keiko*. Alone I would not have succeeded, but with the group, I progressed like magic.

With the hindsight of experience, I now think that this period was for me the moment of transformation from caterpillar to butterfly. Like a butterfly in the making, I needed to concentrate strongly on myself in a chrysalis, and then, once this moment had passed, something exploded and I transformed. It is this path from hard karate to soft karate that transformed me into a butterfly.

Up until December 1st, 1966 in Nogeyama, we simply wanted to push the limits: higher, lower, further – it was pure challenge. It was only then that the *keiko* became more understandable and that names arrived.

The religious practice

On the other hand, some people started to say "I don't want to go to the *keiko* because funny things are happening there," "What Aoki is doing is not good," "This is not karate." At the Tokyu Dojo, Usami-san was beginning to wonder. There was a room above the Tokyu Dojo in which the senior practitioners met... then there was also worship, religious activity... and there were people who did not like this religious side and went to complain to Egami-sensei, saying "they do weird things!"

At home, my mother and my brother were part of Soka-Gakkai[1]. I was therefore naturally involved in their religious activities. As a child, my mother took me with her to her Soka-Gakkai meetings and, when we were there, she said to me "Since you are here, participate as you can." This is how I bathed in Buddhism.

At Aoki-san's, we talked about the Bible and read it before the *keiko*. The organization of Soka-Gakkai is pyramidal, but Aoki-san's practice was more without hierarchy, no-one was higher or lower. Moreover, we often had a good laugh. When we went to church, we were calm and peaceful. In Soka-Gakkai, there were many leaders: first the group leader, then the director and the president, who gave orders to the people below them. With the Rakutenkai practitioners, we were all equal when we were on the edge of exhaustion. In the beginning, when we went to church, I knew nothing about the world of Christianity. Then, little by little,

---

[1] Soka-Gakkai is a popular but rather radical and proselytising brand of Japanese Buddhism.

I became familiar with its practice. I understood that Christianity was horizontal, without hierarchy, and I returned to Bible school in the evening. What I learned there is still alive in me.

In this Bible school, there was a course in pastoral theology during which everyone preached in turn. When my turn came, I talked about the story of the "Three Little Pigs." One of the three built a house on a solid foundation and the other two built houses of straw and wood without foundations. So, I preached like this, "Just as a house must be built on a solid foundation to weather the storm, you must build your spirituality on a solid foundation." I do not remember in which chapter of the Bible it says "You must build on rock."[1] I also preached on the passage about a wheat seed that falls on good ground and grows into a few tens of grains which will themselves produce hundreds which will produce thousands.[2] This is how I started my Sumiyoshi *dojo* by saying to myself, "This will be my starting grain. The people who grow up there will help others to grow." I asked people who came to practice in our *dojo* not to talk about political, religious or money matters. There were very different people, with very different religions and very different political opinions. When, as the elections approach, I was asked to vote for such-and-such a person or to put up a poster at my house, I always answered "No."

At the beginning of Rakutenkai, I was looking to go all the way, beyond my limits. This was my basic thought. Of course, that was also what Aoki-san asked us to do. As far as I am concerned, even during this kind of extreme *keiko*, I have never had a mysterious or supernatural experience, like "what was invisible to me suddenly appeared to me, etc." Yet, if I think about it, it's still very curious that no one was ever injured during a *keiko*, even if we jumped, ran, or rolled without restraint on concrete. Even if we attacked in *tsuki* as hard as we could and got swept away

---

[1] Matthew 7. 24-27, Luke 6. 47-49, Isaiah 26.4.
[2] Mark 4.3-8, Matthew 13.3-8, Luke 8.5-8.

unceremoniously, no one was hurt. We feared nothing and went all out without any ulterior motives. We ran through the night until our tabis were threadbare, but our legs weren't tired. When I'm totally focused, I'm surprisingly strong.

Opening my own dojo

When the Tokyu Dojo closed on April 30th, 1967, I opened my own *dojo* in Sumiyoshi and it was in the fall of that year that this Heiho-Tenshinkai *dojo* was recognized as a branch of Shotokai. But even after that, I continued to participate in the Rakutenkai group, even bringing a young teacher from my *dojo*, Nakaike, who now works in the computer industry. He was practicing at the Tokyu Dojo but as it closed, he came to practice with me in my *dojo* located upstairs from the grocery shop. Then he worked with my brother selling vegetables and gave two karate lessons weekly for me. As I was going to Nogeyama and the Bible school, I obviously needed help but I also preferred to work in a team. I was going back and forth between my *dojo* and Rakutenkai.

In the Rakutenkai group, we also sold flowers to earn money. One day Okusan[1] brought one of her acquaintances who suggested we sell flowers. Since the flower market is practically the same as the grocery market, I offered to take care of buying the flowers, and then Matsuhashi and I would do the distribution. I believe this was in 1967-68. A little later it turned out that the money from the sale of the flowers had disappeared or that we had been the victim of a scam. We finally stopped this activity and I finished Bible school. Then Aoki-san moved to Fuchinobe while his house was rebuilt. Then he had his fourth child. I attended Rakutenkai until about that time. I still remember going to their new house to learn the tea ceremony with his wife. And then there was the Oshima *gasshuku* [p. 79], in which I did not participate.

---

[1] Mrs. Aoki. "Okusan" means "Madame," used without the name of the person, in the way that domestic workers refer to the woman of the house.

At the time of the Oshima *gasshuku*, I had gone to Izu for three months for a yoga course taught by Oki Masahiro. I knew his book on yoga and I happened to pass by his *dojo* in Mishima. I walked in and asked for information. He then asked me questions in return and when I told him about my flexible karate, he asked me if I would teach it in his *dojo*. I agreed and had them do *kibadachi*, *tsuki*, etc. When I returned, I heard about the Oshima *gasshuku* but I went back to Izu to teach karate at the yoga *dojo*. Following this, I did not return directly but I walked around the Izu Peninsula on my own for two weeks, entrusting my *dojo* to Nakaike.

I realized that there were many things that I did not clearly understand in what I had learned from karate and through the *keiko* of the Rakutenkai. I had opened my own *dojo* and, if I was to teach, I needed to digest all that I had learned. While I was traveling, I therefore took notes in a large notebook, like Aoki-san, and managed to organize and summarize the spirit of what I knew. When I got home, I learned that the Oshima *gasshuku* had indeed taken place and that the karate book had been printed. From the Rakutenkai point of view, I had fallen behind, but I needed to take care of myself and my *dojo* first. This was in 1969 or 1970, I believe. I remember Haruyoshi-san asking me to buy the book. And then, I decided to continue living my life with my own *dojo* as my center.

Egami-sensei

Ultimately, my master or, to put it more clearly, the "master of my life," is Egami-sensei. Last May, during the Yutenkai [1] which brought together many karate clubs, such as the Fujitsu club, Egami Takashi-san, Matsuhashi-san, etc., I told the story explaining why, in my *dojo*, those who become brown belts are asked to clean the toilet. Let me tell you why. When I started at the Tokyu Dojo in 1957, I was a brown belt and was in charge of cleaning the

---

[1] Association of disciples of Master Shigeru Egami founded in 1996.

toilets, which I found very dirty. One day, while I was cleaning, Egami-sensei entered the toilet in his socks! Without putting on the toilet slippers[1] ! Nobody ever does that. I told this story to Sugimoto-san and he said that Egami-sensei had said to him "The toilets have become much cleaner than before. Are you cleaning them?" and Sugitomo-san replied that it was not him but Ito-kun. Well, Egami-sensei had said nothing to me, who was cleaning the toilets, when he had met me there. No "thank you!" or "I appreciate the trouble you're taking," no, he simply came in his socks and left. Egami-sensei was a great master, compared to the little beginner high school student that I was. He taught karate as a master in many college clubs. Ordinarily, a simple word of thanks suffices for the little high school student, even if he tries very hard. But this great master, instead of a simple word of thanks, showed me by his attitude "Your toilets are so clean that, against all conventions, I can enter in my socks." I said to myself "This is the master that I will follow until the end."

That's why I have those who become brown belts clean the toilets in my *dojo*. To those who ask me why, I tell my anecdote by adding: "I want you to return to your original motivation before becoming a black belt. By having this experience with this important person, I was able to understand the heart of the *keiko*. I want you to touch on that a little bit." When you become a black belt, you become a model for others; you do demonstrations, you teach. Going back to something humble, like cleaning the toilets, just before reaching the black belt, enables someone to take with them a precious experience that will always bring them back to the essentials. In my case, the toilets in Tokyu Dojo were really dirty and it was easy to want them to get clean. In my *dojo*, on the other hand, they are routinely cleaned. But no matter, I remain

---

[1] In Japan, there are special pairs of slippers in the toilets that one is supposed to use in order not to dirty one's socks or apartment slippers.

adamant: "She or he who cannot or does not want to clean the toilets cannot be qualified!" [laugh].

Sometimes high school students argue: "Even at home, I never do that. Why do it here at the *dojo*?" As for the parents they say: "I can't believe it!" or "Very well!" If the children come back with a question from their parents, I send them back with my story of cleaning the toilets and my meeting with an extraordinary teacher. And at the end of the day, I hope the parents are happy with what I do for their child and are proud of the black belt I give them.

Haruyoshi Fugaku ITO

H.F. Ito played a major role in the creation of this book. Throughout the weeks of September, 2004, during the travels for collecting testimonies, he made comments in between interview sessions. These remarks were recorded in one way or another. At the end of the trip, a formal interview was conducted and transcribed. The whole was then consolidated into a coherent biographical narrative. Upon resumption of the larger project, including the creation of an in-depth historical introductory section, an additional interview was arranged in August, 2019 to fill in some of the gaps left in the conjunctions of the other biographies. For these various reasons, but also because H.F. Ito has maintained his commitment to teaching shintaido to this day, it is not surprising that the text of his biography is more elaborate than others and may at times even take a didactic turn, especially in the sections titled "The Creation of Tenshingoso and Eiko" and "The Heiho Kenkyukai." Confirmation of the English text was obtained via videophone in October, 2019.[1]

Hiroshima's atomic bomb

I was born in Kure[2], near Hiroshima, on May 28th of 1942, three years before the war's end. I hardly remember anything about the fighting, but I have a very clear memory of the "mushroom."

Especially I remember that we first saw a light very far away, then the sound came. In Japanese we say *"pica pica"* – *pica* means shining. In this case *"pica-don!"* A bright light *"pica!"* then *"don!"* – the sound came... later, and with it a kind of earthquake that made the *tatami* mats flip over suddenly. In our case, we were indoors and we saw some light outside – farmer's houses are quite poorly lighted inside – then the sound and the quake. We rushed out-doors and the mushroom came. We were amazed and frightened. Two days later my mom gave birth to my brother Yoshitaka. No nurse or doctor.

Hiroshima-shi[3] is the capital city of Hiroshima Prefecture. It is surrounded by hills. The pilot, being stressed, released the bomb

---

[1] **Credits:** *Interview, transcription, editing:* P. Quettier. *Proofreading*: L. Ordeman.
[2] The small port city of Kure lies just southeast of the city of Hiroshima on Hiroshima Bay, connected by water but also separated from its larger neighbor by prominent hills. Kure was strategically important as a naval base and center for shipbuilding.
[3] *Shi*: city.

in such a way that it exploded much lower than originally planned. The idea had been to have it explode high so that the scientists could measure how far the radiation would reach, but because of the nervous pilot, it exploded much lower. It was lucky for us, more powerful right underneath but less broadly effective. That's how we got out unharmed! Later, I remember that we were moving from one village to another. My mom had Yoshitaka on her back, and she held me by the hand. I remember people being amazed at such a young child walking the way I did.

Post-war life near a U.S. naval base

During the war, there was strong military control, so people behaved themselves. But after the war it completely changed – it was chaos. Kure-town was a navy base headquarters. This is how Americans and English came to occupy my hometown after the war. The GIs came and with them cabarets, prostitution, black markets, selling of forbidden films, etc. That made, of course, the *yakuza's mizu shobai*[1] businesses flourish. In fact, for a long time after the war the mayor of my hometown was a kind of representative of the criminal underworld [laughs].

In this general atmosphere, I remember that when I was in high school, I got involved in some fight and I ended up fighting with the younger brother of a *yakuza* gangster. The principal of my high school had to stop the fight, and in order to let me graduate, he obliged me to apologize to that boy. I thought I was right, and if they would let me fight, I could beat him. But the principal of my school told me, "If you continue that way, I won't let you graduate!" Well! My mom started crying, and I had to bow my head and apologize. But since then, I always wondered about justice, social justice. That gave me a lot of frustration, but luckily, I passed the exams, and I was able to go to Chuo University in Tokyo.

---

[1] 水商売 – *mizushobai*: Litterally "water trade", generally refers to businesses whose profits are uncertain, fluctuating. It is a traditional euphemism for all sorts of "nighttime entertainment businesses."

University and karate

It was a custom that anyone wanting to have a higher education, shouldn't stay in Hiroshima. You had to go either to Kyoto,
Osaka, or Tokyo. Therefore, it was natural for my mom to let me
go there to get a good education. With the idea of social justice in
mind, I started to study law. I wanted to become some kind of
high-level police officer or justice officer, prosecutor. Thinking of
police, I thought I had to have good physical abilities, and that's
how I started to study karate upon entering Chuo. Egami-sensei
was in charge of the *dojo* and Aoki-sensei was his assistant and
would give *gorei* for him.

Egami-sensei becoming Chuo University Karate Club's coach
hadn't been an easy thing, as he came from Waseda University.
The Chuo UKC had its own tradition and pride, but they hadn't
been able to produce any great instructor. It was a big shame for
them, and that's why they resisted Egami's nomination, but being
affiliated to the Shotokai, they finally gave up. Also, a little while
before, some weird problems had happened, as the *sempai* of the
club had been fired from the university because of some involvement with the *yakuza* world. The *OB-kai* of the club then decided
to name Aoki-sensei as captain, although he was only a third-
year[1]. That's how he exceptionally kept the captain – *shusho* – position for two years[2].

Later on, I became captain of the club. Egami-sensei and Aoki-
sensei were visiting the *keiko* every Monday. The other days of the
week, it was my job to take care of the practices.[3] It had been very

[1] Only after reaching their fourth year, the best of those members, willing or able to
engage themselves, would take responsibility for managing the club, by cooperation
and by appointment by the senior practitioners' group.

[2] The captain's job is to teach the newer members (*kohai*). The coordination of the
group is taken care of by the sub-captain (*fukusho*) and the financial matters are taken
care of by the manager (*kaike*). The captain's responsibility is also to maintain good,
direct communication with the master (in this case Egami-*sensei*).

[3] "...to take care of the practices", meaning to give *gorei*, to teach.

common in university karate clubs that when most of the members reached the fourth year of university only the captain or sub-captain, or even the manager sometimes, would take care of the practice. The rest of the fourth-years hardly ever practiced. But starting with my generation, this completely changed. Even after graduation, the fourth-years loved the practice so much that they kept practicing. For our *sempai*, this was an amazing development. I think that this was because Egami-sensei's teaching started blossoming.

Visiting at sensei's home

It was said that on Wednesdays, it was ok for freshmen to visit Egami-sensei's home after supper time. Then, ten of us would crowd in, packed in a small room, and he would teach us by telling many stories. To get back home, we had to take the last train at 11:30 at the latest, which meant leaving from Egami-sensei's home at 11 p.m., last limit. But he kept talking with a dense, almost impolite, on-going *kokyu*, so that we didn't have any chance to interrupt or stop him. Nearing 11 pm, we started to wonder and glance at each other, then eventually 11 pm was past, and we knew that we wouldn't be able to catch a train home. As we were poor, we couldn't take a taxi, so we went back home by foot or we slept at a not-so-far friend's place.

I would visit Egami-sensei's place about once a month and then gradually twice a month.

Then, around fall of 1962, I started to visit Aoki-sensei's place as well. Onozato-san, an elder of the Chuo club who was mentoring me, was already a familiar of Nogcyama and suggested the possibility. These visits took place on weekends, whereas visits at Egami-sensei's were on Wednesday, so that there couldn't be a schedule conflict.

I was attracted by Aoki-sensei's understanding of western philosophy, music and art. Aoki-sensei's world was very different. Egami-sensei was also very intelligent, but his philosophy was based exclusively on Asian culture. In his generation, most Japanese got a very patriotic education. So even if he knew creators like Beethoven or other western artists, he couldn't really appreciate or understand such things. Aoki-sensei was very different. He was completely free. Great things were great. So, every time I went to meet him, we didn't talk about karate; he talked about his impression of reading Dostoevsky or other things like that. There weren't any other *sempai* or *sensei*, instructors of Shotokai, to talk with about such things. Altogether it was a strong culture shock to me, and at the same time, it was like opening a new world.

Another difference was that with Egami-sensei, we kept listening, while with Aoki-sensei we had interactions. More friendly, more open. We could ask questions. So gradually, my passion started to shift from Egami-sensei to Aoki-sensei. I am sure that Egami-sensei was conscious of it, but as the relationship between the two *sensei* was good, it didn't create a problem.

I remember however that the third captain of this time, named Isayama, was living between Tokyo and Yokohama and started to join me visiting Aoki-sensei. We used to sleep in Isayama's place. Then, his mother went to see Egami-sensei and sort of complained that her son was getting "snatched" by Aoki-sensei. Egami-sensei had then to ask Aoki "please stop 'attracting' Isayama." Most of the others of us were from the countryside and freer to do whatever we wanted, but not him.

Isayama was more talented than me. Many of my colleagues in the third year thought that Isayama was going to be captain and that I would be assisting him. But he passed a test to become an aircraft pilot, and after the summer of 1964, before graduation, he was to go to a special training school to become a pilot. That's why, although everyone knew that he was the most talented among us – a handsome guy, tall, with long legs doing a great *yoko-geri*; he was amazing – I got appointed as captain instead of him. We were very good friends anyway, and he is the only Shotokai person of that time that I still see once in a while. A very nice person.

Anyway, I started visiting Aoki-sensei's place more and more often, and as other people started to come, Rakutenkai gradually happened.

Bible studies

When I was in my fourth year, we got the news of President Kennedy's assassination. That had a big impact on us that the president of United States, who was a kind of symbol of social justice, could be killed like that. Because we had some kind of American post-war education in democracy, President Kennedy was a kind of untouchable symbol. Then I thought, "Whoa! If even he gets killed, what is the meaning for me to pass some kind of local bar to establish social justice in my home town?" I had somehow lost the goal of my life. At that time, I was visiting Aoki-sensei's home, having a lot of nice discussions with him, and many very good *keiko* were also happening. So, these two events happened simultaneously: I lost my aspiration to be a lawyer, and I started to get interested in Bible reading through my contact with Aoki-sensei.

In the beginning Aoki-sensei didn't really talk about the Bible, as we were his karate students, but he was reading it. He would always carry some heavy bag, and whenever he would have some time, he would be reading this big book. At first, I thought that this probably was some kind of text on fighting strategy or something like that. Then on Sundays, before the meal, his wife Etsuko would do some prayer. I thought, "What an interesting couple!" Anyway, I respected them and what they were doing, so I started to read the Bible. Doing so, I realized that it was interesting, and I kept reading it on my own behalf. This is how some kind of encounter happened eventually between my aspiration for social justice, my practice, and the teachings of the Bible.

The practice of Christianity and karate efficiency

In karate there is a psychic technic called *de-o-toru*: being sensitive enough to catch a person's intention to attack. If I tried to do it with some technical intention, I was always late. Then, I discovered that if I made myself completely relaxed and pure, my mind and body would act as a mirror, and it worked much better. So, my *keiko* became focused on one idea: how could I make myself pure as quickly as possible? As I became able to do this more and more readily, I entered in a state of mind where I could catch right away any intention of anyone in my surrounding.

That's how the focus of my *keiko* changed. Originally, I had started karate because I wanted to be strong. But once we started to study this kind and level of mental-sharpening, it wasn't "more is better" but "less is better." Very much like Zen. When we did the *kumitachi* or attack *kumite*, the purer you became, the more sensitive you would be. And once you became more sensitive than others, whether your opponent had power or not, you could enter. In order to be sensitive, the focus of my *keiko* became then "How soon can I purify myself?" Reading the Bible, that is exactly what I found under the idea of holiness. Combining meditation, Bible reading, and the practice of Christianity, I grew in that direction.

Then at some point, I realized that social justice wasn't the point in itself and that there was some kind of energy holding this universe. Another way of saying it is, I realized that there was something beyond social justice. President Kennedy was killed and social justice wasn't the ultimate reference. There was some kind of natural law or natural power which was letting our universe go on, which in the Bible was referred to as "God." The assassination of President Kennedy didn't affect the universe itself. In Japanese we say *kogi* or *uchu no justice*, referring to some kind of environmental justice. From that point, I started understanding what Aoki-sensei was talking about when he mentioned *dai shizen*, natural law or universal energy. Listening to beautiful classical music symphonies, looking at sublime paintings, and sharing impressions with Aoki-sensei, I had sometimes understood what he meant, but sometimes not at all. Then, suddenly, all of these made sense.

After that, the interesting part was that my *tsuki* itself changed. It became so sharp that I could surprise my *sempai*. In daily life, too, I started to become sensitive to unseen things like some vicious guys taking advantage of a crowd to touch women. Anytime something like that started in my vicinity, I would catch it, and, when I looked in that direction, I could see it happen. Originally, I had this psychic ability if someone would attack me, but later it didn't matter. Simply walking, I could catch something going on in my surroundings; pickpockets or ugly happenings would affect me very much. It was like being exposed to a heavy meat smell after a long fast – too strong! That's how I realized that the universe itself is taking care to balance things that are happening. All we had to do was to open our consciousness to this level of justice.

My *keiko* completely changed. Etsuko and Aoki-sensei were so happy when I started to tell them about those events. They said, "Great! Through your practice and the study of the Bible, you've reached such a level!" More than Aoki-sensei's compliment, I was touched and impressed by compliments coming from Etsuko. Aoki-sensei was pretty good at praising people, but I knew that Etsuko wasn't like that. Whenever she saw something, she would say it directly.

The creation of Tenshingoso and Eiko

Aoki had the pieces of Tenshingoso in his mind – they came to him from karate *kata*. I remember that during my fourth year of university, he began to make us practice certain forms with open hands. We knew from Egami-sensei that all these were *mudra*, forms of meditation. In addition, Aoki tested them on us in receiving an attack.

The concept of cutting had always been part of our practice. A samurai who lost his sword had to manage to survive with bare hands, using techniques from karate, for example. But conversely, for Egami-sensei a *karate-ka* also had to know how to manage situations with a sword in hand.

This is how Egami-sensei introduced the idea of cutting, *kiri*, even if the practice of the karate *waza* were more traditionally oriented to the idea of striking, *uchi*. We practiced, for example, a *tsuki* he called *shinku-giri* – empty cut – while passing right near the partner. Punch and block were no longer just strikes but cuts that passed *through* the body of the partner. Then we gradually moved to fully cutting *kumite* with *komi* and *harai* cuts.

Training with this idea of distance, we became very sensitive to each other. So much so that it became very difficult to attack someone, because as soon as the intention of attack came, the body of the partner reacted, and she or he countered even before we could start.

To avoid this difficulty, we were looking for a way to attack "without intention," making our minds and bodies as "white" or pure as possible. And the more we did that, the more we became sort of "transparent" to each other, "one" with each other somehow. That is how, by a beautiful evening of the winter 1966, we became unable to attack, but irresistibly got "attracted up" with every hint of attack. And that's how Eiko appeared.

All the while, Mr. Aoki had begun to have ideas of combinations of the different *mudra* movements in waves, flowing from one to another without a definite order. At that time, the movements were not very large but remained close to the original *mudra*. It was only from the moment he had the focal point of Tenso that the "AH" could be positioned before, and from there the "EH," and so on. He then introduced it into the Heiho-kenkyukai practices and tweaked the details.

Following this came the idea of Tenshingoso-kumite. In the beginning, there too, the movements were practiced individually, either on wrist-seizure or attack. Aoki then asked us to practice the movements in the order of the *kata*, which was not without posing some problems at transitions. Our postures and movement were quite stiff. Thus, the final details of the "OH" movement – the very last one – took a long time to be found, until Aoki-sensei understood that the receiver had to "surrender," relaxing shoulders and letting the body relax back.

After that, I started thinking that we should share those practices with other people and that this could be my project.

Entering apprenticeship in a Chinese restaurant

I remember being impressed by the movie "Casablanca" with Humphrey Bogart. It's about an American living in Casablanca, having his own café, while doing some underground business. He would sometimes help Jewish people to escape from German occupation. That made me think: "Well, I don't need to have a title. I can be some kind of 'local hero'." From that point, in order to develop in that direction, I wanted to find some kind of community – mafia members say "family" – so that I could become responsible for a situation. Humphrey Bogart had become my model for "law making."

After sharing my ideas with Egami-sensei and Aoki-sensei, they said, "In fact, you would like to become owner of some kind of hotel or casino. But because you don't come from a 'family,' you will have to start from zero." Then, Egami-sensei suggested that I could take apprenticeship as a chef and Aoki-sensei proposed to introduce me to a young guy that used to practice in Chuo UKC and owned a Chinese restaurant in Yokohama named Eian-Ro. It wasn't far from Aoki-sensei's house, where I could keep practicing with Rakutenkai, so I accepted.

Working in this Chinese restaurant, under Mr. Cho, I started to study not only cooking but also the Japanese know-how and manners of business. Looking at it now, I would call it a "win-win way": The goal was for everyone to be happy with the deal: owner, customers, workers. I liked it – not just one guy making all the profit from the situation.

I also opened a class in the back room of the restaurant. The class started at 11 pm and most of the participants were the restaurant's cooks.

By the way, as I had just been hired, I couldn't ask for weekend leave to participate in Rakutenkai's official foundation ceremony in September, 1965, nor at the first *gasshuku* in November in Chiba.

The Heiho Kenkyukai

Takeda Sokaku, the founder of aiki-jujutsu, taught [Morihei] Ueshiba[1], and Ueshiba taught his nephew [Noriake] Inoue, mostly through *uke*. As he had a strong body and a lot of fighting spirit, the young Inoue served as a kind of "guinea pig" for Ueshiba in his creation of aikido. Through this intense experience his body could assimilate the essence of aikido [*aiki*] and he later formulated it through the concept of *heiho*.

In Japanese, the expressions 兵法, war method, and 平法, peace method, are both pronounced *heiho*. Therefore, playing with this homophony, Inoue-sensei and then Egami-sensei taught that their respective martial arts were methods – or "ways" – to move from one form of *heiho* to the other; from "war" to "peace." All *waza*, although efficient fighting techniques, were also to be seen and, more important, practiced as techniques to achieve peace with one's practice opponent or in life situations.

As Inoue's disciple, Egami-sensei always spoke of *heiho*. What it was, what it meant. He barely taught us any techniques from Inoue-sensei's art, but having "digested" them and his teachings, he was able to influence the practice of Aoki-sensei in this sense.

---

[1] Morihei Ueshiba, founder of aikido

Rakutenkai members also watched many 8-mm films of Inoue-sensei while we were in Egami-sensei's house, and so did Aoki-sensei.

Heiho is definitely connected to the influence of Egami-sensei, and of course at the same time, *heiho* is, and remains, a mysterious concept that goes far back in time beyond this or that school. Aoki-sensei used to say, "*Heiho* came to me or to Rakutenkai," as a ferment or a fertilizer that would be added to a primary mixture. Later, he said that shintaido was an embodiment of *heiho*. The concepts he developed later on, such as "the world of 'one,'" were an expression of it.

As I see it, Takeda Sokaku taught Ueshiba, who taught Inoue, who taught Egami. All of them had in mind the idea that was finally coined as *heiho* by Inoue. They were talented and very creative artists, but none of them found a specific movement that could convey purely the *heiho* concept, although their arts as a whole contained *heiho*. That's what Aoki managed to do: find a *kata* that embodies *heiho*, war and peace altogether. What is *aiki* in aikido is *heiho* in shin-ei-taido and was incarnated, fixed, in Eiko, then Tenshingoso.

That is how, after the development of Eiko and Tenshingoso, we thought that it would be a good idea to deepen the concept of *heiho,* and we started organizing regular *gasshuku* under the label of "Heiho Kenkyukai." According to the "peace" interpretation of the term, Heiho Kenkyukai meant "research group for peace." Katsuhiro [p. 100] was one of the main practitioners of the Heiho Kenkyu-kai, and during the same period he opened his own karate *dojo*, which he named Heiho Tenshin-kai.

We also studied aikido, individually for some of us and as a group through Egami-sensei's son, Masatake, who was not part of Rakutenkai at that time. He had been studying aikido at the Keio University club with Yamaguchi-sensei, who was known for his ability to use mind control. This *sensei* was a very sweet person, friendly and with a powerful spirit. Also, as son of the Egami family, according to the Japanese custom, Masatake went every year at Oshogatsu[1] with his parents, to pay their respects to In-oue-sensei's house. That is how Inoue-sensei always kept an intentional eye on Masatake. All these were some of the reasons why we asked Masatake-san to teach us aikido during a Heiho Kenkyukai *gasshuku*. He was very good.

All in all, this is how Aoki-sensei and Rakutenkai were able to receive in one way or another the influences of Inoue-sensei and to integrate them into our practice[2].

Then, at an institutional level, working to integrate the *heiho* concept with new discoveries like Eiko and Tenshingoso – which was Aoki's stated intention – was a way for Rakutenkai to enforce our connection with Egami-sensei.

Working for a building company and editing "Karate-do Kata for Professionals"

Around that time [1967], I resigned from working at Eian-ro, and I became the bodyguard and driver for the boss of a building company, Mr. Saito Fuji. He was an acquaintance of Aoki-sensei's sister, Takeko-san. She had a room in the Nogeyama house, and I still remember this very well-dressed lady who worked for a cabaret. When Mr. Saito heard that I had left Eian-ro, he asked Aoki-sensei if he could hire me in Fuji Sangyo, his company, and Aoki-sensei agreed or, one could say, he assigned me there. From that moment, I had my weekends off, and that's how I participated actively in the organization of the Heiho Kenkyukai. In this context, we went to Kujukuri, in Chiba, once a month or at least once every two months, and this is how the photo-taking sessions for the *kata* book edition began. Of course, many members of Rakutenkai participated in this book, but I was the linchpin of it.

---

[1] New Year's festival

[2] On this point, see also the comment of Masatake Egami – in turn Shigeru Egami's son, member of Rakutenkai, head-instructor of the shintaido head-office, and finally Inoue-sensei's late disciple.

We had heard about this book since I was a student. Egami-sensei spoke of it in the typical Japanese way, like, "*Koyu hon ga dekitara ii na!*"[1] and so on. We, who listened to him, thought "I would like to be able to do something for that." And finally, without really knowing how it would finally be published, Egami-sensei asked the one among his students whose *kata* were the most accomplished, Aoki, to take care of the photos. That is how it became a mission for the Heiho Kenkyukai. Around 1969 we did a fundraising campaign, after which I remember going back and forth to the printing company until, by fall 1970, we issued the book.

In fact, I only worked as a bodyguard and driver for the Fuji Sangyo company for two years. During that time, I also studied to obtain a real estate agent license. From the moment I got it, I stopped working physically for the company, but I let the boss use my license. And this is how I was able to devote myself to the publication of the book for a full year.

Becoming conscious of financial issues

I had married Harue [Ishide], the younger sister of Aoki-sensei's wife, Etsuko. At some point she would tell me, "See how much Etsuko is suffering!" and, "Of course, you guys are enjoying it all, getting *satori* or whatever... but look at how much Etsuko is enduring!" I got shocked, and thinking of it, I became the first one among Rakutenkai members to realize – as others did later on – that as far as taking care of finances was concerned, Aoki-sensei wasn't such a good husband.

In the beginning, because Aoki-sensei was the assistant instructor of Egami-sensei and was doing this project for Egami-sensei, the people who kept attending Rakutenkai had the feeling that they were somehow helping Egami-sensei. Aoki-sensei wouldn't think of charging anything. Everyone was contributing

---

[1] "Wouldn't it be great if we could get that book done!"

to a kind of research and development team. He [Aoki] took advantage of our aspiration to grow and, on his side, he was doing the job as volunteer. Besides, Egami-sensei was head instructor of the Tokyu Karate Dojo and as Aoki-sensei was formally working for this company *dojo*, he also got a little salary from the company.

Generally speaking, the money issue wasn't well considered. It was miserable to receive money without any specific reason. When we got issued a diploma, we would pay a registration fee to the Shotokai association, and Shotokai would pay Egami-sensei. Also, when we invited Egami-sensei to our summer or spring *gasshuku* and took exams, we would pay him. But beyond that, the teachers didn't get any formal salary. Of course, another problem of the time was that all the people in post-war Japan were very poor. So, even if we paid an annual fee to the university karate club, it was something like two to three hundred yen, about two to three dollars.

In the case of Rakutenkai, from 1965 to 1971 we were gathered as a kind of community, sharing whatever we had. There wasn't any fee for regular practice, but we would make some kind of donation in material. For example, Japanese have a custom to offer a bag of rice sometimes or specialties at seasonal occasions like *Obon* or *Oshogatsu*. In my case my mom would send some oysters every year from Hiroshima to our teacher. No big deal, but eating was an issue. When I was working in the Chinese restaurant, my boss would always give me the untouched leftovers so that I could bring them back to the people of Rakutenkai.

Thinking of it, it was the time when the "sensei care" tradition started. As everyone was poor, we didn't always eat enough, and neither did Aoki-sensei. For him to have enough energy to give good *gorei*, we ate rice soup, but we provided him with some steak. We kind of force-fed him like a goose to get the "*foie gras*" of his *gorei* [laughs]. Then we didn't have any more money for him to bring back to his home. We just made some kind of small money donation at the end of the *gasshuku* – gathered by one person – to cover his expenses.

That's how Aoki-sensei's wife, Etsuko, had to support their family, doing tea ceremony and flower arrangement. A poster shop too. She would even take care of Rakutenkai members by sharing anything she would have, and many of us innocently accepted. That was a kind of model of Christianity. That is why we were always so impressed by this great woman. On the other hand, beyond Christianity, that had always been a kind of traditional [Japanese] household custom... same as in a Chinese family... people coming to the house are taken care of. Eating together, sleeping together, and always there was a big mother caring for everyone [laughs]. Young guys innocently receiving. Then, if one became successful, one would share resources back or forth. That's the Asian kind of tradition, and it is true that Etsuko did a lot in that way.

Anyway, as far as I am concerned, understanding through my wife's admonition how innocent Aoki-sensei was with financial matters and how much Etsuko was enduring, I came naturally to think, "I have to help this guy," or, thinking of Etsuko, "I have to help this family."

Sogo-budo Renmei

Having become conscious of the problem, I did the best I could to contribute to the community life in materials, and then, as we all got older, I finally set up the Sogo-budo Renmei organization, after we had published the karate book. Accordingly, I started to charge some kind of monthly fee to the people willing to keep studying with Aoki-sensei, including Rakutenkai people. Of course, some of them were not happy because in the earlier Rakutenkai days they always got a free ride; they just had to go along with Aoki-sensei. That's how I got some hard criticism from those people, but it was okay with me as long as I thought I was doing the job properly. My problem started when Aoki-sensei started [laughing] ... kind of cheating. For example, he would teach for free, beside the workshops I organized for him ... [laughing]. Of course, people started to go there and not to the one I organized [laughing]. Later on, I think he did the same thing to my brother Yoshitaka. If he would have gotten paid, we would have been okay somehow – we could have "closed our eyes" to it – but he was teaching for nothing! How could I understand that?

As it went, many other things happened, not only financial ...well, I don't want to talk too much about these sorts of things, but he could do some kind of juggling with people ... using one person to discourage another person, etc. His relationships with different people ... thus raising moral issues to me ... [laughing]. Our relationship became loose the last years of my time in Japan. Finally, in 1975, I left for the United States in order to develop shintaido practice in that country. But that's another story.

Yoshitake MATSUHASHI

The initial interview took place in September, 2004 on the premises of Yoshitake Matsu-hashi's company, and in a particular atmosphere because H.F. Ito and Mr. Matsuhashi had not met since the latter had left Rakutenkai, when Mr. Ito created Sogo-budo Renmei. In addition, Mr. Matsuhashi had recently suffered a stroke that damaged part of his memory. The interview began in a somewhat formal way, warmed up as it went on, and ended in a rather friendly atmosphere. The confirmation of the transcription was conducted by Mieko Hirano in May, 2019 on the same premises of Mr. Matsuhashi's company, of which he had, by then, become honorary president.[1]

Practice of karate

I was born in Odomari, Karafuto Island [Sakhalin], and entered Chuo University in 1961.

The reason why I started to practice karate is particular. My father often talked to me about how amazing this thing called karate was, that karate was a technique to win with a single attack. He practiced karate by himself in the middle of the mountains. He died when I was in high school. We were very close to each other. I even named myself after him, Toranosuke, for a while, to keep his memory alive. I tried to do whatever he would have wanted to do, like some kind of hope for my own life.

That's how I joined the karate club, affiliated with Chuo University's physical training groups. As all the guys close to me left the club before graduation, I didn't keep any friends from there.

Chuo's physical training groups, such as the judo club, cheerleading group, etc., had a "right-wing" feeling, which ran contrary to the general tendency of the students at large. Our group did karate in the Egami style and we were proud to believe that it was different from these other groups. These human relationships helped me and led me to Rakutenkai.

---

[1] **Credits:** Interview: H.F. Ito, P. Quettier. Transcription: K. Hokari. Editing: M. Hirano, P. Quettier. *Translation*: P. Quettier. *Proofreading*: A. Weber, L. Ordeman.

The *keiko* at the time was really demanding. So, I would give myself a good rest and take a day off or even two days if it was really bad. Of course, on that third day when I returned to the *dojo*, I'd take a beating and get tossed out. I was often knocked to the floor of the *dojo*. That probably had something to do with my stroke [laughing]. To tell the truth, I was not invested as much as the others in the *keiko*. But Ito-san, for example, practiced with all his might. His karate was exemplary.

Onozato-sempai took good care of me. I don't know why, but he took me under his wing. He often invited me out to eat, even if nobody believed me when I told them about it, since he had a reputation for being very stingy about his money. His mother ran a small restaurant where I felt at home. I was in my first year when he was in his fourth. Fourth-year students are like parents and role models to the first-years, so much so that the good and bad habits of the fourth-year practitioners are often reflected in those of the first-years. In contrast, first-year and third-year guys usually don't get close to each other.

I also remember being very close to [Tokuhiro] Nishiyama [p. 356], even though we often fought. He was under a lot of pressure as an engineering student. He had to attend classes diligently if he wanted to graduate, unlike me in the law school. I was, in fact, in a situation of relative ease, and probably I tended to impose my ideas on others. I remember him getting angry when he felt cornered.

Tokuhiro and I were the same year, and when he was named the next captain, I thought it was appropriate.

Participation in Rakutenkai

Rakutenkai, which did not bear that name yet, was formed when I was in my fourth year of university. Egami-sensei was then the *shihan* and Aoki-san was his deputy. We saw him as an older brother. Aoki-san was doing a sort of avant-garde *keiko* in a group that included not only us from Chuo University but a lot of other people from other groups as well. I was in my fourth year of university and the deputy captain of the karate club. So, I intentionally devoted my time and energy to Rakutenkai's *keiko*, rather than Chuo's. In a way, I intended to bridge the gap between my karate club and Rakutenkai. I obviously found a lot of pleasure and interest in the *keiko* of Rakutenkai. I was part of it for about three years.

We also practiced the tea ceremony. I remember tea ceremonies in Gumyoji, Yokohoma, and in the Sagamihara Garden. At that time male practitioners were rare. We progressed, and I even obtained the levels of Satsubako and Karamono from the Omotesenke school[1].I remember several *keiko* in the concrete-floored gymnasium of Mitsuzawa. In preparation for the tea ceremony, we practiced holding a bowl of water, filled to the brim, with both arms extended forward. We were ordered to keep it flat with our concentration, but of course, the water spilled over. So, Etsuko-san and Aoki-san passed between us to fill our bowls. By the time we were done, our bodies and the floor were soaked.

I remember another *keiko* running with our *bokuto* somewhere in total darkness. When daylight arrived, the place seemed so strange and dangerous to us that we could not understand how we had done it.

One day we ate a lot of eggs to maintain our stamina, but I have no idea where those eggs came from.

Around then we had a *gasshuku* on the beach of Kenzaki, on the Miura Peninsula, where we also had baptisms for the Rakutenkai church. We started out as a kind of Bible reading group, as far as I remember. I remember visiting Shelhorn-sensei. He was very happy and prepared a large amount of *inari-zushi* for us[2]. No one

---

[1] To understand the levels of the Omote Senke school, see https://fr.wikipedia.org/wiki/Omotesenke.

[2] An inari-zushi is a small pocket of fried, vinegared, and sweetened tofu, which is stuffed with rice and various other ingredients.

dared eat because we were fasting. But since we couldn't be rude, I stopped fasting and ate a lot of it.

Remembering these stories, I get a warm feeling deep down. I have no memory of difficult times, even though I spent days and days without any income, relying on everyone in Giwakai to take care of me. In a way, I was richer then than I am now, truth be told. In fact, I retain a more intense memory of it than that of recent events in my memory and even more so in my thoughts.

No, I really didn't consider other people that much. I took care of myself without worrying too much about others. I dealt with my opponents or partners by relying on my own feelings and my own vision of the world. I truly believed that people around me would change if I changed. I was young. This approach stemmed from my character, which was somewhat unbalanced, I think.

One day Aoki-san told me that Suda-san, his friend, had pointed out to him that he could be playing the role of a father for guys like us who had lost their fathers at a very young age. Aoki was upset about it and repeated it to me several times as we walked together.

Although I appear in some photos of the karate book[1], I didn't take part in the actual editing phase.

I am confusing the first Rakutenkai *gasshuku* with the first *gasshuku* for graduates. They both took place on the beach in Iwai. I only remember negotiating the location.

I have no idea what happened in Rakutenkai after the creation of the Sogo-budo Renmei, in which I did not participate.

Odd jobs and businesses

As I did not continue *keiko* very long after the end of my university studies, my mother never took a dim view of my involvement in Rakutenkai. Anyway, she had great confidence in me.

---

[1] *Karate-do for Professionals* by Shigeru Egami

To earn money, we sold encyclopedias but also sewing machines and knitting machines. I still remember asking Egami-sensei to buy a Brother sewing machine. It was Harue-san who presented this work to us, and we took it as a kind of *keiko*.

We also worked as longshoremen. Longshoremen were hired by the day, early in the morning in Kotobuki-cho or the Noge shopping district. We had to stand on certain street corners and wait to be hired. Today Yokohama Port has completely changed and is filled with many container ships.

I also remember working part-time with Aoki-san at the Sapporo brewery in Ebisu. We stacked cases of beer, which arrived one after another on a conveyor belt, onto pallets to be transported by a forklift. Manual labor was used where machines could not operate. Aoki-san had probably lost his job when the Tokyu Dojo closed, although at the time I didn't think about it. This was after I had graduated from university.

We also set up a flower business. We wanted to build a church with the profits. I must say I did it with hesitation. I neither initiated nor directed it. I think it was a business brought about by Harue-san. Nishiyama was also a part of it. He sold flowers at motels every week. Once we had complaints about cosmos flowers that didn't last for the week.

After graduating from university, I attended the Musashino School for a year. It was an establishment intended to help people in difficulty become independent. After a year I was hired by the Brother sewing machine company. At that time Aoki-san was living in Shioiri, Yokosuka, and I was at the Brother sales office in Yokohama.

About Giwakai

The founder of Giwakai was Mr. Ishikawa. He had practiced karate continuously since high school, first at the Denen Coliseum and then at the Tokyu Dojo. Sometime after entering Hosei University, he got together a group of guys like him and founded a karate club called Giwakai. It must have been during his third year of study. After his graduation the following year, Giwakai needed an instructor and Aoki-san was appointed.

Personally, I started going there about a year after it was founded. Aoki-san said, "Let's go see an interesting group." It was probably during their summer *gasshuku*. After that, I was considered Aoki-sensei's assistant for Giwakai.

I remember Minagawa. He was a key member during the club's fourth year. I also remember Iwase. Minagawa was full of energy. At that time, I asked students to jump in *usagi-tobi* with an outstretched *bo* at arm's length. We thought then that real *keiko* only started after all physical energy had been exhausted. But in Minagawa's case, he couldn't exhaust his energy in a limited time with a single *bo*. Therefore, I had to give him a handicap by making him jump with three *bo* instead of one.

As far as I remember, Kato-san replaced me after I left Rakutenkai. But since the special atmosphere of Giwakai did not match Kato-san's approach, the members kept coming to consult with me. Subsequently, the club broke off its relations with Rakutenkai, and no one retained them.

Giwakai's *keiko* was linked to Egami-sensei's style of karate. But Giwakai was never really admitted as a regular Shotokai group. The participants were, however, recognized as members of the Shotokai student federation, affiliated with the Shotokai, and they had a seat on the board of directors.

Moving forward

I took over the building materials business that Onozato-san ran, but it went bankrupt. At that time Onozato-san was suffering from kidney failure which eventually won out.

After graduating from university and embarking on a working life, I could no longer continue to attend Rakutenkai because my pace of life no longer allowed it. Also, I had learned incidentally that Aoki-san let it be known that Matsuhashi had "graduated" from Rakutenkai, which in diplomatic terms meant that the door was now closed to me. My role in Rakutenkai had been a supporting one, and I didn't think it would be a problem if I left. I am grateful to all Rakutenkai members, especially Aoki-san. Egami-sensei also supported me a lot.

The launch of the Sogo-budo Renmei was quite shocking for Egami-sensei. He would say that he was abandoned by those he thought were his successors. Looking back, it probably could have been handled better than it was, but it is possible that the conditions at the time did not allow it.

I participated in the religious activities of Rakutenkai, but without much enthusiasm. Although baptized, I had nothing more to do with Christianity after my departure.

Kazuo HOKARI

K. Hokari played an undeniably important role during our training [p. 21] and we have maintained a fairly traditional *sempai* to *kohai* relationship. The interview took place in September, 2004, in English, and then the transcript was sent to him. He immediately returned it to us, corrected and enriched. Certain parts of the reworked text had taken on a somewhat argumentative and invigorating turn. His insight into his role first in Rakutenkai, and for eight years in the development of the organizations that continued it, is nevertheless extremely valuable because it allows us to understand some of the invisible processes at work from the outset. After several rounds of proofreading and a translation into French, we were able to grasp the essence of what K. Hokari had wanted to say and proceed with a slight editing of the whole, aiming to facilitate reading while preserving the integrity of his ideas and their context. The final version translated into Japanese was sent to K. Hokari, who approved it in May, 2019. The changes to the Japanese version were then transferred exactly into the English version and then into the French translation.[1]

Childhood and schooling

My parents were born, raised, and trained in the suburbs of the city of Nagaoka, Niigata prefecture. After graduating from college, my father went to Tokyo to work in a grocery store. He then became an independent manager of the store and married my mother. They had five children. The eldest was a girl, followed by four boys, of whom I am the second. I was born in Tokyo in 1943, during the second half of the war. A year after I was born, Tokyo was heavily bombed by the U.S. Air Force. My father feared for his family in the face of such an attack and decided to shelter us all in his hometown until the conflict was over. This is how I came to be raised and educated in Niigata. When I arrived, my parents had nothing more than a fairly large nest egg. My father could have bought a lot of rice soil with this money, but he preferred to leave it in the bank in anticipation of a return to Tokyo, once things had calmed down. Unfortunately, that money was reduced to nothing because of the hyperinflation that hit Japan immediately after the

---

[1] **Credits** : *Interview/Transcription*: P. Quettier. *Editing*: K. Hokari, P. Quettier. *Proofreading*: D. Richardson.

war. Each being the last child in their respective families, my parents could not count on any inheritance, and they had to restart from scratch with their five children. My family was reduced to a state of extreme poverty.

Where I grew up, it was normal to enter the workforce immediately after receiving a secondary school certificate. Most, about 70%, of the students did this, and I was supposed to do the same. However, since our siblings were doing well in school, a teacher recommended that my parents send us to high school. My older brother was already enrolled in high school and, as I was just after him, my parents did not have the financial means to support both of us. This is why I was told to prepare for a job after secondary school. It was a terrible prospect for me, but what could I do at the age of 15? Fortunately, during the year of my certificate, the regional administration set up a competition that allowed any selected secondary student to receive a scholarship to continue to high school. I was lucky to succeed in this competition, along with fifteen other children, out of the twenty or thirty thousand who had presented themselves in the prefecture of Niigata. I was able to go to high school, and I later won another scholarship, which allowed me to enter the University of Niigata in April, 1962.

In fact, the amount of my scholarship made it possible to pay not only my expenses but also those of my older brother [laughs]. It was only three thousand yen a month — about thirty thousand in today's currency — but that small amount was enough to change my life. When I entered university, I rented a small studio. It was my first experience of living independently.

University year and practice of Shotokai karate

As I needed to exercise, I looked for a sports club, and that's how I got interested in karate. The Niigata University Karate Club was attached to the Shotokai school run by Egami-sensei. At that time, 1962, Shotokai was in a period of transition. Egami-sensei introduced a new way of practicing, assisted by Aoki-sensei as future Shotokai leader. But there was a time lag between the innovations taking place in Tokyo and when these changes reached the University of Niigata. When I joined the club, some of the alumni resisted the introduction of new ways of doing things, and I didn't know what to expect. Even practitioners a year older than us were hesitant, and this is how we beginners were immediately exposed to these dissensions. Being isolated in Niigata, we lacked reliable information about this new system being developed in Tokyo. Nor did we have any good instruction. That is why we had to get closer to Tokyo.

The Mecca of the Shotokai world of the time was the Chuo University Karate Club, where Aoki-sensei gave *gorei* under the supervision of Egami-sensei. I went there, and that's how I got to know Aoki-sensei, as well as Ito, who was one of the pillars of the Chuo Club at that time. Another of Shotokai's bases in Tokyo was the Tokyu Karate Dojo, where Kato, Okada, and Jugoro[1] practiced.

In our club, in the absence of strong leadership, we were relatively free to do whatever we wanted. Our senior members were not very seriously involved and as we, the juniors, were very eager to learn this new system, they did not oppose it. In fact, at first, the new system was not that different from the old one, so we didn't have any problems. Over time, our *sempai* finished their university studies and left. We took the reins decisively and implemented the new system. When we entered the fourth year, in the spring of 1965, I became a leader of the group, and at that point we fully joined the new Shotokai movement.

Later, in September, 1965, Aoki-sensei began to develop an even newer *keiko* — more innovative than that of Shotokai — at his home in Nogeyama. At Niigata, we still didn't know about it. After obtaining my university diploma in March, 1966, I pursued postgraduate training until March, 1968. Having passed the torch to the practitioners of the next generation, I was now part of the

---

[1] Yoshitaka Ito.

senior practitioners' circle and could no longer practice with them. However, I continued on my own. After my postgraduate work, I found a full-time job in Tokyo and was able to join Rakutenkai in Yokohama. It was two and a half years after Aoki-sensei initiated his innovations.

How the Niigata University Karate Club joined the practice of Aoki-sensei

Having been very active, our generation had achieved record-setting exam results. But after the hand-off, the next generation did not maintain as strong an educational link with Shotokai headquarters. Not surprisingly, their exam results were miserable. After this collapse, the captain came to ask my advice on the best way to remedy it. I suggested he ask headquarters for the appointment of an experienced Shotokai instructor who had full knowledge of the new system; a system that we senior practitioners had picked up by ourselves in Tokyo. They sent a delegation to Tokyo headquarters to make their request, and that is how Aoki-sensei was appointed as the main instructor for the club at the University of Niigata. It was the beginning of a lasting relationship between Aoki-sensei and the Niigata club.

In a way, the Shotokai school did not strictly control its own education system, and Aoki-sensei was able to use his position at Niigata as a kind of laboratory for the new *keiko* system developed in Rakutenkai. At that time, university clubs were the strongholds of Shotokai karate practice in Japan. Aoki-sensei was only one instructor among many, and the others were not very open to the innovations coming from Rakutenkai, which were so very different from what Egami-sensei had taught them.

Clubs such as Chuo, Gakushuin, and Tokyu resisted the Aoki way. The Niigata UKC did not have the same problem, because it was seen as different, far removed from the headquarters, and Aoki-sensei was already accepted as the main instructor. As for me, I had no personal connection with Shotokai headquarters, because the NUKC was considered marginal, unlike the Chuo or Tokyu Clubs, which were foundational. A few rare people had been chosen by Aoki-sensei, or they had approached him themselves, asking to study with him. But the vast majority of the other members had nothing to do with his new *keiko*.

Being part of Rakutenkai

Whatever the difficulties, I was actively practicing karate at the university. At that time, the *keiko* was so hard that you had to be really motivated to continue, and I often asked myself, "Why is this so interesting to me?" and "Why do I keep going?" I didn't have a clear answer to these questions. I didn't understand what gave me the strength to hang on, and I was wondering "why, but why?" I couldn't find a satisfactory answer. Then, after having participated in the Rakutenkai *keiko* for a while, I began to understand the reason for my enthusiasm: The *keiko* of Aoki or Rakutenkai relieved me of a lot of tension in my everyday life. After *keiko*, I felt relaxed, free from everything. This *keiko* was very demanding, it pushed us to the limit. But over time I understood that this is what provided this liberation from our constricted selves.

It was also around this time that I began to believe in Jesus Christ and was baptized. Aoki-sensei was a Christian. He taught the faith that came to him from the Bible through *keiko* and recommended its study to the members of Rakutenkai. He told us stories from the Bible and sometimes even preached. Many people who came to Rakutenkai had accepted Jesus Christ. I gradually understood that the purpose of *keiko* was to bring me to a condition entirely different from that of ordinary life, and to lead me gently toward my true self. The purpose of *keiko* was to release myself, through body movement, from the tensions, preconceptions, limitations, and obstacles that kept me trapped in everyday life.

Obviously, shintaido is a martial art, and therefore a combat art, but unlike other martial arts, it rests on an essentially religious base. In the end, I was no longer drawn to combat techniques as much as to this aspect, which I experienced both physically and mentally in the practice of shintaido. Beyond the martial technique, which I always liked, I found answers to my big questions: "Why am I here?" "What is the meaning of my life?" shintaido had gradually changed the nature of my questioning, and the theoretical basis for this change was in the Bible.

Christianity and martial arts in Rakutenkai

At that time, and even now, I thought that to be totally free I had to be myself. When you live and act as yourself totally, then you free yourself. And it seemed to me that I could do this through shintaido *keiko*. It could bring me to myself and set me free.

We are born naked and innocent, without preconceptions. As we grow up in the world, we accumulate the knowledge we need to live, grow, and survive, and thus form the basis of our thinking. In doing so, we also develop many thoughts that are not essential to us. These "other thoughts" only serve to satisfy our egos and make our little lives easier. But these ideas take on a dramatic reality when they make us sacrifice living things more than is necessary. When we see a documentary in which lions hunt and eat zebras, we don't feel akin to the lions, do we? Why is that? Because we are *a priori* not predisposed toward this kind of wild killing. However, a lion needs to eat other animals to survive. In the same way, a zebra eats plants, and all the sentient beings on this planet must somehow take life to perpetuate their own. The vegetable plankton feeds the animal plankton, which feeds the small fish, which feeds the big fish, which humans eat. Plants feed herbivores, which feed carnivores. Everything that lives enters a great food chain, and we humans are at the very top. Right thinking teaches us not to kill, but we must, whether plants or animals, because otherwise we could not stay alive. Even vegans must kill plants that have their own life instincts and emotions.

Under such conditions, the least we can do is kill only what it takes to keep us alive and thank the creatures we sacrifice. We must also prepare to sacrifice ourselves one day so that others may live.

When we consider these sacrifices and the pollution that we cause, we must appreciate these things that allow us to live, whatever the quality of our existence, good or bad. But instead, we prefer to forget, and we feel that all these things are owed to us. What is more, we want more than what is necessary out of pure selfishness and lust, which leads to even more sacrifice. All these desires are an expression of our self-centeredness. The more we go in this direction, the more we encounter limits, impediments, and obstacles that generate stress. We move away from our real selves without realizing it, but we want even more to alleviate the stress.

To get out of this vicious cycle we must simplify our lives and get rid of what's useless. The more we reduce our lust and get rid of what's useless, physically and mentally, the more we free ourselves from any barrier, limitation, or impediment and come closer to our true self. However, it is almost impossible to free ourselves from our excesses by sheer will; whatever effort we put into it is still a form of clinging. That's why shintaido *keiko* is such a good tool to tackle this biological atavism. Shintaido transforms our mind through our body and frees us from the unnecessary desires we have accumulated in our life. To keep this spirit of simplicity strong in us, we must continue to polish ourselves through *keiko*, or by any similar means, and keep our ego instinct under control.

Well, I'm sounding a bit heavy or didactic here, but I say all this to give an understanding of what underlies my approach.

I interpret the Bible by considering that the words of Jesus were intended for poor and uneducated people, two thousand years ago, and that he illustrated his words though example so the people could understand what he meant.

"Jesus said to him, I am the way, the truth and the life; no one will know the Father, except through me." [St. John 14:6], means "what I [Jesus] tell you is the way to reach yourself, your true self, and your real life. No one can do this without doing what I have done myself."

And, *"Whoever seeks to save his life will lose it and who will lose his life will save it."* [St. Luke 17:33] means "if you seek to maintain your life with unnecessary care, you will lose it; and if you are ready to give your life as soon as necessary, you will save yourself."

Aoki-sensei, an enigma

Such ideas came from Aoki-sensei, who often gave us food for thought during meetings. In this sense, he was a good guide. On the other hand, he was himself a great problem for me and an obstacle to achieving this goal of self-liberation. Since we were very close to him, we always tried to copy what he was doing. This copying constitutes the very basis of *keiko*[1]. But in many cases, what Aoki-sensei said and taught was different from what he did. So, I always found myself embarrassed by what Aoki-sensei actually did, while I was trying to conform to what he was teaching. His theories and ideas were very good, but when we witnessed his actual behavior [laughs] we could only see the contradiction, and we were troubled by it. As his students, we had to accept everything — lessons, ideas, and behavior — but that left us in complete confusion.

I think many people have been disappointed with him and have left shintaido because of this difference between his behavior and his teachings.

---

[1] From 稽 *kei* « think » et 古 *ko* « ancient matters », used in the practice of traditional arts.

I myself was disturbed for a long time because I couldn't make the distinction, and I finally had to face the facts: Aoki-sensei's actions were not in harmony with his thoughts. They differed in many cases. The problem was that he demanded approval for everything he did — technique, teaching, ideas, behavior, art, and everything else. This left many people in a great state of confusion.

One of the points of his teaching was that we should always work to purify ourselves. We had to free ourselves from everything. But in ordinary life, I could not accept some of his actions, and especially his morality, which was particularly unacceptable to me. I'm sorry to say, but it was not acceptable by the standards of morality that he himself taught us. His actual standards of morality were different from those he taught us. He was too irresponsible and devoid of ordinary morals. In Japan, some twenty or so years ago, this sort of thing was not as tolerated as it was in the United States or Europe. People weren't liberated in terms of sexual and other morals. So, he did certain things in secret, but rumors eventually spread, and they disturbed us enormously. I think many people have left shintaido and Aoki-sensei because they could no longer bear to accept his teaching being so obviously contradicted by his behavior.

To say it from a more distanced perspective, when Aoki-sensei established Rakutenkai, to which an elite group of people devoted themselves, the aim was to create a completely new *keiko*, for the benefit of people living in modern society. One could therefore consider that Rakutenkai was a place of experimentation, in which ordinary morals, rules, and common sense had been abolished in favor of the "chaos" of creativity. That's why there were no belts, rules, formal memberships, or membership fees in Rakutenkai. It might have been acceptable in this creative space for Aoki-sensei to act openly as he saw fit, without regard for ordinary rules.

However, when he and his management team set up a new organization in order to offer this new practice, shintaido, to the greatest number of people, it was no longer a question of creativity but rather of popularization, and everyone then had to respect the value system in place in society. This is why Shintaido Kyokai was established with rules, a *keiko* curriculum, and a diploma system. From then on, no one, including Aoki-sensei, could afford to behave simply as one pleased.

But these kinds of constraints ran counter to his creative and artistic inspirations. That's why he couldn't help but violate the rules and morals, and why he did it in secret. It would have been ideal if Aoki-sensei could create the new *keiko* within Rakutenkai and disseminate the results in the Shintaido Kyokai, keeping each of his roles distinct — creator in Rakutenkai and reverent master of the Shintaido Kyokai. In any event, we would never have had enough staff to divide responsibilities into two separate groups and, even if it could have been so, it is unlikely that Aoki-sensei would have succeeded in distinguishing his two roles.

Development of an international shintaido organization

In 1979, I found myself at a turning point in my life due to a very serious traffic accident. After I recovered from this accident, my physical condition no longer allowed me to engage in demanding physical practices as I had in the past. This is why I had to abandon the idea of becoming a professional shintaido instructor. Until then, I hadn't really chosen between becoming a professional instructor or continuing in the corporate world. I had a full-time job and it was getting harder and harder to do both. I had made up my mind to make the choice before my fortieth birthday. The accident forced me to choose when I was thirty-seven.

Although I was no longer able to fully invest myself in both *keiko* and full-time work with heavy responsibilities, I still wanted to make myself useful in one way or another. Aoki-sensei had already decided that Egami[1] would be his successor as the main

---

[1] Masatake Egami

instructor in Japan, and Minagawa assumed the role of manager. Shintaido Kyokai was in bad financial shape, and no one had the business skills to run it as an independent organization. I thought I could use my knowledge of management and administration to contribute to the common good of shintaido.

In the end, however, I was never able to get involved in the Shintaido Kyokai, because it was placed, surreptitiously, under the direct control of Aoki-sensei. Fugaku was abroad — in America, France, and Britain — to propagate shintaido there. I chose to invest my energies in international shintaido activities. In 1980, we organized the first international *gasshuku* in San Francisco. The second one took place in Great Britain in 1982, and the third one in France in 1984. I coordinated these events as manager of the International Shintaido Federation [ISF], and I was also on the front line for the implementation of its statutes and the development of its organization. Ito, for his part, was the initiator of a complete review of the technical curriculum, in collaboration with Aoki-sensei.

This is how I distanced myself from the Japanese organization, which represented, from this standpoint, only one national group among others. Japanese shintaido was then led by Jugoro, who was very competent. His opinion, as I understood it, was that in order to lead the organization of shintaido in Japan, the manager had to put limits on Aoki-sensei's desires and actions. Until then, Aoki-sensei had been able to act as he pleased. But shintaido could not be run as a healthy organization by continuing to allow that. For shintaido to be run as a business, Aoki-sensei had to operate within certain boundaries. But he couldn't bring himself to do that, and that's why he maneuvered Jugoro's dismissal, or, to put it another way, why he made Jugoro give up the idea of being the leader. This happened after the international *gasshuku* in 1980.

Another reason for Jugoro's departure was his dissatisfaction with the development of the international shintaido movement. He believed that, as the manager of Japanese shintaido, he must be the de facto leader of International Shintaido. But Ito [Fugaku] and I had implemented a different system. That's why the first international curriculum was prepared without him. Not surprisingly, he complained that his role was not being respected. And since, at the same time, Aoki-sensei was putting strong pressure on him to break free from the limits imposed on him in Japan, Jugoro decided to stop managing the Shintaido Kyokai.

Upon reflection, it is clear that Aoki-sensei started Rakutenkai and created shintaido, with the help of the elders of Rakutenkai. It was he who had initiated the founding of the Shintaido Kyokai, with the idea of spreading shintaido. He was the engine of the Shintaido Kyokai and, in a way, its owner. That is why, quite naturally, he was the *de facto* leader of the organization. Understanding this, we had repeatedly asked him to assume an official leadership position. But he always refused, saying he did not feel competent. Therefore, others had to do it for him. But behind the scenes, he maintained strict control over the management, taking advantage of his position as founder and *sensei* of all the members.

When Aoki-sensei said something, everyone listened to him and followed him, even if it differed from what had been decided in the meeting. In this way, he placed himself above the rules and the organization, deflected any interference, and did what he wanted with Shintaido Kyokai. If problems did arise, he would step back and position himself so that he was never held responsible. This is why, as I speak[1], incredible as it seems, Shintaido Kyokai still does not have any legal standing in Japan! It is not registered with tax authorities. It is simply a *de facto* association that brings together a group of people with the same hobby, without official status. I proposed that it be registered as a nonprofit organization [NPO], but Aoki-sensei never wanted that. My feeling is that he feared being constrained by statutes and having to assume certain responsibilities in this NPO.

[1] September 15, 2006

When Jugoro took over management after Minagawa, he carried out an uncompromising audit of the financial situation of Shintaido Kyokai. Based on his findings, he entered into an official agreement with Aoki-sensei, stipulating his roles and functions in the organization, as well as his salary. I was there to witness this agreement between Jugoro and Aoki-sensei. Obviously, this was not enough.

I can understand Jugoro's departure. At some point, people like Fugaku, Jugoro, and me had to establish a way to continue our relationship with shintaido. But Aoki-sensei's domination made it impossible. So, we could do it our way, we could leave Japan, or we could resign. Jugoro was very competent. He protected the organization in Japan from Aoki-sensei's interference. In establishing the International Shintaido Federation, our idea was to do the same for shintaido overseas. Obviously, we couldn't say it out loud, but that was the hidden goal [laughs].

In fact, it would be difficult to run Shintaido International from Japan because, while people were enthusiastic about the project at the time of the international *gasshuku*, they would not care much about it when they got home and became preoccupied with their everyday business. Aoki-sensei did not like, perhaps even abhorred, seeing this international organization run so independently. He was its Honorary President, and we had created a position for him as Director of Research, paying him some kind of license fee. But the management of everything else was done without him. We had done internationally the same thing that Jugoro had attempted at the national level. Such a course was necessary if we wanted to ensure the growth of a shintaido dissemination system. Fugaku and I agreed to such an arrangement in order to separate the theoretical Aoki from the practical Aoki [laughs]. It seems clear that he did not like being put in such a position and, later, when I abandoned my position as chairman[1], he

---

[1] See under.

immediately volunteered for the post [laughs] at the international meeting that took place in Boston in 1990. At that point, the ISF began to lose shape and eventually stopped working [laughs].

Departure from shintaido

Since I was still eager to learn Aoki-sensei's shintaido, I had to change my position depending on what I wanted to achieve. I was sometimes chairman of Shintaido International and sometimes a student of Aoki-sensei. This put me in a difficult situation because he had never been able to clearly distinguish between the two positions. It had become particularly difficult for me to remain a student in the "Aoki world." I told myself that I had been able to grow up in this world as if in a sanctuary, an area protected from danger, the way young animals are protected by their parents. However, just as young animals are eventually set out on their own, exposed to the world, the shintaido practitioner must emancipate himself according to the *shu*, *ha*, and *ri* steps of the traditional process in *keiko*.

So, sometime after a *gasshuku* in France, around 1985, I started to feel cramped in my position. However, I was not sure how to get out of it. At that time, we had regular *keiko*, two to three times a week at the Headquarters *dojo* and the Tokyo Gymnasium. One Saturday, while I was lying on my couch, half asleep, listening to classical music, I suddenly had a clear vision in which I saw two images floating separately, one of the Tokyo Gymnasium and another of my office at work. These floating images gradually approached each other in the air. They grew closer and closer, until they merged. I understood that the image of the office symbolized my work life and that of the gymnasium my life in shintaido. They had been separate activities, and in my vision they were becoming one. It was an epiphany, a kind of enlightenment, a *satori*: "Oh, I no longer need to continue practicing shintaido." Working in business and practicing shintaido became one and the same activity for me. They melted and united within me. "Now I can do away with shintaido *keiko* and dedicate myself fully to the business." My everyday activity had become my *keiko*. I thought, "The purpose of *keiko* is to reach your true self and express it; you can do the same without the *dojo keiko*. You no longer have to teach in a *dojo*." I suddenly had a clear realization: Twenty-three years after I started in karate at age eighteen, I found myself out of the world of *keiko*! I bought a bottle of premium Cognac and asked to meet with Aoki-sensei. I offered him the Cognac, I told him about my *satori*, and I said, "Thank you very much for teaching me all these years. I have now finished my shintaido studies!" He accepted my explanation and gave me his blessing.

On a practical level, however, I was still the manager of Shintaido International, and I could not rid myself of that responsibility so easily. I had to pass the function on to someone else. In fact, it took me another three years. In 1988, during the international *gasshuku* in Japan, I transferred my management function to Funakawa, and I retired without any regrets!

In my business, my job is to provide the best technical service to customers who use our products. To do this, I teach them how to improve the performance of their factories by using the products and technologies that our company provides. It is about teaching, which is very close to *gorei* in the shintaido sense of the term. This service is "free" because the cost of training is already included in the purchase price. Working to get our customers to get the most out of our products was a great way to bring the shintaido spirit into my work.

Even if I have thousands of criticisms of Aoki-sensei's bad points, I am also aware that the essential ideas of shintaido originated with him. He has two sides: the very good and the very bad. He is quite interesting to observe in his entirety. The good and bad points of ordinary people are measured on this kind of scale [holding his hands slightly apart], but Aoki-sensei requires this kind of scale [holding his hands much farther apart]. I think he cannot be appreciated according to our usual standards [laughs]!

Yasuko SAITO

We met Y. Saito during the 1970s when we accompanied a foreign visitor, who wished to take lessons in ikebana and the tea ceremony, to her home. We remembered her as an energetic and very committed person. We saw her again with pleasure for this first interview in the spring of 2005, conducted through H.F. Ito. We transcribed the interview very quickly, and we took advantage of a subsequent visit during the summer of the same year to submit the transcription to her. Having reading it, Y. Saito expressed her strong annoyance. Two months later, she sent us a new text, which she had heavily rewritten and, we must say, quite "flattened," telling us in the clearest of terms to publish it as is.[1]

My past

I was born on July 26th, 1935 in Kawasaki. My father is from Aomori prefecture and my mother from Niigata prefecture. I have two older sisters and a younger sister. My father worked in an electrical company in Kawasaki and then was relocated to the Hatano substation. Since he was an engineer and designed pylons, he was obliged to go to work to address the problems that arose during severe air raids, major storms, or typhoons. His work was therefore not very pleasant for his family life.

I have very fond memories of the period just before I started primary school. My family was wealthy, and at the school sports party my father was invited and seated in a place of honor. I was referred to as a "corporate girl." When it was time for the big end-of-year clean-up, there were always a few young men from my father's company who came to help us. I remember it as a time when I was loved by people around me. Then my father was transferred to Hodogaya Substation in Yokohama when I started primary school and our family moved nearby.

With the arrival and intensification of the war, many employees of my father's company were called up, so my father had to

---

[1] **Credits:** *Interview*: H.F. Ito, P. Quettier. *Transcription*: H. Hokari. *Editing*: Y. Saito, P. Quettier. *Translation*: P. Quettier. *Proofreading*: G. Bullen, L. Seaman.

work harder and with heavier responsibilities. He finally died of overwork in June, 1944, having succumbed to tuberculosis.

The war ended in 1945. My father had saved a lot of money for the education of his children and the construction of a house. But the city had been completely burned down during the war. The money in the bank could not be used because all the banks had been blocked. Moreover, the banknotes stored in the cupboards, as well as the government bonds, had become only paper without any value.

It was from that moment that our family became poor. After the war, there was nothing left in the shops. To eat and survive, we went to the peasants to obtain rice and vegetables in exchange for clothes, pottery, etc.

I had never been able to speak with my mother about the disappearance of a certain doll bought by my father for me and my sister. And then, a few years later while we were visiting an acquaintance of the family, I was surprised to find my doll. It was dressed in different clothes but it was mine. In exchange, we had obtained a backpack full of rice and sweet potatoes. I left there with a heavy heart.

I was in middle school when my family became even poorer. I was forced to stop my studies because my mother could no longer pay for my schooling. My older sister had gone to girls' school and then to normal school. My other older sister had gone to girls' school and then to nursing school. My mother wanted her daughters to graduate and to be economically independent.

As for me, after my last year of middle school, I entered high school by attending evening classes, and during the day I worked in a small sewing machine company. I was sad to leave my middle school friends who were going to normal high school. My mother suffered from this situation even more than I did. She felt so guilty for not having been able to provide for the education of her daughter.

My little sister was able to finish high school in Yokohama thanks to the work of two people, my mother and me. However, she died of an intestinal obstruction at the age of twenty. From that moment, my mother and I lived together. Life was getting a little easier but I was starting to wonder if it was a good thing to continue like this.

After graduating from high school, I found a job as a receptionist and tuition collector at a sewing school. It was possible to take evening classes there and work in exchange. Unfortunately, the teacher in charge made me work like a real maid and I had no time left to study. So, I left this school to go to another sewing school, the Juji school, and take classes during the day.

Then, as I had to work, I finally left this school and found a job in the offices of a small company making *sembei*, Japanese rice cakes. It was around this time that I met a very reputable floral art teacher. I started taking his classes, and later I met Etsuko-sensei there. One day she invited me to her house, and that's how I started to see the Aoki family. I made rapid progress in floral art, became a teacher, and taught two courses for my own teacher.

A little later, not long before 1965, at the suggestion of Aoki-sensei, I also started to take a tea ceremony course with a master of flower arrangement. I liked it and I thought I could dedicate my life to it. I then heard about a wonderful tea ceremony teacher who lived in Kamakura and was well-known in tea circles in Kanagawa Prefecture. He had a reputation as a very strict person. When I walked into his house, I felt something very powerful that I couldn't put into words. I then asked very formally that he would accept me among his students. From there, I took his classes without missing one for decades.

And then it happened that tea classes fell at the same time as flower classes and I had to make a choice. I had begun to realize that this world of floral art did not really correspond to me. I felt more attracted by the study of the tea ceremony which, as we know, includes floral art, but also the culinary arts, clothing, pottery, in short everything. In the end, feeling more in tune with this way of tea, I chose to devote myself to it and left the path of floral art.

I followed the lessons of my tea teacher until his death in 1987. I am truly grateful to him for his teaching.

Meeting with Aoki-sensei

When I started going to Aoki-sensei, I met people there who had come to learn martial arts, most of whom were university students. Then, without really knowing how, I started to be part of the group. I just wanted to be there, and I often came there after my day's work. It was a time when Aoki-sensei's house was always open and there was always someone there. The first thing that surprised me was that everyone called Etsuko-sensei "Madam,"[1] whereas for my part, I considered her a master.

We engaged in various activities: martial arts, Bible study, and church services. As for me, as I had a job, I did not attend everything. I was also surprised that everyone sat in a circle. Even at the end of a martial practice, we would sit in a circle and bow to the center. In Japan, in general, the teacher sits in front, the students sit in rows at some distance, and then we bow to each other. Even at my house, when my father was still alive, he sat in the upper seat[2], especially on special occasions such as New Year's Day, etc. I once asked Aoki-sensei about it. I think he replied that it was because there was God at the center. I was really surprised, and at the same time it allowed me to understand why Etsuko-sensei was called "Okusan." I felt unable to leave this group anymore.

After the *keiko*, we ate a meal that Etsuko-sensei had prepared. Most of the time the meal was rice, cooked in lots of water with vegetables. It was a very simple meal, but how good it was! When I watched Etsuko-sensei cook, she cut the hard cabbage stalks

[1] Okusan.
[2] Called the *kamiza*.

into small pieces and cooked them with the rest. I'm sure she was having a hard time "making ends meet."

During and after meals, we talked a lot with Aoki-sensei. Of course, the conversation was mostly about *keiko*, how to do *kata* and *waza*. Everyone was crazy about *keiko*. Looking back, I think that having lived together and shared this experience was a wonderful moment, etched forever in the memory of those who participated in it. A conversation about Van Gogh prompted me to go to the museum. Then I went to listen to a concert conducted by Seiji Ozawa, attend a Noh theater performance, or even visit the Imperial Villa of Katsura in Kyoto with Aoki-sensei. It was from this time that I learned to see things for myself, in my own way.

The group grew larger and larger and began to call itself Rakutenkai. This name seems to mean that, "We suffer in this world; therefore, we rejoice in paradise," A little later, a youth group was formed, high-level students began to teach, and much later an office was opened in Shinjuku. Each person began to walk freely on their own path.

As for me, I wanted to progress in the way of tea ceremony, but at the same time I realized that Rakutenkai was for me an important and joyful place of learning, as well as a precious place for prayer. Everyone in the group was warm and positive. Here was my base, my "base camp."

Rakutenkai practitioners

Over time, I got to know each person in the group and made friends. I met some wonderful people there, either through the practice of martial arts or through the tea ceremony.

With regards to the tea ceremony, one day a person I liked to watch making tea arrived late for class. When I asked him why, he explained to me that he had arrived at Sakuragicho station, the closest to Etsuko-sensei's house, without having been able to prepare himself and that he had therefore taken some time to do this before arriving. I knew that one had to prepare before attending a lesson, but I had never met a person who took it so seriously. This renewed my way of attending lessons.

Another episode is about the practice of martial arts. On my way to the edge of the Tamagawa River to practice, I met a practitioner standing by himself and holding a long stick in front at arm's length for a long time without moving. However, he continued to chat with me non-stop until the end of his practice. And then one day he led a tea ceremony at my house. I was then surprised to see how elegant, light, and clear his gestures were when handling the long-handled bamboo ladle. Here is someone capable of learning with all his strength, without sparing himself, while keeping a good figure and grace, and whose whole personality was thus deeply influenced! A strong personality produces a strong *kata* and *waza*. I then heard that this person had started a business and was continuing to give it his best.

My experiences

I remember a *gasshuku* in which we did a strange exercise: first, we stood in two lines looking in the same direction, then each person in the back line did *tsuki* toward the back of the person in the front line. If the person in the front line felt it, they moved to avoid the *tsuki*. I didn't sense anything. Then Aoki-sensei came and did *tsuki* behind my back and, to my surprise, I could feel his *tsuki* coming. As this worked well, he moved on, and again, I felt nothing.

Being the oldest of the practitioners, when we did *usagi-tobi* I could not continue like the others did. And then one day, I suddenly felt very light and I could continue without stopping! And when I turned around, I saw that Aoki-sensei was right behind me. This kind of mysterious thing happened to me another time and there it was a *goreisha* who was behind me. I wondered, "so this is body energy! He sent me his good energy." Since then, when I visit sick friends, I shake their hands to send them good energy.

From the moment I started to understand this kind of phenomena, I could see mysterious things. For example, one night, when I had been looking at the vertical index finger of my hand for some time, I could see a kind of white smoke coming out of it. I immediately told this to Aoki-sensei and he said to me: "Ah well, you will become different. It would be good if you did more *keiko*." After that, I often saw this white smoke, but today I don't see it any more.

A long time ago, when we did *keiko* at night in Nogeyama Park, we practiced Tenso as was often the case at that time. This is a technique that consists of raising your arms towards the sky with your hands open, palms up, and continuing to push towards the sky as if you wanted to push it higher and higher. That night I was in a lot of pain and I couldn't hear anything, not even the order to stop, but at some point, I stopped suffering and I saw a white corolla above me. It followed me when I moved and, looking at the others, I saw that everyone had this same white corolla. It was a truly mysterious experience. And then, at some point, I noticed that Etsuko-sensei and Aoki-sensei were sitting not far from us and watching us. After that, I talked about what I had experienced to Aoki-sensei and he quietly told me that it was normal: "We call this white corolla a halo, like the one worn by the Buddha and the Christ." This experience dates from a very long time ago, but I remember it very clearly.

From that time, something inside me kept growing and I started to be interested in things outside the world of *keiko*.

Tetsuo HANAKI

At the start of the study, we had known T. Hanaki for a long time without this relationship ever going beyond the formal stage. For their part, H.F. Ito and T. Hanaki had maintained a brotherly relationship since their Rakutenkai years, and had often visited each other during trips to the country where the other lived. The interview, in the spring of 2005, greatly benefited from this mutual friendship, which greatly facilitated its conduct. Later, T. Hanaki facilitated the meeting with T. Koyama [p. 191], whom H.F. Ito knew very little at that time. The Japanese text validation interview took place in May, 2019 in Toyama through Mieko Hirano.[1]

Family, childhood, and training in Toyama

I was born in 1945 in Shinminato in Toyama Prefecture.

The family on my mother's side was wealthy. She owned a lot of land and ran a *geisha* house and a Japanese restaurant. My grandfather came to live with his wife's family[2]. My late mother had studied teaching. Before the war, my father worked for a shirt store in Tokyo. Since he was the second son in the family, I assume that his parents asked him to earn his own living. Then he was called up for war, and when he returned, he got married immediately, even before the war was over. It was around 1948 that he set up his own roofing business, at the age of twenty-four.

The city where I live, Shinminato, has changed a lot. It is a city full of history, and there was a time when it was more prosperous than Kanazawa or Niigata, especially the Kitamaebune district. In the 8th century, the poet Otomo no Yakamochi stayed there and

---

[1] **Credits:** *Interview*: H.F. Ito, P. Quettier. *Transcription*: S. Watanabe. *Editing*: M. Hirano. *Translation*: P. Quettier. *Proofreading*: G. Bullen, L. Seaman.

[2] In Japan, which is a patriarchal society, it is more customary for the wife to go and live in her husband's family home (if the husband is the eldest, the couple then ensures the continuity of the "house"). In some cases, however, as here, it is the husband who goes to live in his wife's family home. This can happen if the "house" has only daughters, in which case the eldest daughter's husband adopts the name of the "house" (as in the case of Takeo Handa, in this book, p. 197).

worked on the Man'yoshu[1]. An emperor also stayed there. The city prospered until the 13th century and was a bright spot culturally, as evidenced by the castle of Hojozu. Economically, it is a fishing town whose inhabitants are known for their frankness and generosity. This temperament is quite atypical in Toyama prefecture. Maybe that's why the residents of Shinminato are so excited about high school baseball.

In college and high school, I was in fragile health, but I did not have a complex about it. I liked studying, and I don't remember fighting. There were of course strong gang leaders, but they did not persecute the weak; on the contrary, they defended them. By playing with my comrades, my health gradually improved and I became stronger. Sometimes I even had the upper hand during our sumo games.

I entered Takaoka High School, the best school in Toyama Prefecture. I didn't really want to go to high school, but my relatives strongly encouraged me to. I would have preferred Shinminato high school, but a middle school teacher begged me to choose Takaoka, which had a better reputation. Later, I realized that he mainly encouraged me to raise the college ranking. In the end, my high school life held little interest for me.

University years and practice of karate

After high school, many of my classmates entered state universities[2]. I didn't really see why I should go to university. In high school I had taken classes seriously but sometimes wondered what I was doing there. When I had to choose a university, I

---

[1] The Man'yoshu 万葉集 (literally "Collection of ten thousand leaves") is the first anthology of Japanese poetry dated around 760, containing 4,516 poems (divided into 20 volumes) composed between the 4th and 8th centuries, on various subjects such as nature, love, or travel and finding their inspiration in traditional Japanese legends.

[2] In Japan, state universities and private universities coexist. Some private universities, such as Keio or Waseda, are highly rated, but the most prestigious are clearly the state universities, which are also less expensive; the first being that of Tokyo (Todai) and the second that of Kyoto (Kyodai).

vaguely thought of astrophysics or geophysics, but my teacher told me that I was not good enough for these disciplines. At the last moment, I opted for letters, took the exams for Chuo and Keio Universities, and passed Chuo. Then I was made to understand that it would be foolish not to also try to enter a state university. So, I applied for Niigata University, where I was admitted. I chose to read law, like that, without thinking.

In college, I wanted to play rugby, but I was not accepted because of my small size. As I would have liked to be able to protect people, I thought, "Why not practice a martial art?" I was invited by members of the karate club, and I went there to have a look. They also offered judo and kendo, but I had an additional reason to prefer karate. There was a very cute high school girl in my household who was being courted by a 3rd dan judo boy and another 2nd dan kendo boy. To attract her attention, I therefore felt compelled to choose karate. If I have taken up judo or kendo, I could not have become their rival. Karate was more difficult, but I couldn't give up in front of these two boys.

There was a big earthquake in Niigata in 1967. It was a shock to me. I said to myself "My parents raised me up until now, but from now on I want to be able to take charge of my own life." This earthquake was a trigger. Every cloud has a silver lining.

Training at the karate club was very tough for me. The captain at this time was Keiichiro Suzuki. His style of *keiko* was identical to that of the Chuo University club. To our eyes as first-year novices, he seemed like a god. The karate practiced in this club was completely different from what I had imagined. At that time the club was practically split in two. There were two fourth-year students, Minagawa and Kita, who had practiced Shotokan karate for three years in high school. Minagawa had even been the captain. These two encouraged us to hit the *makiwara* as well. This lasted until a visit by Aoki-sensei, during the summer course in my third year.

Minagawa and Kita knew the basic techniques of Shotokan. As I wanted to become strong, I had taken them as a model and, by training seriously, I had been able to obtain a black belt in two years, instead of the normal four. In the end, we had three black belts, and all the others were white belts. I must say that I was not happy to sometimes have to follow the *gorei* of a lower-level person, even if they had more seniority in the club. At that time, there were about sixty newcomers to the club each year, but we lost some with each *gasshuku*. There was a *sempai* named Kamiya, who came to give the *gorei*. He was a distinguished man, who reminded us of Nemuri Kyoshiro[1]. He said proudly, "I can avoid the first cannon shot." His Taikyoku-sho was very good, and we wanted to match him. This was before I met Aoki-sensei.

Among the club members, we often wondered, "Is our karate good?" or "Is it real karate?" while drinking *sake*. I remember we referred to a karate book published by Otsuki-shoten Publishing as if it was a Bible.

How Aoki-sensei managed the club

More than anything else, we needed a leader. One day, we went to a *gasshuku* in Haguro, run by the Chuo University karate club, to take exams. We wore dirty *keikogi* because we thought that a dirty *keikogi* was proof of intensive and hard practice. That's where I first met Aoki-sensei. It left me with the impression that he loved drinking *sake*. But he failed almost all of us, saying, "Niigata University is filthy! Your atmosphere is too dirty!" During the *gasshuku*, he asked me to attack him in *tsuki*. When I did so, I had the impression of receiving a huge log of wood on my arm! I thought to myself, "This guy is amazing!" Cho-san, who had passed the exam, then invited him to the Niigata club's summer *gasshuku*. I was in my third year at the time.

---

[1] Nemuri Kyoshiro is a samurai character from Renzaburo Shibata's novels. He embodies the figure of a nihilistic dandy, wielding the sword with great dexterity.

Before the arrival of Aoki-sensei, the elders and the fourth-years taught us during the courses. We impatiently looked forward to these courses. The summer one lasted a week, including travel. For a two-hour *keiko*, we started with a two-kilometer run, then *usagi-tobi* for twenty to thirty minutes. Then came the *kihon-waza* and finally the *katas*. Actually, we only did Taikyoku because it was the only one we knew, especially when Kamiya-san was leading. Of course, sometimes we also did Ten-no-kata and Chi-no-kata.

After Aoki-sensei took over the management of the club, the *keiko* became extremely rigorous. At one point in my third year, I thought to myself, "Okay, you are starting from scratch!" I had been thinking that I was finally a bit of an authority with the younger ones, but in fact, I was starting from scratch! [laughs] In general, it was a third-year who took care of the *jumbi-taiso*. Then Aoki-sensei took over and we started with *kaikyaku-sho*, followed by five hundred *moro-geri*. It was extremely hard to whip both legs together straight ahead. However, I was sure that I had made the right choice and I had complete confidence in him. I found there the novelty that I was looking for and I was impressed by this extraordinary way in which he had swept aside my *tsuki* ... but above all I had seen his own *moro-geri* facing Egami-sensei: really high, up to Egami-sensei's head. This is how naturally, very slowly, I began to believe that our karate was the strongest and most effective; we were training so hard. I also began to testify without any complexes to those around me.

At that time, I was able to do *usagi-tobi* for four kilometers. Those who practiced a lot gradually became indifferent to the question of which karate was stronger. Those who did not practice seriously knew theoretically that this karate was good but did not know it with their body; so, they were tempted to look elsewhere, to other types of karate, "just in case." Aoki-sensei's karate, if you practiced it seriously, made you efficient and strong. I felt I was in the right place. The more *moro-geri* I did, the more flexible my body became and the higher I could jump, a bit like in the photo of *moro-geri* published in the book *Karate-do Kata for Professionals*[1]. And there were several of us who became capable of doing it, like Koyama and Kaneda. Moreover, thanks to Aoki-sensei's *keiko*, our club opened to others. When we went to Tokyo, we met incredible people, and that encouraged us to progress.

I was enjoying getting stronger, so I forged ahead without questioning myself. At one point, Hokari-san's younger brother went to Tokyo for a while and came back wearing a white belt[2]. This shocked many members of the club, but as far as I was concerned, I didn't care; I was simply enjoying the *keiko*. Just like when we collectively failed, it encouraged me to practice more seriously. My life was essentially centered on the *keiko*. It was a great time!

Each time Aoki-sensei came, he taught different things. When he taught Tenso — in 1967 or 1968, in my fourth year — we did it like everything we did, hard and relentlessly until we were exhausted. Afterwards, I may have felt a weird feeling in my *koshi* or funny thoughts going through my head, like "Why do we have to do this?" But the feeling "Whatever, just do it and that's all!" won out every time.

Participation in the Rakutenkai

From my fourth year, I started going to Nogeyama to practice in three-day/two-night sessions. I remember those *keiko* well. We attacked each other with the *bokuto*, we did Eiko with the *bo*, or we meditated while carrying containers full of water at arm's

---

[1] EGAMI S. (1970), *Karate-do Kata for Professionals*, Rakutenkai ed., p.94.

[2] The members of Rakutenkai had decided by mutual agreement to return to wearing white belts, to ensure equality between the members (some of whom did not come from the world of martial arts) and in the spirit of a "new beginning." Takeo Handa had devoted three months of his student life to an intensive practice session with Rakutenkai, and had returned proudly wearing his white belt. This testimony from Hanaki indicates the staggering effect that this measure may have had on some of the karate practitioners. For more details on this episode, see T. Handa's account.

length. I would sometimes say to myself, "Why did I come from so far away to do such a crazy thing?" When I think about it now, I see that it was the foundation for what subsequently made my life, but I didn't understand it at the time...and I wondered what I was doing, paying my own travel expenses, and practicing at times of the day when I should have been in bed!

It was also the time when all the members of the group were Christians. So, I seriously read the Bible, to understand Christianity and believe in Jesus Christ, too. But the more I read, the more questions and doubts I had. I was still surprised to see that Hokari-san was completely invested in it! I really liked Bertrand Russell, perhaps because he was agnostic. I also liked Hiroshi Suekawa, professor of Ritsu-meikan University, in particular his book "The path where he walked." I wasn't really receptive to Christianity, I'm afraid.

During the Kenzaki *gasshuku*, on the Miura peninsula, Aoki-sensei told us about the "world of zero" or "the world of one," but I didn't understand anything. I had gone to this course, even when I was overwhelmed with work in my company, because it had been presented as "purely martial."

At the Kujukuri-hama *gasshuku*, a year after finishing my university studies, we spent an hour in *seiza* at night facing the sea, watching the lights of the fishing boats. I had chosen a room with foreigners, so I was able to talk with them. They had traveled to quite a few countries, and their way of thinking was completely different from mine. This convinced me of the need to get out of Japan, and in 1972 I went to the United States for the first time.

My parents let me go as often as I wanted to Rakutenkai. I think they said to themselves, "That's the way it is!" At that time, my father was still healthy and running the family roofing business. People said that he was rather lucky.

Over time, the *keiko* and *gasshuku* with Aoki-sensei at Niigata University engendered impressive changes in Suzuki-kun and

Koyama-kun, especially Suzuki. When I started, the captain was Suzuki Keiichiro. Then there was Cho-san, who invited Aoki-sensei to come to Niigata for the first time. Then I remember that Hokari-san taught as a *sempai*, and two years later I became captain, followed by Suzuki and Koyama.

I also remember Ito Toshio from the Faculty of Civil Engineering, with whom I went to Rakutenkai. In my fourth year, I liked to do the *ki-no-nagare keiko* in a café with Ito and Suzuki: one attacks mentally and the other indicates when he perceives the attack. Ito almost never seized the right moment, but the very sensitive Suzuki seized it very well. Ito was really not technically gifted and he could be very critical. He was like that until his third year and then during the spring *gasshuku* of my fourth year I was surprised to see him change drastically. I think he was influenced by Aoki-sensei, as if he resonated with him or something. In fact, it was not so much his *tsuki* that had changed as his *uke* [receiving]. The *uke* requires sensitivity, rather than body technique. Even if you are not technically gifted, if you capture the moment of attack, you can avoid it without any particular technique. He did it really well, even better than Koyama.

Among the members of the Niigata University karate club, I was able to train some people as *sempai*: first Koyama and Suzuki, then Nishiya from the medical school, and then a year later came Nishina and Miyazawa, and again a year later Kaneda. It was during their time that the club's karate technique reached its peak. And then it continued until the year of Mukoyama. I think they had much better technique than we did, in *tsuki* or *keri* for example. It was thanks to the *jumbi-taiso*, the exercises developing fundamental physical strength, which were still powerful, but also because they had been able to build their own relationship to the teaching of Aoki-sensei.

In Niigata, only the technical side was transmitted - karate as a martial art - leaving aside the Bible, the religious or spiritual side. Technically everyone respected and trusted Aoki-sensei, but on a spiritual or religious level many found themselves in contradiction, even in conflict, with his ideas. As for me, I moved away from the *keiko* of the Rakutenkai from the moment when I found myself more and more absorbed by my work.

Taking over the family business and practicing at Shinminato

In working life, we have a lot of opportunity to drink, and we don't have much time for *keiko*. I ended up suffering from this, and really wanted to practice. It was then that I met Kaneda, who worked at the Shinminato Police Station. We then started to practice together, in the martial arts room adjoining the police station. As he had just left university, he could move very energetically but I had lost a lot, it was a real disaster! I immediately went back to *keiko* at a rate of two to three times a week and three to six months later, I had recovered my initial form.

It was at this time that Bruce Lee became fashionable and the neighborhood children came to ask to be taught karate. At first, we refused because we thought they would not appreciate our rigorous practice. But in the end, we accepted. In the same room, there was a group from the Shorinji-kempo. Their technique was limited and their bodies hard. Next to our acrobatic technique, the difference was obvious.

Later, we changed to the Toyama county *dojo*. Here there was a class of aiki-kempo, one of the schools of aikido. Their practitioners were surprised by our movements, which they felt completely incapable of. So, our *tsuki* seemed very soft but it took you off the ground. In the same way, we were able to easily do a hundred *moro-geri* without stopping. We started sharing about our practice, but our techniques were so different that it didn't work. So, we took lessons from each other. As far as we were concerned, when we tried our *kote-gaeshi* or *shiho-nage* techniques[1] on them, we had no success. They easily countered us, and threw us very

---

[1] Large expansive throwing techniques.

hard, because they had a good knowledge of these practices, in a much more precise, concrete, and combative approach than we did, with joint techniques. These techniques do not work without great precision of execution. We learned their way of doing things, and then we were able to receive their attacks and throw them very easily. I learned a lot from this experience. There are many approaches and ways to do it. Aiki-kempo teacher Tani-san had a good personality. This is perhaps why many nurses came to learn aiki-kempo. We also did some *gasshuku* together.

Then later, with Kaneda, we founded a shintaido club, Shintaido Hokuriku. We advertised on Toyama TV. Egami-kun came to help us with the promotion. We made a brochure with a photo of Fugaku-san's Tenso and I also demonstrated Eiko in the street in front of the castle. Kaneda and I invested three or four hundred thousand yen[1] each in this operation. And so, little by little, people came to learn shintaido.

Coaching high-school baseball teams

And then one day, the owner of the gas station near my house, who was a former student of Shinminato High School, suggested to the manager of the baseball club that I become its coach. At first, I refused, because it was a time when my body was soaked with alcohol and cigarette smoke. Then I asked for a month to get back into physical shape, and we started on January 15th, 1986. Everyone started to train seriously under my direction, and the club won fourth place in the spring tournament for Toyama Prefecture.

Because we had succeeded in the spring, we naturally tried the summer tournament, and we ended up winning the Toyama tournaments twice in a row. This gave us the opportunity to participate in the national tournament, the Koshien, but we lost narrowly against Tenri High School. We then said to ourselves, "Next time, we will be champions!"

---

[1] Between $2000 and $3000.

It was such fun! I remember that when they won their fourth-place, I made them do a victory Eiko. Usually, on the day before the match, the teams trained on side-by-side pitches, but our opponent teams avoided training alongside us because news had spread that Shinminato was doing extremely impressive and powerful things. I can now say it: it was magical! This team had great energy and impressive strength! It was really a good experience.

Then, as I had become friends with the director of Jinsei High School, he also asked me to become the coach of their club. I did this for two years and then Okada-san came to take over, but his practice was too purely shintaido. The high school students had come to play baseball on a baseball field and they saw no point in practicing a martial art on their field, which had become a *dojo*. It was also related to Okada-san's personality. In my case, I cooked up exercises to adapt to the expectations of young people. Everything is in the art of cooking, isn't it?

What I retain from this for today

I remember that, at the Shuzenji *gasshuku*[1], Aoki-sensei told me something that influenced me a lot, then and later: "There are those who understand immediately, and there are those who never understand. In your case, you may not understand anything for decades, but if you ever understand, then everything will become clear to you. Anyway, even if it is possible that you will never understand, practice seriously!" He also told me, "Make sure you practice thoroughly, without any compromise, until you are thirty-five years old, and everything will be easier for you after that." I now completely agree with what he said to me then. This *gasshuku* has been very useful to me.

People often tell me that I have a voice that carries. I owe my vitality to shintaido and to my training. In my childhood, I was

---

[1] Organized by Suzuki M., who was then in his fourth year.

very weak and shy. After the Niigata earthquake, I managed to change and become stronger. That's why I started karate. My wife and I were married in 1972. Today, when she is told how weak and shy I was as a child, she refuses to believe it. During a recent trip to South Korea with other people, I realized that at sixty I was stronger and more solid than everyone else, even in terms of appetite. The rest of the group was very surprised.

I train every morning. Otherwise, I feel the same as if I hadn't brushed my teeth. It's just normal. In the past, I was called "Mr. jumbi-taiso." I still am, and I train to keep learning. When I was a student, I trained my body to be able to face any eventuality at any time. Now, well past thirty-five, all that shintaido training has left me with nothing but good things.

Keeping my body flexible and practicing Tenshingoso or Eiko, what could be more wonderful!? When I do Tenshingoso, I feel regenerated, as if I had taken a sauna or hot bath and then a cold bath. In all circumstances, I stretch myself towards the sky, my consciousness projected towards the universe, at least up to the stratosphere, and I then feel full of energy. That's wonderful!

As for Eiko, it is the feeling of "going through," vitality itself, which gives me the courage to go beyond the limits. Tenshingoso gives me a well-ordered energy, but Eiko is stronger. Eiko is free and without order, like an explosion, and we can do it as we want, without worrying about the tone. I run in Eiko and I love it. Tenshingoso and Eiko are my treasures.

I am past the age of jumping, and it is the state of my body that tells me what to do. Morning *jumbi-taiso* makes me feel good; it allows me to organize my day. I wear more clothes than necessary in order to sweat. With the sweat, the alcohol leaves my body and anything bad as well. First, I walk two kilometers to get to the stadium. Then I do a kilometer and a half of gentle running followed by a hundred meters at full power, in Eiko if my condition allows it. Then I go home walking quietly, with a few bursts of speed for a hundred or a hundred and fifty meters. I need those full power runs to get me going. I do this every day, rain or shine, except of course when I'm on the road for work. Over time, you can see the traces of my passages on the grass of the stadium. This is how, thanks to shintaido, I keep myself in good health.

However, since last year, my hip hurts when I lift my leg as if to do *mawashi-geri*. I can lift my leg, but it is painful. I feel like it's not for me anymore, and so I don't do it anymore. Even Taikyoku-sho now hurts my hips. But all that doesn't matter because I still have Tenshingoso and Eiko.

What's the use of living to be eighty if you're not in good health? I tell anyone who wants to hear me, you have to stay healthy [laughs]. I continue today to do what my *sensei* advised me as a pure dream of youth, because I want my *sensei* to remain Aoki-sensei. When I do Tenshingoso and Eiko, I have the image of Master Aoki in mind from time to time. And then I say to myself, "That's enough, leave him alone!" Yes, that's it! shintaido occupies an important place in me. And then, as time goes by, everything changes, everyone must find their own way.

Toshio ITO

The initial interview was conducted in September, 2004 through H.F. Ito, with some direct exchanges in English. During the validation appointment in May, 2019, T. Ito asked us to send him a copy of the text by email. A few weeks later, he sent us a revised and very heavily watered-down text. Six months later, in November, 2019, we decided to ask him for a new interview to propose a version closer to the original text, putting forward our reasons for doing this. He agreed to this with good grace.[1]

Youthful years

I was born in 1943 in Aichi prefecture, where I stayed until the end of high school. We were a family of seven children, four brothers and three sisters. My father worked for a wholesaler affiliated with a cotton processing factory. Shortly before I entered university, he retired and one of my brothers took over.

I didn't pass the college entrance exam on my first attempt. The following year, at age nineteen, I tried again and passed the entrance exam for Niigata University. I was interested in mechanics, and in order to become an engineer I entered the Faculty of Engineering.

Karate

I showed up at the karate club to practice in December, right in the middle of the academic year. As I was behind the others, I looked around to know what to do, trying awkwardly to punch or kick. One of the senior practitioners — who in fact was not a student but a taxi driver — then took me aside: "What are you doing there in the middle of the *keiko*?" I realized that it was a waste of time to start so late in the year, and I promised myself to come

[1] **Credits:** *Interview*: H.F. Ito, P. Quettier. *Transcription*: M. Minagawa. *Editing*: K. Hokari, P. Quettier. *Translations*: K. Hokari, P. Quettier, M. Hirano. *Proof reading*: J.F. Dégremont. *French/English translation*: P. Quettier. *Proofreading*: G. Bullen, L. Seaman.

back the following year with the other beginners. That's what I did.

When I joined, Watanabe-san was the captain of the club. Looking at the *keiko*, I wondered if I was going to be able to endure something so rigorous. However, as I wanted to become strong, and especially since it was Egami-sensei's Shotokai karate, which was more flexible than other styles of karate, I hung on. Two years later, it was Kamiya who became the assistant captain of Kinoshita, of Nagaoka University of Engineering. Kinoshita, Ito and Hokari took turns giving the *gorei*. That summer we went to a *gasshuku* in the Nagano area, in Zenkoji.

The following year, the summer *gasshuku* was held in Nikko. Cho was captain, assisted by Kato and Hyoki. This is where we learned that Yanagisawa-sensei had been assigned as our instructor on the recommendation of Igarashi-san. That same year we also participated in the last two days of Chuo University's *gasshuku* in Aizu-Wakamatsu. The members of Chuo, who were already exhausted, resented us for arriving late.

And then Aoki-sensei became our instructor. He first appeared at the Nikko *gasshuku*, led by Cho, Hyoki, and Kato. Aoki-sensei had a high opinion of Cho. Eventually, Kato and Hyoki had to withdraw because they were from the engineering faculty located in Nagaoka. Cho, who was from the Niigata College of Education, took the lead[1].

Then came the time of promising people like Koyama, Suzuki, Kamata and Kamishima, also called the four musketeers. Aoki-sensei paid a lot of attention to Kamishima during our summer *gasshuku* in Nikko. He made him hold his *bo* horizontally either running or in *kibadachi*, all the time during the course. I also remember another guy called Kurata who was also very good. Either way, Aoki-sensei made a kind of fixation on Kamishima and

---

[1] Ito Toshio hints at the real reason for Hyoki and Kato leaving: a difference in perspective with the club's new instructor regarding practice.

wanted to see him progress. He also took special care of him during the *gasshuku* the following spring. I was entering my fourth year, just as Kamishima, Koyama, Suzuki, and Kamata were entering their third year. Kamata, who was entering medical school, had to drop out. Later, when Aoki-sensei met Kamishima at the time of the summer *gasshuku*, he is said to have muttered, "What a strange look, his eyes look dead; maybe a problem in his private life?" Later, I heard a rumor that Kamishima was entangled in a special relationship with a girlfriend and couldn't get over it. He left the karate club soon after.

The following year, when Kita and Hanaki took over the club, we went to a *gasshuku* in Hakuba. I remember that at the first *keiko*, we jumped in *usagi-tobi* for about an hour and a half, waiting for Aoki-sensei to appear. But he and his assistant, Matsuhashi-san, were sleeping, because they had counted on us to wake them up. In the end, they didn't show up and this first *keiko* only consisted of an hour and a half of *usagi-tobi*.

From that time, the Niigata Karate Club progressed through several levels, as we received a lot of attention from Aoki-sensei. He also taught in clubs at Gakushuin and Toho Universities. As for me, after graduating from university in March, 1968, I moved to Tokyo to seek employment and participate in Rakutenkai activities. At the very beginning, I stayed in the room that Hokari rented in Aoki-sensei's house.

Rakutenkai years

I then found a job in Tokyo and a room in Ichikawa City. From March to August, 1968, I went to Yokohama every Saturday and Sunday to practice with Rakutenkai. The trip from Ichikawa to Nogeyama took two and a half hours. So, I finished my work on Friday at 5:00 p.m. to take the train at 5:30 p.m. and arrive at Rakutenkai around 8:00 p.m. At work I didn't do much, and sometimes I even slept in the warehouse. So much so that in August the manager told me, "This job does not suit you, you are fired!" But I immediately found another job in Shinjuku, closer to Yokohama. It was an oil wholesaler that a friend had recommended. I lived in Shinjuku for about a year and a half. I had a regular income and I came to Rakutenkai on weekends. We practiced on Friday and Saturday evenings, and then we slept at Aoki-sensei's house packed like sardines. On Sundays we did a short *keiko*, and I went back to my apartment on Sunday evening without doing the night *keiko* because I had to work the next morning.

I bought a "Jigen Ryu" style *bokken* that I still have. From then on, I became more and more involved in the practice. It was like a pleasant extension of student life. I also liked being part of a group. We humans like to be in groups. Once people join a group, most of them want to stay there, feeling a kind of harmony, unless, of course, the group becomes extremely strange. I can't justify what I was doing at that time any better.

Later, I got a job at Teraoka Corporation in Tokyo. We practiced in the park and at Ipponmatsu Elementary School. I remember Ho was around most of the time and he got really good. We also went to practice at Tokyo High School in Shimo-Maruko and near the Tama River. I vaguely remember someone renting a room on the second or third floor of a building. We did the *keiko* on Saturday or Sunday and we returned from the *dojo* in the middle of the night. We made a lot of noise — ten to fifteen people rushing into a small room, talking and laughing while preparing the meal — and the neighbors complained loudly. At that time, Okada-san and Kato-san gave the *gorei*, in terms like, "Run from one end to the other!" Aoki-sensei always came later.

Cho-san, former Shotokai and owner of the Chinese restaurant Eian-ro, was at that time a kind of patron for Rakutenkai. One day, when I was still a student, we were brought to Eian-ro where we were served a meal. I ate everything that was served to us in quantity because at the time I rarely had the opportunity to eat well. After the meal, Aoki-sensei said, "Let's go," but no one, Aoki-sensei included, pretended to pay for what we had eaten. I then realized that it was Cho-san who gave us this meal and I felt very sorry for him. Anyway, I thought to myself, "Okay, let's go home!" but instead we went to Yamashita Park, where we ran Eiko for two or three hours. I wouldn't have eaten so much if I had known such a tough *keiko* was waiting for me.

Another day, when Hanaki and I were both in our fourth year, Aoki-sensei took us to fill our bellies at Eian-ro and then said, "Let's go for a run," and then we did Eiko continuously from eleven o'clock in the evening to two o'clock in the morning! As I was running slowly, I was constantly overtaken by Hanaki as we went back and forth. Halfway there was a small bridge that bothered us a lot. I fell several times while stumbling over the edge of the bridge in the dark. The course was a kilometer long and we couldn't see the other end. I remember a tramp sitting by the road who finally asked, "What the hell are you doing?" So Hanaki, who is a very serious man, explained very carefully to the tramp what the *keiko* consisted of.

I subsequently had many opportunities to do this same *keiko* in Nogeyama Park. I couldn't tell if Eiko was a good or a bad practice for me. But Aoki-sensei explained things perfectly: "This is good, this is bad," etc. and I accepted it, although I had some doubts. He said, for example, "Energy is like a white blade that comes out of your body and projects through your arms," or "If you practice sincerely, you will see white energy coming out of here." After that, I could not help seeking to see such phenomena.

Kat-chan's mother[1] ran a fruit and vegetable store. He always brought a lot of vegetables, radishes and other things, which we cooked at Rakutenkai. Everyone but me seemed to get incredible energy from it. When you think about it, where did the Rakutenkai guys get so much energy from? Personally, I was different and I always kept a certain distance.

---

[1] Katsuhiro Ito.

I was baptized in the spring of Showa 43 [1968] in Kenzaki. The water was still a bit cold. I was at the top of my form at that time. Aoki-sensei was constantly coming up with new ideas and he would say, "Let's try this or that" as soon as they came to him. One day he found *shikko-zuki*[1] and asked us to practice it immediately on the tatami or wooden floor. I remember having thus ruined the tatami[2] of a small annex room of Eian-ro, where Fugaku Ito worked as a cook.

Some guys tried to make me believe in Christianity to better understand the way of Rakutenkai, based on the spirit of Christianity. But I had trouble with that, because it seemed to me that associating a religion with Rakutenkai's activities could cause problems. Of course, no one ever said that anyone who didn't believe in Jesus Christ couldn't be part of the Rakutenkai. However, there was a certain atmosphere that suggested it was best to adhere to Christianity.

For example, one person told me that after reading the Bible a lot and immersing myself in Christianity, I could experience a great satori: "If you believe in Jesus Christ, you will suddenly see what remained invisible to you," or "Unless you believe in Jesus, you will not be able to access what you are really looking for." At least that's how I interpreted it. Aoki-sensei meanwhile never said such things.

In the end, rightly or wrongly, I felt that if I refused religion, I should stop coming to Rakutenkai. Afterwards, I said to myself that I could only see things clearly after I joined Christianity: "It is my life after all. I might see things in a new light after being baptized; let's try!" And that's how I was baptized by Shelhorn-sensei. Kishida-san was baptized with me there and two or three others. Rakutenkai had asked Shelhorn-sensei because Okada-san, still in training at the Bible school, couldn't do it for us. Thereafter,

---

[1] *Tsuki* while moving on one's knees.
[2] The usual (non-martial) tatami are covered with a fragile straw mat.

Okada-san baptized the members of Rakutenkai. After being baptized, I said to myself, "Wow! I finally jumped into Christianity by being baptized. I don't see the difference!" I always had mixed feelings about it, and I was never really able to devote myself to religion.

A dozen people trained on Saturday evening. We got home at two or three o'clock in the morning and, after a short sleep, we got up at six or seven o'clock to study the Bible until nine o'clock. Then we had a meal consisting mainly of bread brought by Kat-chan, which we filled with fried vegetables. It was really delicious, because everyone was hungry, although it would be considered rather poor food nowadays. Regular members were Okada-san, Kato-san, Hokari, Matsuhashi, and Ma-chan[1]. He was still a student so he only came in the evening or in the morning. I heard his father wasn't happy to see him in Rakutenkai. Some people, whose parents were not in favor of their joining Rakutenkai, received from Aoki-sensei, in a roundabout way, the suggestion to formally separate from their parents, in order to become fully involved in Rakutenkai.

Kat-chan, Ho and Jugoro were there too. Takeo and Minagawa joined later. Some women too, like Tsuchiya-san, Kato Etsuko, Kishida-san, and Harue-san. Afterwards, the Ishide brother and sister, Tadashi and Kazuyo, became regular members. When Ishide Kayoko, at that time called Shimma-san, came, she invested all her energy and was deeply drawn to Rakutenkai.

Anyway, I continued on this path until around the spring of 1970. I then returned to my hometown for a semester before returning to Tokyo where I worked part-time for an exporter in Funabashi. When I went back to Rakuten-kai, I saw that Ho and other people were gone.

In one of Kenzaki's *gasshuku* that I attended, Ma-chan was there. We all ran two to three hundred meters in Eiko under

---

[1] Masatake Egami.

Fugaku-san's *gorei*. Aoki-sensei was running ahead and everyone was following him, except Kato and Okada who were watching Ma-chan. Unfortunately, he hit an obstacle - some kind of debris from a boat buried in the sand - and injured himself. Aoki-sensei's face went very pale. He didn't want to show it but he was angry. He claimed to treat all members equally, but in fact the more promising members were treated differently. As far as I remember, Ma-chan must have broken a tooth. Afterwards, Okada-san and Kato-san got a real dressing-down by Aoki-sensei. This is not a rumor, as I heard it directly. That was the only time I saw Aoki-sensei get angry. You know that Mr. Suzuki, consultant of Seven-Eleven[1], once said, "I am only dancing on the palm of Mr. Ito, founder of Ito-Yokado." Well, Aoki-sensei is stronger than Mr. Ito when it comes to controlling people. Not only Ma-chan, but everyone had been goaded to run at full speed. When I heard such harsh words, I couldn't help but feel great frustration, even though no one else seemed to be affected.

We started Kenka practice[2] at the Ipponmatsu school gymnasium. Everyone walked calmly, keeping the soles of their feet in contact with the ground, as if delicately holding flowers in their hands so as not to damage them. It's an excellent practice to get a natural movement, to lower the hips and imagine holding in your arms something precious like a bouquet of flowers or a baby. At the heart of things, there is in Aoki-sensei's approach a deep love for humanity. For example, we hit into our partners hard and then we gently help them fall, even though "attacking with love" sounds strange. On the other hand, I did not feel any love from him, but I guess he has this idea as a kind of theoretical backbone. When I think of him, there is an atmosphere that can be disturbing... something uncompromising. I don't know what he was aiming for. Sometimes people approached him, and then later moved

---

[1] Very popular chain of stores for essential items, open from 7am to 11pm, hence its name.
[2] Technique subsequently named Kenka-in-hoko.

away sooner or later. For example, M. Ho left him quickly. I always wondered why things happened like this. And finally, all this Rakutenkai world dispersed shortly after. What a strange group, right?

My journey to the USA and Europe

I wanted to see different places outside of Japan, especially Europe. Several of us had this idea of traveling, and Aoki-sensei, without encouraging us directly, often traveled abroad himself. He would tell us about interesting places here and there, New York, etc. When I told him of my intention, he advised me to go to the United States rather than Europe: "America is really energetic, you should definitely see it." Of course, I wanted to go, but he encouraged me to go there first. So, when I was around thirty years old, I left Japan for the United States. I was thinking of going to Europe if I was able to get by in the United States for a while and gain some leeway there.

I entered Los Angeles, to find that my passport had been stamped "Not extendable after 3 months". The guys around me said, "That's funny. You're the only one with that kind of stamp. Did you do something wrong?" It was incomprehensible. For want of a better idea, I said to myself "I'll go to an English class; I'll find a lot of information there." There were about ten students, including eight Japanese people. How do you study English properly with so many Japanese? However, it contained information intended exclusively for the Japanese. This is how I came to look for a job. One of the school staff introduced me for a vacancy at a Korean restaurant run by a Korean man married to a Japanese woman. I worked there, but the daily wage was very low and there was nothing left after paying the rent and the food. As my three-month visa was due to expire soon, I found another place to do the washing up. And then I went by bus to Canada and immediately returned to the United States; but by plane in order to avoid any problem with the immigration services, and this worked.

I went to collect my luggage in Los Angeles before backpacking on a two-week bus trip. I first went to Arizona, where I met Takeo in a community recommended by Aoki-sensei, then to Chicago, where I met Minagawa who was doing Eiko with his *bo* in a park, and finally I went to see Niagara Falls, via Pittsburgh, before arriving in New York.

Once I had got there, I took two weeks to visit different places in the city, before being hired as a dishwasher in a Japanese restaurant called "Benihana," managed by the famous "Rocky Aoki." I found and shared a room with three other guys in a cheap hotel, very popular among penniless people, the "Barcort Hotel" not far from the restaurant. Since the salary was good and I had almost no expenses, I saved up to a million yen in four months. I was planning to go to Germany with this money, because I wanted to study the German language. But eventually, I went to the "People of the living God" community in New Orleans. I arrived there around December 10th and stayed until spring. Then I returned to New York and flew from Kennedy Airport to Dusseldorf, Germany. I settled in a small town called Arolsen, west of Kassel. I chose the place hoping that there would be no Japanese in this small town, but there were actually a lot! There were also many independent Christian churches. I worked as a dish washer until September in a restaurant with other Japanese employees and took two German courses. Then I moved to Hamburg where I stayed until March of the following year, still as a dish-washer. Then, I returned to Arolsen before returning to Japan. In total, I had stayed abroad for two and a half years. I was thirty-two years old.

Leaving Christianity and Rakutenkai at the same time

My father died of stomach cancer forty days after my return. I had not been informed of his illness while traveling because my family did not want to worry me. When I came home saying, "Here

I am!" there was a sign on my father's door: "No one should enter this room." I said, "What does 'Nobody should come in this room' mean?" So, my mom said, "Well...actually..." and she explained everything to me. I walked in and saw that he had changed terribly. He looked like a skeleton. I was so shocked that I couldn't hold back my tears.

As he was very psycho-rigid, my father had not gone to the hospital for fear of hearing bad news there, but he continually complained of a stomach ache. As time passed, he became thinner and thinner; so thin that he ended up becoming skeletal. Finally, we transported him to the hospital on a stretcher and he was diagnosed with inoperable stomach cancer; he was doomed. I felt like he had been waiting for me to come back so I could see him alive again.

On the day of my arrival in Haneda, I had stayed in a hotel to take stock of my life: "I have to make a clean break right now." The next morning, I went to see Aoki-sensei and he was there. I said to him, "So far, you have taken good care of me. I am however sorry to tell you that I have stopped being a Christian." Then I went to the church in Kawasaki and said to Shelhorn-sensei: "I have ceased to be a Christian." He was left dumbfounded. This was in July, 1976.

Having come out of Christianity – what a strange thing to say – I would have had a hard time staying in Rakutenkai. It was suggested to me that I talk about it with Hokari-san. I returned to my hometown in August and came back to Tokyo in November. I worked at the Sannoh Hotel for American soldiers for about a year, during which time I visited Hokari-san. He had moved to the Aoba district of Yokohama and married Handa Hideko-san. The visit did not change my position.

For a short time, I had thought Christianity was good, but that was now finished. Buddhism and Shintoism recognize divinity in everything, don't they? But in this case, you have to worship everything, which is complicated. I had thought that from this point of view, a monotheistic religion is practical; such simplicity is good. Now I think all is well if we keep love in mind. I do not need to follow any religion, and to some extent I am free from religion.

Maintaining contact with members of Rakutenkai

I wasn't particularly close to anyone during the Rakutenkai days. Later, I had the opportunity to meet Matsuhashi. One day, a guy called Sato, who was junior to me at Niigata University, called me and asked me to meet Matsuhashi. I agreed and we visited him in his office near Hamamatsu-cho station. We greeted each other, "It's been a long time!" He told me that he was helping his brother dig sand near Nokogiri Mountain in Chiba Prefecture and sell it. He clearly remembered having participated in the photo shoot for the book of karate *kata*, which was to be published by Egami-sensei, but he had left before publication. It seems that he had had a disagreement with Aoki-sensei. Later, I read in an article written by Mrs. Egami, that Egami-sensei had been upset to see the book published under the name of Rakutenkai rather than Shotokai and also that there had been a disagreement between Aoki-sensei and Egami-sensei about copyright. I don't know how much Matsuhashi knew at the time, but he felt resentment toward Aoki-sensei. It was he who introduced me to this memoir written by Mrs. Egami. I bought it and, after reading it, I said to myself: "People are always fighting among themselves!"

Masashi SUZUKI

M. Suzuki is Emeritus Professor of English Literature of Kyoto University. His was one of the first interviews, in May, 2004, because the circumstances lent themselves to it, but also in order to obtain his opinion as a researcher on the study to come. For this reason, more than half of the interview, conducted in English, was devoted to a discussion of the context of the study; this part was not included in the final text. Moreover, once a first draft was written, it was missing an introduction and a conclusion. A second interview was conducted by video-conference in August, 2018, and the final English text was approved in May, 2018. The Japanese translation was then approved through M. Hirano, during a visit we paid him at his place of residence of Sendai in May, 2019.[1]

Childhood in Niigata

I was born in Niigata in 1946. My mother came from Tokyo, and my father was born and brought up in Niigata. We were six brothers and sisters, and I was the youngest one of all. As a child, I was interested in English, and when I entered Niigata University in 1965, I took an English literature course. My elder brother, who is the same age as Hokari-san, was a member of the Niigata karate club. I was looking for some side activity to my studies, and he told me that the practice of karate was quite good. About a hundred freshmen joined the karate club in 1965, but after the summer *gasshuku*[2], the number was drastically reduced to only five or six. Hard training might have been the main reason for the reduction. But *sempai*, or senior practitioners, were very kind to freshmen. And in my second year, Aoki-sensei came to coach us, and I found his *gorei* excellent, giving me further reasons to keep going.

---

[1] **Credits :** *Interview/transcription/editing/translation*: P. Quettier. English-French *Proofreading*: D. Richardson.

[2] In Japan, the beginning of the school and university year take place in April, and the summer *gasshuku* happens just a few months later.

Karate in Niigata University Karate Club (NUKC)

Our karate was old-fashioned, and we thought something should be changed, but we didn't know what or how to change. We felt that our karate methods and body movements were somehow ill-suited for the times. That's why we were looking for something new or different or, you might say, more fun in our practice. But how would we find that? From whom should we ask advice?

I wasn't really aware of what was going on, but my *sempai* Hokari-san, a fourth-year, and Hanaki-san, a second-year, were then looking for a good coach, *shihan*, or master. At that time, our group, Niigata University Karate Club, belonged to the Shotokai school. Our *sempai* got information from the Karate Club of Chuo University in Tokyo, which was the Mecca of the Shotokai school. We had tests every year at Chuo University to get elevated to a higher rank [*dan* 段]; I got a black belt of the first dan [初段] during my second year of university. Ikarashi Toshihiko-sensei, our *shihan* of NUKC, admired and paid high respect to Aoki-sensei, although he was much senior to Aoki-sensei. He would always tell us how strong Aoki-sensei was and about his personality as he knew it. He might have also thought that his own karate was getting too old-fashioned or outdated, I don't know. At some point, when I was a second-year university student. he said, "Well, I am too old to teach you now, but I'd like to introduce you to a very talented master, Aoki," and he urged us to accept Aoki-sensei's guidance. Ikarashi-shihan was very liberal, open-minded, and proactive.

The evolution from karate to shintaido, seen from NUKC

It was at a summer *gasshuku* in Nikko, Nagano, in 1966 that Aoki-sensei came to coach us for the first time. Aoki-sensei's *gorei* was soft and enjoyable, it was fun. When he saw us practicing with clenched teeth, he used to say, "Laugh, laugh!"

The Rakutenkai task force had started a couple of years earlier. That's what Aoki-sensei told us soon after he came to NUKC. Since the beginning, the *keiko* had constantly changed in style, body movement, and feeling. For example, we were told to open our palms. We wondered why, but nobody could tell us. Aoki-sensei was very young. In fact, he is only ten years older than me. I remember us taking a bath together[1] during a *gasshuku*. He used to talk a lot, and it was always very interesting and stimulating. Aoki-sensei had a radical effect on my — our — way of thinking about karate. Everything he said was so new, so provocative, and so inspiring. Some of what he said we understood, but some things we couldn't understand at all. In Aoki-sensei's view, everything around us was inevitably connected to karate. But how that could be so, perhaps nobody else could fully understand.

One of the most impressive things I remember him saying was, "Well, Suzuki-kun, everybody thinks the concept of karate is limited to this [picking up an object from the table as a symbol of karate] ... everyone thinks that this is karate but ... it is not karate! Nowadays these [taking a second object from the table and holding up both] are karate!" The old-fashioned idea of karate was therefore only a part of the new idea of karate. This was quite a revelation! He didn't dismiss the old karate but incorporated it by transforming it.

In senior karate members' minds, this must have stirred strong mixed feelings. A fresh recruit like me wasn't concerned at all about the old-fashioned karate. But perhaps older members were confused by the new karate. Aoki-sensei deconstructed the old concept of karate and expanded and reformed it. Everything and anything around us had meaning from the viewpoint of the new karate.

---

[1] Village or neighborhood collective baths have traditionally played an important role as places to exchange information and ideas. The traditional hotels in which the *gasshuku* are held maintain this tradition, which plays an important role in the internal communication of the working or learning groups that they host.

For some people, Aoki-sensei's way of thinking might have sounded contradictory, but in fact it was not. His thought expanded and contracted, and became a spiral. In my opinion, expansion and contraction are intertwined with each other within him, forming a spiral in his way of thinking. The evolution of shintaido reflects Aoki-sensei's personality, and the origin of his philosophy was deeply rooted in the times. He was the right person to express the tenor of the times, of the country, and of the universe. He was very talented at expressing those things through karate and body movement. For him, karate was a medium, or a means, of expressing his aesthetic, religious, and philosophical ideas.

Karate or *budo* is unique to Japanese culture. Nowadays people are saying that *budo* is a very important part of Japanese culture. We have to pursue it earnestly. Many essential things are expressed through *budo*. *Budo* could be considered a way to integrate, develop, and transmit essential elements of Japanese culture. If we take *budo* as a metaphor, we could expand it endlessly. Depending on how we define *budo*, it expands or contracts infinitely! It occupies a very small space indeed, but it contains the universe.

Personal interests and evolution

When I started to practice karate, I wasn't interested in using it to fight, nor was I trying to become a strong man. I was looking for something different to which I could devote myself, my whole energy, my intelligence, my money, or whatever. Appreciating this, my elder brother advised me to join NUKC. He was also a senior member of the club.

I enjoyed moving my body. A year or so after I started, I began to think that something serious might be hidden within karate. I wanted to delve more deeply into the philosophical meaning of karate. I didn't care how hard the *keiko* was, I was full of energy. *Keiko* always made me feel fresh and different. For me, karate practice was a moving medium for self-expression. For example, when we did a *kata* like Taikyokuken or Heian as a group — we had about 50 or 60 members in those days — the expression of the *kata* was entirely different from one person to the next! My *kata* and other members' *kata* were quite different from each other. "What does this mean?" I wondered. Seeing us performing *kata*, Aoki-sensei would correct this or that, and I wondered, "What does this *kata* mean?"

One day, Aoki-sensei showed us his famous text about the trace of the sword: "The locus of a sword is a sign." It intrigued me enormously and gave me a great clue for thinking about body movement. It stretched and vibrated my brain very much and gave me a starting point for deepening my thought about karate. I could think of a sword as a killing tool, but that phrase, "the locus of the sword is a sign," forced me to ponder the meaning behind it. That's how I became interested in what was happening in Rakutenkai.

Participating in Rakutenkai

The body movement of karate was so refreshing that I always felt different after *keiko*; it inspired me to consider something religious, aesthetic, or philosophical behind karate. It removed the veil from my eyes, and I felt as if something new had appeared before me. *Budojo* became a school for me.

Hokari-san was a very influential person. I was a freshman when he was a fourth-year student. After graduating from university, he did post-graduate study. When he went to work for a research institute, he kept practicing with Aoki-sensei, Fugaku-san, and the others, as a member of Rakutenkai, the elite group of karate men and women that was founded on September 23rd, 1965. As a student, I had no spare money, but Hokari-san bought me a ticket from Niigata to Tokyo and said, "Why don't you come to practice with us at Rakutenkai?" That's how, as a fourth-year University student, I went three or four times a year up to Yokohama, where Rakutenkai was in residence at Aoki-sensei's house, and stayed for a few days of practice.

Rakutenkai *keiko* was very stimulating and inspiring. Aoki-sensei made it a strict rule to never repeat the same *keiko*. I loved the energetic expression of opening palms. I also practiced bojutsu, running for hours in Eiko, and *kumitachi* fascinated me. I felt I was involved in the process of the new karate that was coming into being.

About religion

I come from a Buddhist tradition, meaning that, like most Japanese people, I put the palms of my hands together and pray or meditate in front of a grave. But my parents had no particular religious inclination, and they never tried to force their own religious ideas on me. Karate or *budo* is in essence religious, so you might say Rakutenkai *keiko* was religious, but if you ask me whether it was Buddhism, Christianity, or something else, I cannot answer. I cannot classify it. As I clearly remember, Aoki-sensei once told us that the Bible was an excellent guidebook for karate. During the Rakutenkai period, I think I knew that some people were studying the Bible seriously. Perhaps their activities were inspired by the teachings of the Bible, but I personally didn't mind them at all. Aoki-sensei never tried in any way to lead me in that direction.

The end of the Rakutenkai period

At the beginning of its history, Rakutenkai was a kind of esoteric society, in which the members could concentrate on creating a new *budo* for humanity in the future. But at some point, Aoki-sensei, Fugaku-san, and some others decided to open the door and make the Rakutenkai *keiko* known to society at large. They formed a new organization, Sogo-budo Renmei, and the end of the original Rakutenkai was the start of a new Rakutenkai practice.

Soon after graduating from university, I got a job at Yamaguchi University, first as a lecturer and then as associate professor. About ten years later, I moved to Kyoto. I never taught shintaido to anyone, but I tried to include what I got from shintaido *keiko* into my academic activities. Being at the core of my way of thinking, these ideas had a deep influence on my research and teaching.

Nowadays I do Tenshingoso once a day for personal enjoyment.

Shintaido might not be a commercial success, but it is a *budo* in the broad sense and occupies a unique place in Japanese and international culture. Its humanistic, aesthetic, and religious philosophy is really worth studying.

It has changed a lot and still keeps changing.

Akihiko KOYAMA

A. Koyama was introduced to us in the spring of 2005 by T. Hanaki [p. 159]. The interview was held at the premises of Mr. Koyama's company and conducted with the help of H.F. Ito. The verification of the Japanese text transcribed from the interview was carried out in May, 2019 with the help of M. Hirano, when Mr. Koyama was already retired from company management.[1]

Childhood in Niigata

I was born in Niigata Prefecture on January 2nd, 1947. My father was first an office worker at a small company, then, in 1958, he set up a small business manufacturing paper bags. I was about 11 years old at the time. My parents were both the last children of farming families and could only rely on themselves. Initially my mother worked as a door-to-door cleaning-product saleswoman. Then she worked with my father for the family business.

After that I felt that my family gradually freed itself from poverty. Of course, the whole Japanese society was poor at that time, but in my eyes as a child, we were poorer than our neighbors. My parents come from farming families, and I don't remember that we ran out of food. I rather felt the poverty in our way of dressing. And then, when television became popular, around the time my father was making paper bags, my parents bought one along with the neighbors, and it was through things like that that I got the impression we were doing better.

As a child I had a good constitution, and I never had a serious injury. Moreover, until today, I have never been hospitalized. My mother was very keen on education. In my neighborhood no family employed a tutor, but my mother insisted that I have one, at some sacrifice. Unfortunately, I did not live up to her expectations

[1] **Credits:** *Interview*: H.F. Ito, P. Quettier. *Transcription*: S. Watanabe. *Editing*: M. Hirano, P. Quettier. *Translation*: P. Quettier. *Proofreading*: A. Weber, L. Ordeman.

academically. I was "only" in the top twenty percent of the class. And I wasn't great at physical education either.

Niigata High School was the top high school in Niigata Prefecture. I was able to enter despite my average grades because nationally Niigata Prefecture generally did not have a very high academic level. My middle school teacher told me: "There is no need to try to enter this high school with these grades because the level is too high for you." However, I was admitted, by chance it seems. And for the university entrance exam a high school teacher told me: "No need to try for this university with your grades, the level will be too high." But somehow, I got in there too. I have been very lucky.

Carefree college life and entry into working life

In high school, I was part of the table tennis club for a year, but I wanted to become strong and that was not enough. I gave up table tennis to study karate on my own. During elementary school and middle school, physical education had never been my strength. I could have done judo, but I could see that the judo club was full of boys with big bodies. As for me I was tall, but skinny. I weighed about 50 kilos. As there were quite a few short people in the karate club, I figured out that even a skinny or short person could become strong there. As we say in Japan, "Although small, the Japanese *sansho* pepper has punch."

I don't remember being bullied or anything like that, but when I was in elementary school, there was a tramp in my neighborhood who was bigger than me. My neighbor's big brother, a junior high school student, was crying because he was beaten up by the man, while I was just hanging about, unable to do anything or help him.

I entered Niigata University in April of 1965. There I chose to specialize in civil engineering, and ultimately, I chose the precision engineering section in the engineering department, not because I wanted to do anything in particular, but because I wanted to see what I could do. And I simply preferred things related to science. I was not good at all in geography, history, or literature. Obviously, I could have chosen the faculty of science rather than that of civil engineering. But the faculty of science aims to train teachers, while engineering is useful for the economy. I entered the precision engineering department of the faculty of civil engineering.

I didn't do much during my years at university. I did just enough to get the necessary credits for the diploma. My parents were very busy with their work and had little time for me, so I took advantage of the pleasures of university life, dividing my days between *mahjong* and karate. In the morning, I would ask my mother to make me a bento box for lunch, then I would go to the *mahjong* establishment, and from there to karate training. And the days, months, and years went by like this.

I am the eldest of the family. I have a little sister, two years younger than me, and a little brother, three years younger than her. Three children in all. My sister is now married and lives in Kameda, near the city of Niigata. My brother also got married and works with me. Previously he studied at Meiji University and worked for four years for Taiko Bank in Niigata.

After my father fell ill with low blood pressure, I left the steel company, Niigata Tekko, where I had worked as a draftsman for a year after university, and I joined the family business. Until his death at the age of 63, my father directed Koyama Seitai. I then took over management at the age of thirty-three.

About fifteen years ago I changed the type of production of my company. This was four or five years after my father died. We have moved on to manufacture toys called "capsule toys." These are small toys included in a capsule that is placed in a dispensing device. When you put a hundred yen into the machine and turn a crank, a capsule comes out of it. I made them as a subcontractor for the Bandai company[1]. These machines, called *gashapon*, were installed in supermarkets. As a result, I offered to these same supermarkets other goods priced at ¥100 — small utensils, etc. I positioned myself as an intermediary wholesaler. Large wholesalers sell large quantities of goods such as washing powder, toilet paper or tissues. I made sure to occupy the consumer niches left open by these large wholesalers. Currently, I employ ten people with annual sales of about ¥270,000,000. I have two sons. The youngest works with me in the family business, and the eldest works for the UFJ bank branch in Shizuoka.

Is this karate the right one?

When I was a high school student, I did karate by copying others. When I entered Niigata University, I immediately joined the karate club. I saw karate moves there that were completely different from those my high school classmates were doing. The movements were soft and flexible, and the stance very low. The *tsuki* swooped straight ahead, so their *keiko* was already that of the Shotokai style. Of course, they no longer used the *makiwara*. Since there was only this club for all of Niigata University, I had no choice. Outside of the official practice hours, I continued to train on a personal *makiwara* that I had set up outside the *dojo* — telling myself it couldn't hurt. The *sempai* of the club did not say anything, neither for nor against. It's not that I had a contrary spirit, but I felt like doing it, and therefore I did it without fear of upsetting them. Among the group there was some questioning, especially from Hashizume-san. Another one, a year older than me, I think, was going to practice in town in a different karate *dojo*. I imagine that he, too, must have had doubts. For my part, I asked Hanaki-san, who was in his second year, "What do you think about our karate? Can it make us strong?" He replied, "I don't know any more than you. But no one is strong at first. First, we

[1] Bandai is the third largest toy producer in the world.

practice, and then we'll ask ourselves this question once we have a black belt." I still remember that conversation.

There was a person who had trained in Shotokan karate in high school, and he had a brown belt. He didn't want to be part of our club, saying, "This is not karate!" I then invited him to do a *jiyu-kumite*[1]. I only informed Hanaki-san and the other first-years. In our first year we only wore the white belt. We only knew *oizuki*, but we practiced experimental training such as *jiyu-kumite*. As we were only in the first year, we never had the upper hand over our *sempai*, and I often happened to be touched by kicks. So, I didn't have much of a chance of winning. However, Hanaki-san often had the upper hand, even if he only did *tsuki* in *zenkutsu* just like us, but very direct and fast. He was also able to receive *keri* in *ko-kutsu-dachi*. In short, he was very strong. As it turned out, none of the brown belt's Shotokan techniques worked against Hanaki-san. Even his *keri* was not strong, and I received it myself afterwards without any difficulty.

Suddenly, after having noticed that our type of *keiko* worked rather well, we had the heart to continue. I don't remember Suzuki being there. Was Hanaki-san especially agile? I didn't think it was particularly that or that he was special. I just felt like it would be great to be able to move like him. I believed that he was strong simply because he trained a lot and not because he was particularly agile or had better stamina.

Aoki-sensei's keiko

I first met Aoki-sensei at the Nikko *gasshuku*, I believe, during the summer of my second year of university. He gave me an impression of robustness, audacity, and speed. I wondered what was required to achieve such fast, strong, and solid movements. His movements were completely different from those of our *sempai*. It was impressive. I remember that Aoki-sensei hardly explained

---

[1] Free-form sparring.

anything and that he made us do hours of *renzoku-waza*[1]. The third- and fourth-year members of the university club also practiced Eiko. After these trainings, we'd be completely dead; but we were told that the real training started precisely from that point onwards. It was very hard and rigorous. I did not understand at all why we made these funny *keri* continuously and in a circle; a bit like jumps. I did not see at all how this *keri* could be effective. Aoki-sensei said, "*keri* in this relaxed way is the most effective and strong." However, I thought that for a *keri* to be more effective and stronger, you had to start from a stationary position before kicking; I kept thinking that for a long time.

All the same, I immediately felt that Aoki-sensei's technique was superior and effective. But I wondered how come the technique of the others was not like that, even though they trained in the same way. In the end, what impressed me the most about Aoki was the image he presented, his personality. I wanted to experience for myself the sensation that emanated from his movement. I did not understand anything about the relationship between the movement and its result, and I have to admit that I had trouble doing what he asked of me without giving any explanation. In the end, I said to myself that "one day maybe I will understand...," and the training continued like this without me seeing the meaning. Sometimes our arms were blue with bruises after the long sessions of *gedan-barai*. What could it be used for? Aoki-sensei never explained it to us. This discouraged more than one practitioner who left the club.

Anyway, at that time I myself wasn't very clear in my head about it. I seem to remember once hearing Hokari-san say that "those who train must follow their master without asking questions. "On another occasion I overheard Suzuki make similar comments, saying that "in teaching trainees, you don't have to explain each technique according to your own understanding" and that

---

[1] Technique practiced repetitively and continuously

"even if I give a detailed explanation, I don't think it will make much sense to them." It was from about this time on that Suzuki trained seriously and followed Aoki-sensei without question. But I always wanted to know why; I was argumentative.

Getting closer to Rakutenkai

I don't remember being able to discuss techniques with Suzuki at the time. There was something wise about him, and I had the impression that he thought differently. After university I nevertheless had a few opportunities to talk about karate with him, concerning the result that one could expect from such and such a *keiko*. For instance, Hikari, this technique that allows access to the *wakame-taiso* state: my understanding was that it was a way of acquiring the ability to feel the *tsuki* attack of my partner. I face my partner, then when they attack me with a *tsuki*, I quickly avoid them thanks to Hikari. But Suzuki said to me, "Oh well, for me it's different." I think he saw Hikari as a way of working on human relationships. My understanding of *keiko* was more practical, more materialistic than Suzuki's. I always reasoned in terms of *tsuki*, *keri*, or *kumite*, even when thinking about Hikari.

Eventually, after many experiences, I began to appreciate this way of practicing. I thought Aoki-sensei was extraordinary on a physical level and in the way he moved. I remember him teaching me *mae-geri* for the first time. I was in second year. While telling me "*keri* must be done like this," he did it very quickly. I was flabbergasted, as his *keri* was extremely fast, strong, and different from anything I knew. I had been taught that *keri* was done in a sequence of movements — first raising the leg, then whipping straight with the toes up — but he didn't bother with any foreplay. His *keri* swept away everything I had learned.

I came to think that Suzuki was right. That was the right way to teach karate. He did exactly that. In my case, even in my last university years, when I practiced with Aoki-sensei, in Niigata or in Tokyo, I did as he taught me, but as soon as I practiced by myself, I was filled with doubts. Well, I didn't use the *makiwara* anymore, nor did I move in the old way, but I still wanted to give a logical, mechanical explanation for my movements. For example, Eiko is useful for making the *tsuki* stronger and that's why you have to run Eiko desperately until the whole body becomes a sword. I needed that kind of practical justification, even to run.

Another example: I remember a Rakutenkai *gasshuku* where we did Eiko or something like that and suddenly someone started shouting "Oh, my heavenly father!" For me, who had come to do karate, I said to myself, "What the heck is this?" For my part, I imagined Eiko as a very useful technique for fighting on a large plain, armed with a stick. When I told Suzuki that, he said, "We don't need that kind of explanation. Doesn't this way feel better?" In fact, I don't recall discussing it with Suzuki during the *gasshuku* itself. I rarely attended — once or twice — but when I heard the cry "Oh, my heavenly father!" I figured it wasn't for me or I didn't belong in this world, and I stopped going. Aoki-sensei must have had his reasons, and I wanted to become as strong as him, but on the other hand, "Oh my heavenly Father!" No way, not for me!

Days as manager of the Niigata University Karate Club

After I left Niigata Tekko to succeed my father as head of the company, Aoki-sensei at the same time asked me to become the manager of the Niigata University karate club. Previously, at age 26, I had opened my own *dojo* in town to give substance to my reflections on Aoki-sensei's *keiko* and mine. I wanted to prove that our karate was the best but didn't know how to do that in the absence of a tournament or a big convention of practitioners. The other types of karate held tournaments, at least student tournaments, but not ours. I really wanted to show that the karate I practiced was authentic and the best there was. As I was fairly self-confident, I myself awarded the black belt to the practitioners of my *dojo*. Some were progressing well. I taught in the university club and in my *dojo*. I sometimes took the *dojo* practitioners to train at the club. And then, after a while, my job suffered and the business went into decline, even though I was working hard at it. In the end I had to close the *dojo* in town in order to concentrate on work.

In my *dojo*, we did *usagi-tobi* and *moro-geri*. I adapted an open-legged *usagi-tobi*. I also used other techniques that were unique to me. We tried *mae-geri* from the crouching position or continuously. It was quite hard. I tested the techniques one by one. I had also installed a punching bag because I saw it as a good way to check the effectiveness of our karate. I asked practitioners to do *harai*, *tsuki*, or *keri* on it to feel for themselves what was going on in their body. However, I asked them to keep their hands flexible, in the ordinary *seiken* way. I made them do a lot of experiments and tests. In the beginning the students were incapable of good *keri*, because they had never used the punching bag to improve on their own. Their feet slipped on the bag, they missed the timing, or placed themselves at the wrong distance. I made them do a lot of practice of this kind so that they would get a really good *keri*.

We sometimes received visits from all kinds of people. One day a former boxer came, whom I asked to hit me as hard as possible, but I didn't feel anything at all.

We also happened to participate in a kind of mutual demonstration with a group of Kyokushinkai. People who came to watch were unable to say which of the two karate was better. They simply said that Kyokushinkai karate looked effective because of the noise they made when hitting the *shinai*; we didn't do that kind of stuff.

I talked with my students about the particularities of our karate or what it meant to be "strong" in karate. We also talked about the lack of *jiyu-kumite* in our karate. I explained to them that it was like the difference between kendo and iaido[1]. In our

---

[1] A martial way that features the study of the numerous, different ways of drawing and returning the sword to its scabbard.

time, we no longer fought a duel with a real sword in order to find out who was strongest. So, if our *tsuki* wasn't really strong — just as a *shinai* isn't — there would be no danger in testing it in real combat, but then what's the point? On the other hand, if it was really strong, we couldn't afford to really apply it to a person, could we? I invited them to practice to get a really strong *tsuki*, which they would never have the opportunity to test on anyone. I believe that this kind of exchange helped them understand the reason for our *keiko*.

There was a practitioner in my *dojo* to whom I awarded a black belt and whose movements were closer to those of Aoki-sensei than to mine. He was the only one. I was very happy about him. He didn't have such precise movements as another equally re-markable one, named Mukoyama, but he was sturdy and strong. He is now in his fifties and works as a salaried office employee. We have maintained communication for some time, but currently we only exchange New Year's wishes.

Decline of the Niigata University club

Niigata University Karate Club was known to have no outside activities, such as tournaments and so forth, only training. The other martial arts clubs, like kendo or judo, participated in tour-naments and brought back prizes, but not us. And then a Shito-ryu karate practitioner entered Niigata University and founded a club. This club grew very quickly and participated in tournaments. Later a Wado-ryu karate club was set up. There were only women who practiced in this club. Finally, a Kyokushin-ryu karate club opened up. Eventually there were four karate clubs. Each year there were about forty students who wanted to do karate, about ten per club, but in our club there were the fewest.

To choose a club, the freshmen wanted to see the practice. We tried hard to attract them, but those who came to watch our prac-tice rarely stayed. The people who joined the club tended to have a personal connection, such as being from the same hometown as upperclassmen. I now think that it was our organization at the time that was unsuitable. People only understand a club by practicing there for several years, but not at the beginning.

When I entered the club, we were thirty-six newcomers. In the end only Suzuki and I stayed. At that time there was graffiti on the wall of the *dojo* that said "Why such a rigorous *keiko*?" As a club we should have been thinking about all the factors that were causing people to leave.

As our club had decided to practice Aoki-sensei's way, the practice was really rigorous, and we resigned ourselves to people leaving the club. Yet these people had come to practice karate. So, there was definitely a problem. When I asked some of these people why they left the club, they replied: "I don't want to become a professional *karateka*, nor make a living out of it. I simply wanted to do karate as a university sports activity. So why continue such a rigorous practice?" Our club should have been able to retain some of these people while satisfying others ready to go after a rigorous *keiko*. Obviously, without the creation of other karate clubs, we might have survived even without questioning ourselves.

Well, in my time and in Suzuki's time, the club worked well. It was even able to produce excellent people like Kaneda-kun and Mukoyama-kun. I had the opportunity to speak with Mukoyama. He told me that, despite the torments, he had come to understand a lot of things, thanks to the training. Aoki-sensei is a kind of path-seeker, an austere practitioner. He came to teach in our club, but I also had the impression that he was using us to test research tracks. If we had practiced an old-style karate, a little hard, and had participated in tournaments, our club might not have declined. But on the other hand, it is thanks to this rigorous practice of Aoki-sensei that people like Kaneda and Mukoyama emerged, although many others never really took off.

When the practice is rigorous and without explanation, some will continue with the hope of understanding one day. It would have been difficult to scoop up all of them, but couldn't we have explained a bit more anyway? On the other hand, explaining too much is not good either. So where to start, and where to stop? Sometimes we thought we could do hard karate in the first year, hitting the *makiwara* and getting calluses on the hands. Then, in the second year, we would ask to remove the tension from the technique. Or, we imagined a progression over four years starting from Shotokan karate, then moving on to flexible karate and ending with shintaido karate. Or, we could have allowed first- and second-year practitioners to participate in tournaments, but not after – something like that.

Even if you don't understand what Aoki-sensei is doing right from the beginning, if you keep at it, you'll understand after about three years. Practicing like this from the beginning, you progress faster. The *sempai* have practiced and experienced enough hard karate to understand what it is, and to protect the younger ones from having to redo the whole process. They should start directly with flexible karate. Aoki-sensei used to say: "In order to watch TV, you don't need to study the principles of how television works. Just switch it on." And yet, an insect like a dragonfly or a butterfly metamorphoses. It starts out as an egg, then a caterpillar, then a chrysalis, and finally a butterfly. The butterfly goes through all these stages during a lifetime. A butterfly cannot be born directly into a butterfly. What Aoki-sensei told us seems to me today to be kind of theoretical, scientific, to be honest. I think that's fine. I understand it up to that point, but I don't understand from there. I sent a letter to Aoki-sensei to ask him about that. I don't remember getting a response.

What I understood, what I learned

In my case, I was one step short of becoming the "real thing," and I had drawn a line for myself within the scope of my understanding. In Suzuki's case, I think he was able to go beyond that and acquire the way of thinking by properly inheriting the influence of his teacher, absorbed most of the essence, and was able to make use of it in his own world. In Hanaki-san's case, he loved pushing himself. For my part, I did not quite understand what I was doing. I remember doing Eiko for the first time in Nagaoka; it was foggy and I took the opportunity to cheat. It's silly when you think about it.

I was not particularly aware of what I learned from *keiko*, as for example, working on interpersonal relationships or on a way of thinking, etc. But sometimes I had the feeling of understanding. For instance, when Aoki-sensei explained *irimi* to us, he said that it was also useful outside of the *dojo*. Sometimes I remember it and understand how to use *irimi* to receive the feeling of a person, partner, or opponent, to deal with or go along with the person. Other than that, I don't see any karate influence in what I do on a daily basis. I don't do any health practices, but when I need to refresh myself, I naturally do Tenshingoso. I was taught through Tenshingoso how to open things up by cutting in front of me and then how to offer up and devote all of myself and return to the earth. In my daily life I am not really aware of such devotion. I understand Tenshingoso as stretching gymnastics. Well, I feel like I learned something good. A technique like AH-UN or a principle like *ichigo ichie*, I learned from Aoki-sensei in the first or second year. For me, AH is liberation and UN silence. For example, while running a marathon, I tried AH when I was going through a very hard time and was able to enter this state of AH.

Matsuhashi-san is the first Rakutenkai member to have come to Niigata University's karate club. He came with Aoki-sensei and I saw that his movements resembled those of Aoki-sensei. Kato-sensei, another member of Rakutenkai, also came and gave me a different impression than Aoki-sensei and Matsuhashi-san. At that time, I was no longer the captain of the club. I don't remember if Okada-sensei also came to Niigata. However, I clearly remember him somewhere running Eiko at full power. I also remember Aoki-sensei's wife, she left an impression on me. She was remarkably supportive and had her own work and otherwise her own path[1]. I keep the image of her as a bright and joyful person.

One day, I don't remember exactly when, I happened to stay over at Aoki-sensei's after an intense *keiko*. It seemed a natural continuation of the program, something genuine. A thought then crossed my mind, "If I lived with Aoki-sensei under the same roof and I stayed next to him, something extraordinary could happen." I thought about it, but I didn't do it. I trusted Aoki-sensei then; I totally respected him and admired him. It was like that, and I think I kept that feeling.

---

[1] "Her own path"/ "jibun no michi" (自分の道)

Takeo HOKARI-HANDA

The initial interview with Takeo Handa took place in a Tokyo café in September, 2004 without an interpreter, in a mixture of English and Japanese. After transcription and translation of the Japanese parts, the text was written in English and then in Japanese. In December, 2019, when the interview for the validation of the Japanese text was held, Mr. Handa and his wife, *Keiko*, both then retired, received us in the Handa's beautiful family property in Nagano, where they had just taken over management of family business interests.[1]

University of Niigata

I was born in Niigata Prefecture in 1948. There was one girl and four boys in my family. I am the youngest and there is a brother between Shiko[2] and me. This brother is currently taking care of our parents in Niigata. Shiko's real first name is Kazuo. "Shiko" is just a shintaido nickname that I no longer want to use. I went to Niigata University, and that's where I started practicing karate. My brother Kazuo was five years older than me and already living in Tokyo.

I stayed in college for five years instead of the usual four years. All my fellow practitioners of the same generation from the karate club also had to repeat a year and do a fifth year. We loved karate so much that we went to the university compound to practice [karate] at night instead of going to class.

Between the first and second year of university studies, I spent six months in Yokohama. I had missed a single teaching unit in the academic program, but since I could only make it up from September to March, I had to wait six months to re-enroll[3]. So, I took the opportunity to spend this semester in Yokohama and practice with Rakutenkai. I was 20 and 1/2 years old. After this period, I returned to Niigata University and its regular karate practice.

---

[1] **Credits:** *Interview:* P. Quettier. *Transcription of Japanese parts:* S. Iida. *Translation to English:* K. Hokari. *Editing/translation:* P. Quettier. *Proofreading:* A. Weber, L. Ordeman.

[2] Kazuo Hokari was nicknamed "Shiko."

[3] In Japan the academic year ends in March.

I considered karate as a form of *budo*, a strong way. But after I graduated from college, I didn't have much interest in strength anymore. I rather had the feeling that through the practice I could have access to a different world. This world did not seem to me to be made up of visible, palpable things. I felt that our world was like a shadow of another world which I could enter through practice.

Being part of Rakutenkai

At that time Aoki-sensei was already visiting our Niigata club twice a year for spring and autumn *gasshuku*. He came with Matsuhashi-san, and they allowed me to go deeper into karate-do. Because of this missed semester, I suddenly had the opportunity to go see them and get a direct, more in-depth perspective on their practice. I went there without hesitation.

Senior members like Matsuhashi-san, Okada-san, or Nishiyama-san were trying to start some sort of cleaning business for schools and other such facilities. So, I worked with them. I also cooked because Matsuhashi-san told me that "cooking is a very good practice." This is how I understand things, and so I cooked for them and practiced with them in the evening. It was a crazy time but so interesting.

Questions about the meaning of the practice

Like I said, I didn't start practicing to get strong in a martial sense. I considered such an idea to be not very serious. Instead, I firmly believed in the spiritual qualities of the practice. I also practiced aikido.

I no longer have a precise memory of this six-month stay with Rakutenkai nor of what I was able to gain there, but on returning to the karate club of Niigata University, I was surprised by the impression of "children's games" which emanated from the practice of my fellow students. From then on, along with a few other club members, I began to promote a more sincere approach to the practice and became more and more invested in *keiko* itself. This led me to ask myself seriously, again and again, the same question: "What does the practice of sogo-budo or that of karate bring to me?" Frankly speaking, I still had no desire to get stronger, nor did I have any proof that such a *keiko* had made me stronger, not even that I had gained anything from it.

At some point though, I started to feel things I had never experienced before. But that was much later. Right after my six-month period with Rakutenkai, I didn't feel like I had had a special experience, something that would have made me say, "That's it!" I was still very deeply in search of myself.

Entering deeply into the keiko experience

I vividly remember the day my brother Kazuo said to me, "You have become clear and transparent." I had been taught that you could see other people's bodies as "transparent," but I had never seen such a thing or experienced anything new. I simply had, by observing the practice of my comrades on their return from Tokyo, the feeling of seeing it as child's play, and I interpreted this as a deficit to be made up for in terms of honest investment and concentration in practice.

I understood that the technique could only be effective on the condition of having invested very seriously in the *keiko*. Progress brought more efficient techniques but also increased sensitivity and the ability to see things that were otherwise invisible. All these phenomena amounted to the same thing, just different ways of expressing it. In my case, this realization made my practice much more enjoyable. Rather than a process to gain something, the *keiko* had itself become a pure pleasure.

For example, our generation of Japanese was the first to make exclusive use of chairs for sitting down, starting from early childhood. We had no experience of sitting in the *seiza* position. So, I was very bad at *seiza* at first. But as I progressed in the *keiko*, I began to calm down deeply and to feel good. I then took pleasure in meditating as long as possible in *seiza*, and I began to experience various spiritual worlds that I entered by practicing different forms of *mudra*. I could travel from one spiritual world to another, appearing to myself as a vision, depending on whether I was using one *mudra* or another. I remember seeing myself one day suspended like a star among others in a starry sky, contemplating the cosmos and the earth from very high. I have had many such experiences.

During *keiko*, while in motion, I got to the point of not feeling tired anymore, even if, for example, I was running in Eiko for a very long time. Regardless of the distance covered, I never had the urge to stop because of my fatigue or because I had difficulty breathing. I remember such a practice of infinite round trips of Eiko with my *bo* at night in a park along the port of Yokohama. It was as if I had lost the sensation of my body. Such experiences were truly joyful.

Another *keiko*, very popular at the time, consisted of going individually to a Shinto shrine in our vicinity in the middle of the night, and many nights in a row, to engage in a meditative practice of moving our *bokuto* up and down, slowly and without interruption. This practice is called *age-oroshi*. I was doing 1,000 lifts and descents every night and felt really good. As I was alone in the middle of the night, a rumor eventually spread in the neighborhood that a ghost was visiting the shrine every night [laughs]. I really liked this *keiko* which allowed me to enter a spiritual world of high concentration.

Extensions of spiritual experiences

One day, after I graduated from university, Aoki-sensei played music records for us at his house. Ma-chan[1], Toshima-san[2], and a few others were there. Aoki-sensei had a lot of music records. He started with modern jazz, then rock'n'roll, the Beatles and others.

---

[1] Affectionate abbreviation for Masatake Egami.
[2] Maiden name of Shigeko Ito.

I can't remember the precise order, but at one point he played traditional African music, concluding with a Bach violin concerto. The effect on me was absolutely extraordinary. Until my dying day, I will never stop thanking him and thanking shintaido for giving me the opportunity and the sensitivity to live such an experience. Every time the violin string sounded "gyunn!" it was like an arrow of light shooting into and through my body. I suddenly understood the value of art and that of music to the highest degree. It was not so much the technique of the musician as his understanding of the work being played, in a state of such high concentration to the point of becoming one with the very mind of the composer. This enormous shock of artistic emotion allowed me to understand how important music was for us humans. I had never had such a profound experience in *keiko*. We had heard this famous story of the "birth of Eiko," during which seven people had a very special experience. I had never experienced anything like it myself, but this musical experience was really something!

A few years ago, I traveled to Italy with my wife. At one point we visited St. Peter's Basilica in Rome. In the Basilica there is a special room called the "prayer room" into which ordinary visitors are usually forbidden to enter by the guards. Anyway, the guard had left, and without realizing it, I walked into that room. Everyone present was praying from the depths of their hearts. I then had the feeling of a very strong spiritual presence, like very thick snow falling hard in the room, healing these people and all the others in the room. I did not want to leave that room.

Although these two experiences were very different, each has made an extraordinary impression on me. This was especially true for the music experience. To this day nothing comparable has ever again happened to me. The true value of shintaido is to make possible these kinds of situations in which a person can be marked by simply listening to Bach. Shintaido purifies the mind by purifying the body, expands our consciousness and allows us to simply accept everything and make our communication with others deeper.

Participation in community projects

After I graduated, things remained more or less the same, as if my studies were continuing. I lived in Yokohama with Ma-chan, Minagawa-san and Okada-san's younger brother, Gan-san. The four of us lived in a six-tatami room, upstairs in Aoki-sensei's house. Our *sempai* were working. We pooled our money. I don't know how long it lasted exactly... I would say about a year. At one-point Ishide Tadashi-san joined us, and then he went on to Hokkaido to learn mink farming with the idea of making a business out of it. With the same idea in mind, we tried selling flowers in order to raise money to support our community. That did not work out, nor did other similar initiatives succeed at that time. Aoki-sensei asked us to form a sort of community outside of Tokyo, in the mountains of Kanagawa prefecture. It was a good place to create a community. A few people went there but soon came back.

At that time, Aoki-sensei was trying to teach shintaido in America and Europe. He had gone to the United States with Minagawa-san. For our part we tried to teach and preach shintaido. I would say that all of this lasted about two years. Of course, we practiced in Nogeyama Park, under the guidance of Fugaku-san. Minagawa-san, Ma-chan [Masatake], Gan-chan, and I formed a gang of four wags. We worked during the day and... [laughing like someone about to tell a funny story] ... Fugaku-san asked us to practice on our own every night. He taught us two evenings a week. In winter, the weather could be so cold that none of us practiced every night, and on some days, no one even went to the park. And so it happened that Fugaku-san's teaching day fell on one of those very cold days, and he couldn't find anyone. Instead, we had gone somewhere to drink coffee and have a cozy evening. Fugaku-san was a very serious-minded person. He said to himself, "Those young guys didn't come because I'm too lazy myself," ... and... he went out in the cold to douse himself with buckets of ice water! When we heard the news from another person later, we were devastated and felt somewhat guilty. We thought, "People of our generation sometimes feel very different from theirs — they are like old samurai and we are lazy!"

Little by little, towards a personal and family destiny

When that time ended, I traveled to the United States on my own for about eight months... at least, less than a year. Upon my return, I married the older sister of my brother Shiko-san's wife[1]. I was then 27 years old, and it was six months after Shiko-san's wedding. Gan-san had returned to his hometown. He intended to found a kind of home for disabled people. As a married man I now had to enter the workforce. This is how I entered the service of a company, and I have been working until today, changing companies twice. I also continued to practice for about five years. I went every week to the Sunday *keiko* at the Tokyo Taikukan and to *gasshuku*. And then from year to year my relationship gradually loosened. One day, I went to a bojutsu *gasshuku* at the end of which Aoki-sensei asked that everyone present take an exam. I had no desire to take such an exam because my intention was only to practice. But everyone else responded to the request, and so I complied; but after that I no longer wanted to continue. It was the right time, anyway! I said to myself, "I have my own feelings and I pursue my own idea of life: I no longer need to participate in a *gasshuku* or anything else." That's how I just quit.

Today I feel that those memories belong to a long-gone past. I have found my own path of spiritual development, and I want to stick to it.

---

[1] By marrying the eldest of the family, Takeo-san took her name, to ensure the continuity of the name.

Final thoughts

My feeling is that each person must strive to follow and continue on one's own path. Social circumstances fluctuate with ups and downs, but we should move forward no matter what, day by day. Each individuality, each life finds its end, but we continue year after year, generation after generation. Even when death comes for me, I want to continue on my way. I have no interest in the past.

Aoki-sensei goes his way. Each person pursuing his own path is happy. This is a good thing. He's a very special character. He strives to create, then to destroy, in order to create again. I'm too weak to stay close to him. Getting out of his perimeter has made me happy.

Masatake EGAMI

M. Egami was our first instructor and we have maintained a constant relationship with him over the years through the exchange of greeting cards and visits during our trips to Japan. The interview was conducted in English during such a visit, in September, 2004. The work was then put on hold for 14 years, and we refrained from meeting him, as well as most of the other members of the Rakutenkai. Finally, M. Egami's English text was approved in the spring of 2018, followed by approval of the Japanese translation by M. Hirano in November, 2019.

The significant position occupied by M. Egami, as the son of S. Egami and between the different generations of the Rakutenkai, including H. Aoki, obviously made him cautious in his expression. The insertion of the parenthetical [laughs] — as a Japanese way of indicating embarrassment and as an invitation to non-verbal communication on a delicate subject — is therefore particularly important in his case. We have noticed that for this same purpose, M. Egami also used short and sudden interruptions in speech, giving it a very characteristic prosody. Simple ellipses have been inserted to mark these occurrences.[1]

Childhood in a martial arts environment

I was born in 1947 in Kyushu. Later, I moved with my parents to Tokyo. When my father was a university student, he studied karate. After graduation, he wanted to be a businessman, in Kyushu ... but he didn't succeed. When I was three years old, he went bankrupt, and we had to "escape" to the Tokyo area. We kind of stayed hidden in a very remote place in the countryside of Chiba Prefecture. There, he still wanted to be a businessman. He had many ideas and did many things, but nothing really worked. He would arrive one day late or that kind of thing. Sometimes, when his business was successful, we were quite rich, and then suddenly we were incredibly poor again. I was very young, so I don't remember very much ... just a few things. Finally, as he was already famous in the karate world, some people who lived in the area came to him and said, "Please stop trying to go into business. Please teach us karate." That's how they pulled him back into the karate world again. Meanwhile, he was still a little ashamed as he didn't think that karate was a proper job. He couldn't think of it as

---

[1] **Credits:** *Interview/transcription/editing/translation*: P. Quettier. *Proofreading*: D. Richardson, L. Seaman.

a business to make money for himself. He was that kind of person. But as we were very poor, he decided he had to teach karate.

As time went by, my father taught in various places. That eventually led to his meeting Inoue-sensei from shinwa-taido. Before that he had been studying karate for a long time and was strongly pursuing a personal quest about the effectiveness of karate. This story about him is quite well known. When he was young, karate was supposed to be effective. But when he watched people and received different people's attacks,[1] he had to admit that he couldn't feel anything. Then he went to see many famous teachers and, although it was very impolite to do so, he asked them, "Would you please attack me and let me feel your attack?" And indeed, he honestly couldn't feel anything. Those from whom he felt a little effect were boxers. Those from whom he felt the most effect were ordinary people. Their attacks moved him. From then on, he continued to pursue this quest to understand what made certain attacks effective: "Why, why, why do these supposedly deadly attackers have an ineffective attack when faced squarely?" he asked himself. Around that time, a junior member of the Waseda University karate club asked him to look at his *tsuki*. Seeing it, my father was suddenly struck by something different and asked, "Where did you learn that?" It appeared that this *tsuki* came from Inoue-sensei. So, my father decided to go see him.

There is a story about their meeting. In karate my father had learned something about a technique named *sankaku-tobi* from Funakoshi-sensei. Funakoshi-sensei had mentioned it while he watched his own son doing *kumite* with my father one day. This technique was considered a secret in karate. As my father was one of the strongest practitioners in karate, he knew the secret. Later, when he met Inoue-sensei's teaching, he could see that in the shinwa-taido school, *sankaku-tobi* was taught to newcomers right

---

[1] This technique consists of receiving a fist attack (*tsuki*) directly into the stomach with little or no protection. This is done in order to measure the effects of the impact on the body by its displacement.

from the start. In due time, he talked with Inoue-sensei about *sankaku-tobi* being taught to beginners. Then it was Inoue-sensei's turn to be amazed at his knowledge. In fact, Inoue-sensei had thought that people in karate didn't know about *sankaku-tobi*. He was greatly impressed when he heard my father point it out in the shinwa-taido *keiko*.

Those are the circumstances through which my father asked to be accepted and entered into Inoue-sensei's *keiko*. Having thus shown his understanding, he thought he had been accepted as a disciple, and from then on, he did every necessary thing, such as cleaning, taking care of shoes — even when a large party of people gathered, he knew which shoes belonged to which person, even though all the shoes looked almost identical — and so on. But in Inoue-sensei's mind, my father wasn't a disciple yet. My father realized this when Inoue asked him one day, "Would you please become my disciple?" Martial arts are this kind of world. After that, there was an introductory ceremony, and for the first time ... Oh! [showing surprise] I am not telling my story but my father's! Well, that is to explain how my father was able to start changing the karate *keiko*.

He had come to Inoue-sensei in search of techniques, but you cannot steal a master's technique. A technique isn't a "thing" that can be given or taken. One has to "fill oneself," or reach a proper level of accomplishment by practice, and then one will be able to master a certain technique. So, at some point, my father stopped trying and just accepted things as they came, naturally. That is how his karate changed. It's not that karate changed, but the way of life in karate changed. Inoue-sensei's *keiko* wasn't only a matter of technique. My father practiced like this almost every day for three years. Financially, he was still totally broke, so he wasn't paying much for tuition. This might have made some other members jealous. Anyway, every New Year, we would visit Inoue-sensei's home to show our respect[1]. I was in elementary school at that time, and I remember Inoue-sensei as being very big — he was small but made an impression of being very big — and it was nice to be near him. His movement and his speech were very interesting.

Personal apprenticeship of aikido and shintaido

I began to be interested in martial arts ... [laughs] ... we are gradually approaching the core of the history: How I began the practice of shintaido. When I was in late elementary school or my first year of junior high school [about 13], ... Mister A.[2] [laughs] came to our house. Many people had been coming to our house. My father would sit and people would talk. It was so interesting to listen to them. Sometimes they would practice. My father never told me to leave, so I stayed and watched. It was very interesting. Sometimes, I would serve as a guinea pig for my father's experiments. When Mister A. came, he was like a brother. He would stay. He was very earnest and eager to learn. About that time, I was in university and, as there was no other practice there, such as karate or shinwa-taido, I started to practice aikido. It was very interesting. Morihei Ueshiba was an impressive person, and he was Inoue-sensei's uncle. Aikido was a bit strange, as it used power. I could see that I was already influenced by my father's and Mister A.'s *keiko*. Still, I practiced aikido even though it created a dilemma for me. This was three years before Ueshiba's death. One day, he came to the *dojo* in Shinjuku. He lived in a building near where we were practicing. I remember him shouting at me, "This is the way a *jo* [short staff] should be used!" He shouted so much

---

[1] The traditional practice discouraged a direct financial relationship between master and disciples. Instead, a custom was established that once a year, at New Year, the disciple and his family would pay a ceremonial visit to the master's home to show their respect and present a gift, in money or in goods, in gratitude for the teachings.

[2] At first, Masatake Egami used the expression "Mister A." when talking about Rakutenkai leader and founder of shintaido, Hiroyuki Aoki. Later, he would sometimes, use "Mister Aoki" or simply "Aoki," in the way historians do.

that the elder members tried to restrain him. I remember another occasion when I had gone to aikido right after coming back from a Sogo-budo Renmei *gasshuku*. After the class I happened to meet Ueshiba going up the stairs. He was ahead of me and I was following him when he turned suddenly and shouted, "Who is this guy?!" My energy must have been different and strange to him. His assistant told him that I was one of his disciples, but he didn't seem to believe it. All in all, aikido was interesting, and I progressed to *nidan*.

Then, I gradually grew attracted to the sogo-budo "cult" [laughs]. My life was trouble-free. Just before my graduation from university, Mister A. came to my house, and before leaving he asked, "Would you please come and teach us aikido?" It might have been manipulative on his part, but it made me proud, and I led an aikido *gasshuku* for them. Later, I went to a *daienshu* in Asama, after which I started to practice. I did it very seriously. What I was especially interested in was what happened outside *keiko*, in daily life.

When I was about 23 or 24, I wanted to be a Christian, but I couldn't invest myself fully in the religious aspect. I remember that when I was 24, Mister A. came to me and asked me to put together a group that would be the second generation of Rakutenkai. We held many *keiko* and *gasshuku*. Five of us decided to live in Shinjuku together as a commune, which we called the Nihon Juku. After Gan "graduated" from studying with Mister A., he left the group. Then Takeo got a job, and Minagawa took an apartment with Pam. We all separated. The Nihon Juku was not a success. Maybe Mister A. had expected something big, but it ended very small. At that point, around 1976, I was about 29.

When I was around 26 years old, every day I would experience many different states of mind, some very mysterious. That's a fact ... but ... anyway.... when I am alone, I am happy. When I'm with people, I am more tense. I was doing shintaido like a religion. I remember a special meeting in Nogeyama: One after another, everyone was called to talk with Mister A. I thought I might be asked to be a disciple, but there was no sign. Something wasn't stable. I was wondering, "Why doesn't he say anything?" In the end, that was probably a good thing.

Teaching the Honbu keiko

In 1975, Mister A. asked me to lead *gorei* at the *honbu*, the main *keiko*. Kato-sensei and Fugaku-sensei had stopped. Previously, after graduating from university, I had gone to Nogeyama, and I got the impression that there was some kind of dead feeling. The feeling that something had already finished. Matsuhashi-san wasn't there. "Why isn't he here?" I wondered. Dead feeling. That's possibly why Mister A. wanted to start a second generation. I didn't understand those things then. Mister A. said it was just that those people were old. At first, it was very hard to give *gorei* ... very difficult. Mister A. warned me, "Nobody will tell you what to do." But even a small suggestion would have been very helpful. One day, Kato-sensei was present when something happened in the class, and I saw things suddenly change. He probably saw it, and saw my understanding, because he said something about it. That was very helpful. Gradually things changed.

[After the interviewer had shared some good memories of those times.] Yes, really, those days were happy days for me. With visions ... that kept coming true. For example, I thought that when one gave *gorei*, one had to be clean in mind. Therefore, every *goreisha* needed to prepare before practice. That's why the atmosphere was so severe for me before each *keiko*. One day, I was so tired that no matter how hard I tried, I couldn't prepare for the *keiko* properly. Still, I had to give *gorei*, so I decided to do an experiment to see what happened when I was unable to prepare. At some point during that *keiko*, I silently said to myself, "*Wasshoi!*"[1] To my surprise, one of the participants in the group answered

---

[1] "*Wasshoi!*" is a kind of cheering-up expression used in Japan to "take heart" (for example by a party carrying a heavy *mikoshi* during a festival).

"*Wasshoi!*" out loud. I had said it just to myself, secretly in my mind, and this person was responding out loud. Again, I said silently, "*Wasshoi!*" and somebody else responded loudly, "*Wasshoi!*" It went on and on that way. That made me realize how deep the link was between us in *keiko*, and how important it was for everyone to be able to influence the community in a positive way. I thought, "Everybody, as well as me, should make their bodies and minds clean!" It was really a fearful understanding; interesting and awesomely fearful. Before that realization, I had thought that only good feelings could have an effect, otherwise, there was no *gorei*. But from that experience, I understood that it is possible to manipulate people. It was really an interesting time.

Another time, I had been listening to a Bach violin sonata and it stayed with me. During *keiko*, we did some movement that was in the same rhythm as the music inside me. It was very beautiful. After *keiko*, someone came up to me and told me about this violin sonata. The connection is so close that we must all be pure, *goreisha* and everyone, because we all influence each other.

Some important changes seemed to happen around the time that Mister A. went to Brazil. After a short time there, he wrote me a letter in which he said that he wanted to stay in Brazil. He asked me, "Would you please take care of the group?" My feeling was, "I can't, I can't!" But I believed in him, so I thought to myself, "If this is how he really wants things to be, then so be it!" I wrote back to him, agreeing to his request. But it seemed that this was not what he really wanted [laughs]. Maybe he wanted me to write, "Please, come back!" [laughs]. Suddenly he *was* back ... just after I had written to him! ... I was very surprised ... [laughs]! But it really didn't matter to me. So, I introduced him to the new members. But I was really surprised that, as I watched him in the Tokyo Gymnasium, he seemed to have become very small ... It was very amazing ... he had nothing special ... he was just like a normal person. Other people were noticing it too.

Then things began to change and ... well, how can I say this? I have kept it secret, OK? Something personal happened. He interfered in a very disrespectful way ... I mean, a spiritual way... a way special to him. It was something I couldn't permit. Really, I wanted to kill him. I was so angry! But suddenly he was nowhere to be found. Of all people, he was the one who shouldn't have done this, but he did it [laughs]... and then he wasn't there [laughs]. Later, he apologized ... in front of everybody [laughs]. Of course, he did it without naming any names. He said, "I interfered too much!" I was the only one who knew what he meant.

At about the same time, I had an inspiration. I was walking from the Shinjuku office, near the two movie theaters on the way to the station, when a strong vision came to me about what was happening, and what was going to happen. I suddenly realized everything! I thought, "If I remain here, I am finished!" I had to get out. But it was difficult because I am Japanese ... very Japanese .... Then I realized that I could go abroad. At that time Jugoro-san[1] and Mister A. had gone travelling abroad... Then I was told by several people ... you [interviewer] told me, as did John and Lee and John Kent and some other people: "Why don't you travel?" Suddenly everyone was telling me something like, "You look tired, what about travelling?" I was wondering about it when John and Lee offered some financial assistance. I wrote to Mister A., "If you agree, I would like to travel." He said, "Then it should be only a personal thing ..." [laughs]. Many things were happening at the same time. There was the urge to go abroad. I was having some problems in *keiko*, too: Giving *gorei* was beautiful and sacred to me ... but I was thinking, "It's wonderfully beautiful ... but it's enough!" I felt a sort of hole inside me. I felt I needed to be on my own to heal it. All those things were happening at the same time. That's why I went abroad with John Kent and Michael Thompson.

---

[1] Yoshitaka ITO

Looking for and finding "a way out"

Well, I am a very serious person, too serious. So, at that point I tried to break my serious self. But I didn't break [laughs] ... or maybe I did, just superficially. Travelling was interesting. I went to Mexico and Europe. I still wanted to be finished with shintaido, but my problem was how to find a proper way out. Even though I wanted to stop, I started to put together a shintaido group in Mexico. After forming the group, I thought I would be able to leave. But that wasn't possible. Altogether, I remained abroad a year and a half. Then, there was the issue of my father's stroke and death. Initially, I didn't think about coming back to Japan., My brother called me and said, "Please come back!" But I refused. Finally, Mister A. called me [laughs]... and he also said, "Come back" ... [laughs] ... I was very surprised. But I didn't have any money to buy a ticket ... Finally, a friend lent me the money so that I could come back, and I arrived in Japan three months before my father's passing. When I visited him in the intensive care unit of the hospital, although he had brain damage, I think he recognized me. When I grasped his hand, he opened it and slowly waved it left and right. I was shocked. I had done many bad things in Mexico and in Europe. I did all of them because I wanted to break myself. So, when my father reacted in this way to my presence, I thought that he was shouting in his heart, "Don't come anymore!" But later I realized that he was saying to me, "Goodbye!"

Coming back to Japan, I still had the problem of wanting to leave shintaido, and I was wondering how to do it properly. If I were to encounter Mister A., he might try to control me again [laughs]. I really didn't want that. So, I made myself quiet ... and faded away. He came into my dreams every day... It was amazing.

[After some general exchange with the interviewer about the subjective influence experience of cult members] Well, it's difficult! There is something in shintaido itself ... some kind of problem. If possible, it should be made clear... It's only a personal thing ... up to the individual ... but I don't know, really. In truth, it can happen in any world ... even in a business company. It relates to the question of using people ... for another purpose. I think that we [educators, managers] must learn to wait ... to wait for people to grow. Otherwise, when somebody wants to make a person into this or that ... it goes beyond human reach ... it becomes "super human." We must wait and allow the person to grow. It's much better that way. *Gorei* is like that ... Mister A. once taught me that there was a better way of giving *gorei* — by standing outside ... not inside ... the group and watching the people growing. He has both! It's really sad, actually, that Okada-san couldn't leave. Sad! Sometime after I quit shintaido, there was an anniversary, the 25th I think. At that time Okada-san called me to say, "Please come to the 25th anniversary." I told him, "Please, take me off your list! [laughs]" .... He got angry and said, "Don't say that! I too want to quit." [laughs] Sad indeed.

Practicing shin-ei-taido and building up a personal way of life

When I came back from Mexico, I thought that I would be finished with any kind of *keiko*, *budo* or anything else. But after my father's death and before I got married, I went to meet Inoue-sensei to give him my greetings and tell him about my projects. He asked, "Are you practicing?" He added, "It's not good to practice alone!" Later, he reiterated, "You had better practice with other people." When I got a chance to meet him again, he said, "You can come to me!" It didn't feel like he was manipulating me, so I decided to go. After practicing with him, I realized many things! I am very sorry ... but I must say that, by his own account, Mister A. thought he would be some kind of successor to Inoue-sensei, but in my opinion, that is not the case at all. I really came to understand that they are completely different people ... they have very little in common!

Nonetheless, I think that in shintaido, Eiko is Mister A.'s masterpiece! Mister A. had a vision, he put things together, and Eiko was born. It's a great and very beautiful masterpiece. My thinking is that the masterpiece was born, right? ... But that and the Eiko we do now are not the same ... you know? This is yet another work of Mister A. The time of birth is the time of birth ... Then follows a *kata* ... it is the expression ... and the birth and the expression are not always the same ... although sometimes it's possible that they are the same. This can be true of many things. It is a process, everything is a process. Birth ... every time something is born ... it's not good or bad. To make it into the form of a *kata* is Mister A.'s work. I think that at the time of its birth it was something very great. Then ... everything went ...! That is not a question of technique ... it's expression ... the world of expression. Technique is another matter.

I found that through shinwa-taido — later called shin-ei-taido — I could heal this hole in myself. Really! But I didn't want the experience of being in a cult again in shinwa-taido. It had been a very rich experience ... but you don't want to do it twice, because, in the Japanese way, it is very difficult to get out. I think that it's up to the leader ... the person at the top. If that person is straight-minded, he can let people be free. Otherwise ... it becomes a cult. *Budo* is a top-down system. Mister A. has been making use of that top-down characteristic ... although he always said that this was not good ... [laughs]. If the leader is straight-minded ... it's OK to go ... to go into ... this is difficult to explain ... To that point, I like the zen world. The zen monk who wrote the calligraphy that I have downstairs, he is one of my teachers ... my master ... so-called master, you know what I mean? He is very talented, and he could have manipulated me, but he never did. Always "pat!" [making a gesture of cutting some string attached in front of himself], he cuts! He never pulls [making a movement like pulling a string], but rather cuts [motioning in front of the stomach]. We talk and then it's finished! Just talking is enough ... This time is this time. Then you cut and go back. I realized that many masters, or so-called masters, do pull. In that case, when I am away from them, I feel, "Ha! I want to meet with him" ... or something like that. In the zen master's case, never! But when you meet him it's very intense ... an intense time. Then, when it is finished, it's over. In Inoue-sensei's case there was a slight pulling, but it was not really a problem. There are three masters inside me: Inoue-sensei, the zen monk Maruichi-sensei, and my father ... I understand that now.

Final considerations

[After some tentative conversation with the interviewer comparing Master Aoki's approach with Picasso's, who's habitual "betrayal" of relationships with close friends or family seemed inherent to the artistic process itself].

Picasso's way is OK for me ... but in Mister A.'s case, it is not exactly the same! I had hoped he would be somebody like that. He called me once about some problem he had. He wanted to explain himself. Actually, it didn't concern me ... but he wanted to tell me ... because ... how to say this? ... well, he wanted me to believe him ... and I did believe him ... but he didn't quite admit anything ... he kept making excuses to me. Well, if he thought that what he did was OK, then he should do as he thought! But no, he wanted someone to approve of him. Really, it was sad! ... Also, on different matters he could come across as kind of envious ... not honest? For example, when I was in Mexico, somebody wrote to me saying, "Well Ma-chan, you are developing shintaido in Mexico, but you should remember that this place was Mister A.'s first!" [laughs]. "Mexico is not your place but Mister A.'s!" I was very surprised and didn't understand what was happening. So, I didn't write back to this person. Instead, I wrote directly to Mister A. Then he apologized [laughs]! Really, I couldn't understand it. It's not manly, is it? If he had written directly to me, "It's not your place," that would have been OK. But why go through another person? This person had been manipulated [laughs].

As a martial art, physically, shintaido is not good enough. Mentally, I think it can teach people how to devote themselves absolutely to the search for truth, or something like that. I have another way, but shintaido could be one way. Physically, it's not enough for a martial art, not enough. The karate part is quite good, I think. Some parts are good and other parts are not martial enough ... just forms. Form is not good or bad, but simply form! As a martial art there is another way. That's why I say that Eiko is a masterpiece. It's good for people to devote their study to some absolute. But such an absolute also has the tendency to grow into a cult [laughs]. Now, I know there is a much easier way... [laughs]: daily life ... we can learn through daily life.

Aikido was mainly created by Inoue-sensei ... very few people know that. Actually, the head of the Oomoto-kyo[1] asked him to help Ueshiba-sensei. As Inoue was a true pupil of the founder of Oomoto, he helped Ueshiba-sensei. Also, he was Ueshiba's nephew. You know the concepts of *ura* [back facing] and *omote* [front facing]? Ueshiba-sensei was the front, visible, part. In 1988, we gave a demonstration of shinwa-taido in Tokyo to which several shintaido members came to watch. Afterward, I was a little bit disappointed to hear that Mister A. had declared, "That's very old!" [laughs]. In fact, Inoue-sensei was very old, that's true. He practiced until he was 90 years old. It was nearly unbelievable. We are accustomed to saying that in *budo* any person can practice to any age. But that is usually not true. In his case, he could. He had not much muscle power, as he was ninety years old, but he showed us that he was still very effective. He was a living proof that there is something beyond physical, muscular technique. Shintaido makes people move easily in a prescribed dimension. In shinwa-taido, we don't try to control ... just do ... cut [gestures].

---

[1] **Oomoto-kyo** is a religion founded in 1892 by Deguchi Nao (1836–1918), often categorized as a new Japanese religion derived from Shinto.

That is very interesting. Shinwa-taido starts from the strongest point ... conditioning. That's all. Then age doesn't matter.

Mister A. is a man with a good heart but with such a complicated inner world. People have opinions about the reasons why his energy left him at some point. Personally, I don't know, but, in any case, he had no energy. When I met him in the early days of Rakutenkai, people were coming almost every day after *keiko*, he was really bright. Then suddenly it changed.

Masashi MINAGAWA

M. Minagawa was one of our first two instructors. He also participated in this project at every stage, helping in one way or another whenever he could. The formal interview took place in July, 2005 in Japanese through M. Hirano. M. Minagawa then transcribed the recording himself, arranging and enriching the text, and providing additional details about certain situations. The final text was validated in Japanese in November, 2019 by videoconference with M. Hirano.[1]

My village and my family

I was born on March 21st, 1949, in Hyakkan-non, Sutama-cho Kitakoma-gun, Yamanashi-Ken. It is a small village located in the middle of Honshu, the big island of Japan, and surrounded by mountains. In the distance, we could see Mount Fuji to the south and the Yatsugatake mountains to the north. I am the first-born son of Kaname, my father, and Yaeko, my mother. I have an older sister and two younger brothers. My parents ran a hair-dresser/barber business. My mother had her own hair salon for a while, but she left that work when I was in elementary school, to assist my father in his own business.

Childhood memory: burns

The great experience of my childhood was an accident that happened to me when I was three years old. The barber shop re-quired a lot of boiling water. It was heated in an earthen cooker located at the back of the house. From there, the boiling water was poured into a bucket that my grandmother carried to the shop. One day, I ran around the corner and bumped into my grand-mother carrying the bucket. The boiling water spilled on me and scalded me. I still remember this scene very clearly. The resulting burn covered half of my body, and the doctor was not sure if I would live. My mother spared no effort to take care of me, but it was a real miracle that I survived. At first, my grandmother would

[1] **Credits:** *Interview*: M. Hirano, P. Quettier. *Transcription*: M. Minagawa. *Editing*: M. Minagawa, M. Hirano, P. Quettier. *Translation*: P. Quettier. *Proofreading*: D. Richardson.

not let me out of the house because of the extent of the scars, and so I could not meet anyone. My scars covered my neck and chest, and I had to hide them by keeping the collar of my jacket turned up and buttoned, even in the height of summer. When people looked at me, I felt like they saw only my scars. This is why I hardly ever spoke to anyone until the age of 13 or 14.

I can still see, in its smallest details, the sequence of events until the accident — from where I started running down the hall, to the corner where I turned before I hit the bucket — I remember it as if I was watching the scene in a film. From that point on, no more memories. I was wearing a sweater, which my grandmother hastily removed ... and the skin on my upper body came off with it. It was a very serious burn. Maybe I'm a better person today for having been peeled like this [laughs]? It's an experience that has taught me a lot.

A special house

It was one of my ancestors who founded this village. He understood that a crossroads would certainly be an ideal place to do business. He set up his hairdresser/barbershop there and offered his services to passers-by, and the village developed around it. Our barbershop was a kind of information center, always full of people. My mother, who was very good at cooking, loved taking care of people. My father took care of a few young delinquents. He educated them while they resisted authority. Lots of people hung around my house like this, so much so that we almost never ate meals simply as a family.

Also, there were not many baths in the houses of the time, so, all kinds of people came to take a bath in our house: actors who came to local productions, tattooed *yakuza*, and others. While observing and listening to these diverse people in this baroque environment, my impressions allowed me, even if vaguely, to discern sincere persons from those who were not. A long time after, during the shintaido era, the same thing happened when Aoki-sensei talked with a group of people and I was only half listening to what was being said. My childhood experience allowed me to see into people, beyond appearances, and to understand what they really wanted to talk about. I thus acquired an instinct to perceive superficial people and to move away from them.

Fighting bullies

As a kid, I hated bullies. When I happened to witness a bully harassing someone, I threw myself on the aggressor and fought until he stopped. It became so bad that my parents were reluctant to allow me to go out, not only because of the burns, but because I put myself in dangerous situations. If I saw an adult, *yakuza* or other, doing bad things using force, being a child did not prevent me from physically taking him to task, screaming to stop his bullying.

At that time, I was confident in my strength because I used to chop firewood for the shop with a big axe and do all kinds of heavy work for my father. But, thinking about it afterwards, I understood that what kept these people from attacking me was the protective shadow of my father behind me, and that of all these young people my father was taking care of, who were considered delinquents. The bullies feared retaliation from these people who seemed to enjoy my home so much. The delinquents felt so good there that, even if my father urged them to leave, they stayed. My father was a kind of big brother, with good advice for all these guys.

About my father

My father lost his own father when he was a teenager. As he was good at studying, relatives offered him financial help to pursue his education in high school. But he refused their offer, preferring to take care of his mother, brothers, and sister. He passed the Manchurian Railways exam — for well-paid jobs — and went to work in China all by himself.

There, he also played on the company's ice hockey team, in order to send more money to his family. At that time, the Manchurian Railways used sports to promote the business. I heard my grandmother say that my father sent her the same amount every month that a school principal earned. Manchuria was a dream country for the Japanese in those times, when the Japanese army occupied China, as shown in the film *The Last Emperor*. The Manchurian Railways were created to build a rapid route to the interior of China for Japanese troops.

Having the support of the military, the staff were treated very well. Even when there was not much to eat during wartime, Japanese workers received more rations than ordinary people. Having too much for himself, my father gave his surplus food to Chinese subordinates. But the military police came and severely blamed him for squandering the company's property on the Chinese. However, when many Japanese experienced the revenge of the Chinese people at the end of the war, my father was spared and evacuated by the same Chinese whom he had fed. This saved him from ending up in a prisoner-of-war camp in Russia. Pretending he was sick, they helped him escape and boarded him onto a boat bound for Japan.

On the return trip, he sadly threw all his savings into the sea because his money was no longer worth the paper on which it was printed. The surface of the sea was white with the notes everyone threw away. My father told me that he had never felt so anxious and sad as when he returned to Japan after having lost everything. Having inherited Yamanashi's hair salon, he started over from scratch, setting up shop as a barber.

When he was young, he had dreamed of traveling the world and settling in a vast region; but the war had destroyed his hopes. For my part, I could not inherit the family business, but by expatriating to England, I sort of fulfilled my father's dream.

My father hated injustice. He always urged me to stay fair and humble. He never judged people. He was open-minded and knew how to listen. In business, if only one side wins, nothing can be concluded. Although he gave the impression of being stubborn, he knew how to listen and take into account everything he knew. When I planned to marry Pam and went with her to see my parents in Yamanashi, we were warmly welcomed, even though foreigners were almost unknown in those times.

Turbulent school years

Since I was constantly fighting, my school teacher summoned me every day to the staff room. I explained my point to him, and I think that, to a certain extent, he did not think me bad. I never started a fight, but if someone provoked me, I answered. Or, when I told a person to stop, he would get angry and the fight would start. My teacher would have me sit in *seiza* in his room, so that I could meditate on my behavior. Even today, I sometimes sit in *seiza* with this feeling.

Eventually, thanks to this teacher, Yamada-sensei, I started to think that being a teacher, which allows you to influence people, was a wonderful occupation. I wanted to become a teacher.

I fought like this until junior high school, and then I had a sudden revelation. I hated violence that hurt people. Consequently, I responded violently to this violence. But in the end, I produced nothing better than what others generation: more violence. It was a turning point, and I stopped fighting.

My shyness made me do extraordinary things. For example, my father wanted me to study English before entering college, and he entrusted me to the care of a teacher who taught private lessons nearby. I would go to this teacher's house every week, but having worked all day in a school, he was always so tired that he was already asleep when I arrived. Since I didn't dare wake him up, I sat in silence all through the "lesson." When he finally woke up, he would say, "Very well, you can go home," which I did, after duly thanking him. Shyness prevented me from voicing my opinion to others.

I was always full of energy. My teacher told me to go fishing every day to calm my unstable temper, so I went day after day to the nearby river. One day, absorbed in observing the movements of the float, I got lost in the moment. Even as night fell, I could see clearly, so continued to fish. And then, suddenly, the surroundings became very noisy. All the village firefighters had been sent to look for me. I was just sitting there fishing, and I didn't understand why they were shouting! This kind of mishap often happened to me. Another day, I went to read in the library during a break. Engrossed in an interesting book, I emerged only when I heard my name being shouted by my mother and my teacher, looking for me in the corridors. Once absorbed in things, I forgot about everything else.

I was what is called a "problem child," so much so that my teacher later admitted to me that he was very worried about my future.

Physical activities

I had a lot of work to do at home, and that kept me in shape. Since my father used sharp tools for his hairdressing work, he took care that his hands remained impeccable for serving his customers, and he preferred not to do heavy work. This is why he entrusted me with the daily task of cutting the wood necessary for heating the boiling water. Thanks to doing this regular physical work from an early age, I developed a lot of strength. No one could beat me at sumo, even the big guys. In junior high school, when I wanted to measure the strength of my back on a special machine, I broke the machine. But apart from helping at home, I hated physical exercise and much preferred reading.

I started to enjoy physical exercise only after discovering basketball in junior high school. There was, by chance, another advantage to this game. The basketball jersey was open at the top, revealing the chest. At first, I was afraid to show my scars, as if everyone would see nothing but them. But, to my surprise, no one noticed anything, despite the open collar. I then understood that I had been worrying unnecessarily. It was a huge relief. This is how my heart was freed at the same time that I discovered the joy of moving my body.

I entered the Nirasaki Prefectural High School. Since I had been playing basketball in junior high school, I thought I would do the same in high school. However, the basketball and judo clubhouses were adjacent, and I inadvertently entered the judo clubhouse. It so happened that one of my high school classmates was there and greeted me. I was so shy that I didn't dare let him down. I practiced judo for three years. Since I had physical strength, I progressed so well that I was even able to throw my *senpai*. One day, a university coach was invited over the summer holidays. When he asked me to practice with him, I managed to get out of his hold.

I often stayed after judo lessons to play with the children of the neighborhood. Much later, when shintaido was opening up in the early 1970s, I happened to meet one of them. Many young people of this era had become disillusioned and were sniffing thinner[1]. We gave a demonstration at the entrance to the pedestrian streets of Shinjuku, which were famous for the youths who frequented them. We thought this would be a good way to recruit young people in the early days of shintaido. Then, this young man with whom I had practiced judo when he was a child, recognized me and spoke to me, and we reconnected. Subsequently, thanks to this meeting, he stopped using drugs and met a good teacher who encouraged him to study to become a pilot. I am so grateful to shintaido for giving me this opportunity to help him.

During the last year of high school, my classmates were busy preparing for university entrance exams, concentrating only on courses that would help them pass these exams. For my part, I wondered what life was about, and what my destiny was. I was

---

[1] Practice, very damaging to neurons, consisting of emptying a tube of glue (thinned with trichlorethylene) in a paper bag and breathing in the bag until getting dizzy.

very anxious. Since I wanted to be a teacher, I was told I could enroll in a teacher-training course at Yamanashi University, and my high school was willing to provide me with a recommendation. But my parents objected, saying I was still too young to plan my future as a teacher. Of course, as the eldest boy, I could have taken over the family business, but my father doubted my business sense. In the end, I trusted him and followed his recommendation to abandon this local university project and try the examination for one of the Tokyo universities. I would thus become the first one from my village to study at a university in Tokyo.

Hosei University and discovery of karate

Although I didn't prepare much, I managed to get into Hosei University to study economics. This is how my Tokyo life started. I was in a state of complete confusion. This transition from a small community, protected by everyone, to huge Tokyo, was brutal. To make matters worse, my local dialect made everyone laugh and consider me stupid.

For my part, I was amazed by these students who invested so little in their studies, preferring to make the most of their brand-new freedom. I was a little disappointed and still couldn't find an answer to the questions about the meaning of life with which I was obsessed. A classmate, Iwase-san, invited me to join his club's seaside picnic in Chiba the next day. Since there is no sea in Yamanashi, I thought it would be a good idea to go, and I signed up. But when I got there, it was not a picnic but a *gasshuku*.

We were immediately invited to rabbit-hop back and forth from one end of the beach to the other. This lasted until the end of the session. At first, I found it really stupid. But out of respect for the *sempai* who encouraged us, I conscientiously tried to go on. Gradually, I found it more and more fun. I felt as if the sounds of the surrounding waves were entering my body, and I started to sing in unison with them. Everyone seemed to be in pain, but I sang. Some people looked at me a little oddly, but I had so much fun that I couldn't help but sing. It was a very physical exercise, however, and when we stopped, I couldn't even walk. And the next day, jumping again! What a strange experience! That's how I came to join the Giwakai karate club.

The Giwakai *dojo* was located on the roof of the main building of Hosei University. We practiced barefoot on the raw concrete, and quickly the soles of my feet were worn out, but I persevered. Ishikawa-san, founder of Giwakai, studied karate with Aoki-sensei at Tokyu Karate Dojo. When he had to leave Giwakai, he asked Aoki-sensei to find a replacement, and we were assigned an instructor named Matsuhashi. Matsuhashi-san's karate *keiko* was very different from our usual practice. It was called sogo-budo, or unified martial arts, and was not yet called shintaido; but the *keiko* was already that of shintaido. I was completely fascinated by Matsuhashi-san, and I went to his house, near Shinjuku Nishi-guchi Park, every day to practice. We invited Aoki-sensei to the Giwakai summer *gasshuku* and autumn *gasshuku*. At the time, Aoki-sensei had already left Shotokai to develop his own style. Giwakai found itself torn between Shotokai karate and sogo-budo.

Meeting with Aoki-sensei for the first time

I first met Aoki-sensei during a very intense summer *gasshuku* in my second year of university. At the time, people from various universities would come to the Giwakai *gasshuku* just to practice with Aoki-sensei. He gave a lecture, and the *sempai* sat in the front rows. As a beginner, I was seated at the rear. While he was speaking, I suddenly felt the people around me disappear; it was as if the master and I were connected by a rope or a path. He was talking to everyone, teaching one thing or another and making jokes but, to my eyes, he was speaking only to me. In a discussion 20 years later, he told me that he remembered very well this experience with this strange boy dressed in a red shirt, with whom he had made sure to make a connection.

The *keiko* of that time was very severe. I was so stiff that I was told that I would have to practice more than the other people just to get to the same level as them. For example, in Eiko practice, everyone else used one *bo*, but I used three. The teacher added his own *bo* to mine. They were thicker than normal ones, and I had to grip very hard in order to hold them together. It was so heavy that I had to run constantly to keep them from falling, which would have offended the instructor. I was made to do 20 laps while the others did ten. Obviously, I found myself exhausted even before the real *keiko* started. I gladly accepted this treatment, however, because I understood that it was the only way for me to keep up with others.

Encountering Rakutenkai keiko

Unfortunately, when I was in the third year of university, Matsuhashi-san stopped teaching us, due to a disagreement with Aoki-sensei. Shortly before that, he had told me about a monthly Rakutenkai *gasshuku* called Heiho Kenkyukai in Kujukuri-hama in Chiba prefecture. I was still a beginner, but I really wanted to participate in this *gasshuku*, and so I went there. I immediately realized that it was not proper to stumble this way into a course intended only for Rakutenkai members, who had gathered to study about *heiho* under the direction of Aoki-sensei.

The course director was Hokari Shiko-sensei, and he did everything he could to discourage me from staying. He explained that mixing beginners into a high-level study group would inevitably bring down the quality of training. As a manager, he needed to inform Aoki-sensei, who nevertheless allowed me to stay. So, I was able to participate in this *gasshuku*, but I was "baptized" with my *sempai's gedan-barai*! It was mostly Ito-sensei and Hokari-sensei who "took care" of me and, in a way, they continue to do so. This is how I got involved in Rakutenkai.

During that time, university club captains would often visit Aoki-sensei in Nogeyama and participate in a special *keiko* based on Eiko and Tenshingoso, especially Eiko. I had heard about Eiko from my elders at the club. It sounded like a strange thing. At Gi-wakai, we were still practicing *kaikyaku-zenshin* a very low *kibadachi* for hours on end. So, when I did my first Eiko during this Heiho Kenkyukai *gasshuku*, I thought it was great. We were asked to get up in Tenso and stay there without ever giving up. It seemed that we were going to stay like that for 30 minutes or an hour, and we groaned together from the difficulty. And then I heard "Stop!" and we slowly lowered our arms. But when I reached Shoko, everything around had turned black, and I saw something like a candle burning in the distance. My body started to run naturally toward this light and ... I hit a wall, which sent me rolling. I got up and got caught up again in the race ... into another wall, and again, and again. Everyone laughed as they watched me, but I couldn't stop myself. In the end, I thought this Eiko *keiko* was really great.

Besides *keiko*, what Aoki-sensei told us was also interesting. We were so enthralled that no one wanted to go home, and we often missed the last train. He talked to us about many things and always in such simple and understandable ways. I remember be-ing especially impressed with his presentation about nothingness. At first, he talked about it using the expression "space of love." This probably served as the basis for what later became the Tenshin philosophy, the Tenchi-hitobito-ware-ittai of today. He talked about it a lot around 1972, developing the idea of "1 + 1 = 0."

Compared to these Rakutenkai *keiko*, the university *keiko* seemed to me more and more boring. Since Ito-sensei had opened the Sogo-budo Renmei office in Shinjuku, I went to help him with various simple tasks. Having heard that I often ran Eiko with my *bo* in the park, he recommended that I start a bojutsu club. This is how I came to create the first university bojutsu club in Hosei Uni-versity.

In 1970, in the midst of the student movement against the U.S.-Japan Security Treaty[1], because of clashes between students and riot police, my university was considered part of the Zenkyoto[2] student power movement. To make matters worse, the suicide of the writer Yukio Mishima, had just occurred at the headquarters of the Self-Defense-Force in Ichigaya, near Hosei University. Consequently, when I was carrying my *bo*, it was confused with a *geba*[3] — a fighting stick used in riots — and I had to undergo extensive interrogation by the police. Finally, because of the various blockades, I almost never went to the campus toward the end of my studies. I went to Rakutenkai instead. Eventually, we created the Zenkoku Gakkusei Renmei [4] with other students from Rakutenkai, from the Women's University of Physical Education and from Niigata University. We met in the Sogo-budo Renmei office in Shinjuku to practice together.

Since Hosei University was private, it needed to maintain its reputation. So, they made sure to organize exams despite the ongoing situation. To pass, you normally had to present a dissertation or work on the exam topics, but in our case, we graduated automatically without having to present a dissertation. Today, Hosei University does have a very good reputation, but at that time, even though it ranked among the top six private universities in Tokyo, it was not well respected. It frustrated me, because I was worried about my future. That is why I only went there to practice karate.

Toward the end of the academic year, members of the Rakutenkai met to prepare the first *daienshu* organized by Sogo-budo Renmei. We practiced late at night and then we had a

---

[1] Treaty of Mutual Cooperation and Security between the United States and Japan, initiated in 1960.

[2] "All Campus Joint Struggle Committee". See the Zenkyoto article on https://en.wikipedia.org/wiki/Zenkyoto

[3] By contraction of the German word *gewalt* (violence), used for weapons by anarchist insurrection.

[4] Unitary Federation of Students

meeting. I remember the members of Rakutenkai seemed to be shining, and I was not able to enter their circle. I felt dirty and saw everything I touched become black. It was as if toxins were coming out of my hands. Seeing this, Aoki-sensei told me, "How about going to do Eiko in Nogeyama park?" I went there and did Eiko as I was told. The moment I raised my arms, it was as if the scales that covered my eyes fell and the dirt was washed away with my tears. And when I returned to Rakutenkai after running, the dazzling circle of light surrounding the group was gone, and everyone greeted me warmly.

During this *gasshuku*, there was an exam session for which all members gave up their black belts and wore the beginner's white belt. The exam to become an instructor consisted of Tenshingoso and Eiko. I was very impressed by the demonstrations by the members of the Rakutenkai, by the beauty and the purity of their Tenshingoso. Immediately after the session, I went to Aoki-sensei to tell him that I wanted to dedicate my life to shintaido. I have always considered this moment as my real starting point.

After graduating from university, I wondered what would become of me. I decided to follow the example of my *sempai* and devote myself to shintaido, so I started working for Sogo-Budo Renmei. Ito-sensei was the manager and had just published Egami-sensei's Karate-do book. I was put in charge of selling it. Kato-sensei was the teaching director, and I also assisted him. His *gorei* was very interesting, although he did not stay in office very long.

Rakutenkai's second generation, opening to the world: the Nihon-juku

At one point, members of my generation started to regroup. I had rented a room in Aoki-sensei's house. Around 1971, Okada Gan and Egami Masatake came to live with me, while the next room was occupied by Ishide Tadashi, Hokari Takeo, and others. And so began a period of communal life that lasted several years.

Previously, the activities of Rakutenkai had diversified into three activities: Rakutenkai Church, the Seisho Kenkyu-kai[1], led by the Reverend Okada Mitsuru; Sogo-Budo Renmei, which Ito-sensei and Kato-sensei led; and the Artistic and Cultural Movement of shintaido[2], led by Ito Harue and Okada Gan.

A project team bringing together young people of the second generation was formed — the Nihon Juku[3] — with the idea of spreading shintaido to the world. To prepare ourselves, we engaged in various training activities. For example, to learn how to present shintaido, we organized a speech contest under the direction of Aoki-sensei and his wife, who had formerly been part of Chuo University's debating club. I was not good at speaking in public, but Egami Masatake and I won the competition. My speech came at the very end and, seeing that everyone was tired, I invited them to move a little and do a few shoulder rotations before speaking. I assumed that was what had pleased everyone. At that time, Egami and I were always working together, while Okada Gan, Ishide Tadashi, and Hokari Takeo formed another group.

Shortly afterward, Egami and I were "missioned" to sell encyclopedias. We had to gain confidence outside the restricted, protective circle of Rakutenkai. We had to gain real work experience. It was a kind of *keiko* that allowed us to translate into life what we knew about *kumite*. And that is why Aoki-sensei one day informed us that he had negotiated jobs for us in an encyclopedia sales company, and that they were expecting us the next day!

We went to the Nihon Tosho Han'bai, located in Sarugaku-cho, Chiyoda-ku, Tokyo. For my part, I did not sell anything during the

---

[1] Bible Study Group.

[2] Hyogen Genjutsu, materialized in 1972 in Kujukuri during an avant-garde festival entitled "Humanity and universe" (*ningen to uchu no matsuri*) by Ito Harue and Okada Iwao.

[3] The *juku* are traditional schools. Also, numerous communities that opened in Japan in this fertile era called themselves *juku*. Nihon, or Nippon, is the Japanese term for Japan.

first two months, but I considered myself in an apprenticeship. Because we sold door to door, we had to work weekends. One day, we asked for a weekend break to participate in a *gasshuku*. But our chief told us that if we didn't improve our sales figures, which were very bad, taking a weekend break was out of question. So, because we really wanted to go to this *gasshuku*, we "changed gears," and that's how we started to improve. Our manager was a good person with a lot of experience and, in the end, Egami and I became "golden members" — among the top 50 in annual sales figures nationwide. Later on, our manager opened sale counters in front of bookstores and department stores. Sales increased, as did our wages, and we continued this way until 1973.

Unforgettable practices

We loved the Sundays of Nogeyama's Rakutenkai, made up of religious celebrations and *keiko*. Aoki-sensei always shared his latest ideas with us. Then, after the Nihon-juku began to form, one of these Sundays became the last. We gathered in full, young and old alike, to practice in the gymnasium of the Ipponmatsu primary school in Nogeyama. During this *keiko*, Aoki-sensei invited us to make our *keiko* a celebration. From there, the shintaido *keiko* itself became a form of worship. The theme of this *gasshuku* was "going out into the world."

From that moment, we initiated different training methods. I remember a special night *keiko* in which we learned how to avoid attacks from behind. The *keiko* took place near the Tama River, and I, doing *sensei* care,[1] had to tell Aoki-sensei when it was time to go. But, having seen the driver of the car, Tadashi-san, leave, I assumed that he had told Aoki-sensei, and so I went to the *dojo*.

---

[1] The "*sensei* care person" takes care of all material aspects of the class so that the teacher can focus exclusively on teaching. These responsibilities include handling the teacher's transportation, clothing, and special snacks and beverages, getting the teacher to events on time, and making sure that materials, and equipment needed for teaching are available at the right time and place.

Arriving at the *dojo*, I saw Tadashi but not Aoki-sensei. He was still in his room waiting for me to call him.

Aoki-sensei was of course very upset, and it happened that he engaged us in a super-severe *keiko*. Obviously, everyone made the link between one thing and the other. It was a special *keiko*, in which we practiced anticipating attacks with plastic baseball bats. To make matters worse, Toshima-san, who had been asked to buy soft plastic bats, had bought hard ones by mistake. Everyone began groaning when we started to strike. Furthermore, one might imagine that the pain would have made us merciful. But no, when we took on the role of attacker, we struck with renewed enthusiasm! As for me, I got the impression that everyone was particularly "generous" with me for having put Aoki-sensei in this severe mood. It was very cold, and I ended up not only with my head black and blue but also with my ears bleeding!

We did many such experimental *keiko*. It was hard, but so interesting.

On another day, members of the Nihon Juku discovered Shoko with a *bokuto*. The gymnasium had a large mezzanine where we were asked to do Shoko, while everyone else was doing Eiko in the main hall downstairs. In my introduction to the *bokuto*, I found it very heavy. My hands sank down, so I lifted them up, but the pain made them go down again. We were told to stay absolutely still, but my arms were shaking, and my *bokuto*, like everyone's, inevitably kept moving up and down. And then we heard Aoki-sensei telling us to "stop fishing," and that made us laugh. Thus relaxed, we got back into it again. Then, I suddenly noticed that my neighbor, Tadashi-san, was completely still; it was impressive. Taking a better look however, I saw that he had gently placed the tip of his *bokuto* on the edge of the railing! I never would have had the guts to do such a thing, so I just did what I was asked to do. Tadashi said that he hated *keiko*, but he was a great guy. In fact, he was doing his best.

End of the Nihon Juku and beginning of responsibilities

After a while, it became necessary to stop being a burden on the Aoki family home. We still wanted to build a community and we had carried out serious research on different examples of living in a community, abroad and in Japan; we even visited some of them. Finally, Gan-san rented an apartment to start the Nihon Juku in Tokyo, and some other people left to find a new life in Hokkaido. In the end, nothing lasted for long. The activities of Sogo-Budo Renmei became more and more significant. Religious activities had somehow "dissolved" in it. And we each went on our own paths.

In 1975, Aoki-sensei suddenly retired. He said that Ito was preparing to go to the United States and that he himself had no energy left. He dissolved Rakutenkai and entrusted shintaido to Egami and myself, asking us to manage it as we thought fit. This is how I became the manager of the Sogo-Budo Renmei office after Ito-sensei, and how Egami Masatake took over the teaching after Kato-sensei.

Under the charismatic leadership of Egami, we went to various universities to offer demonstrations. We gained members, and we created bojutsu clubs in Keio, Chuo, and Waseda universities. Many people also came from abroad to practice shintaido, especially from the UK and France.

In spring of 1977, Aoki-sensei went on a long trip to various foreign countries and finally settled in Brazil for a while. There, in contact with various people, his creativity was recharged. He created a new system for bojutsu and another one for shintaido called Yoki-kei.

When Aoki-sensei was abroad, Rakutenkai activities had been transferred to Hokari-san's home. Meetings and study groups were held there, and thus the Hokari home became the second base for Rakutenkai activities.

Aoki-sensei returned to Japan in 1978, but he left the management to us for a while. It was our custom to hold two weekly training sessions that brought everyone together at the Tokyo Gymnasium in Sendagaya on Friday evenings and Sunday afternoons. Kato-sensei, who had become an acupuncturist and had stopped teaching shintaido, was also invited by Aoki-sensei to teach a special course there every Friday.

Aoki-sensei

When I first met Aoki-sensei at university, he had a great, strong body. His arms were very thick and powerful, and I dreaded his *gedan-barai*. I couldn't believe that such a strong person could exist in the world. Gradually, I started to go beyond the visible and became interested in the invisible world, which fascinated me more.

Aoki-sensei showed me different strange things that he was able to do. For example, for the Rakutenkai night *keiko* in Nogeyama Park, we gathered after work to practice freely with enthusiasm. Aoki-sensei did not give *gorei* but came to visit us toward the end. Since I was the youngest, I sometimes just watched what others were doing. It was one of those days, and I was watching quietly when I suddenly felt a change in the atmosphere. Aoki-sensei stood there, motionless, near the central pond, and all the ducks and other birds were converging on him. Then, seeing me, his concentration changed and, suddenly, these same birds suddenly dispersed in all directions. Later, I heard that from a very young age he had had this talent to make animals come to him or, conversely, disperse.

On another occasion, as I was walking with him in the streets, carrying his bag — he was always carrying a lot of books, and his bag was very heavy — all the passers-by whom I came across converged around me, and I couldn't get through. I then noticed that Aoki-sensei was walking quietly beside me, with a faint smile on his face and absolutely no one around him.

He taught me how to get people to congregate or disperse in *keiko*. Even today, I am having difficulties but, 30 years later, when I give *gorei*, I still remember those many occasions when he showed me how to expand and shrink consciousness.

Aoki-sensei wrote to me during his trip abroad, to tell me about things that were happening for various people. He knew by telepathy. Subsequently, he criticized me for not knowing how to realize these things, even though I was in Japan. This kind of telepathic phenomenon often happened with him, and he would warn me before things happened.

During a *gasshuku* in the countryside, our dormitory was bathed in the sound of frogs singing in the surrounding rice fields. Aoki-sensei asked for the songs to stop, and the frogs suddenly became silent. Then, as soon as he asked, they started again. I have no idea how he did it.

Likewise, he could cause a room, even a distant one, filled with noisy people, to suddenly become quiet. When Sogo-Budo Renmei opened its office in Shinjuku, the floor below was occupied by a rather lively gay bar. One day, Aoki-sensei told us that we were going to take energy from this bar, and we all became very cheerful without having drunk anything. Conversely, the customers of the ground floor became very calm.

I have often been the "privileged witness" of Aoki-sensei's experiments in *toate*.

One day, I was walking in town with him and, as we were waiting at a crossing, he did something, and I was suddenly lying on the ground without being able to move. Thereafter, I had to stay in bed for a whole week. I felt like he had taken all my energy away.

Much later, in March, 1980, a year after I had left the managerial role of Sogo-Budo Renmei, I went to the United States with Aoki-sensei and Ito Jugoro-san. We went hiking in the snowy mountains, and one day, as we came to a gently sloping place, Aoki-sensei pointed to a tree about 50 meters away and asked me to run at full speed. At that time, I was experiencing a dull anxiety about the future, and I took the opportunity to let go of my annoyance by running with all my might. But suddenly I realized that Aoki-sensei was walking quietly by my side, laughing out loud. I thought I was running hard and at full speed, but the more I tried, the more I slowed down, like an engine running out of gasoline, and I ended up falling down 20 yards from the tree.

He often played such tricks on me. Of course, he also showed me different types of *toate* during many *kumite*.

After returning from Brazil, Aoki-sensei underwent some sort of rehabilitation for about a year. Pam and I had just married, and we lived in Noborito, near the Tama River. Aoki-sensei came to see us every day, during or at the end of his training, completely exhausted. I felt a bit guilty to be living a comfortable married life while my teacher was training so hard. He had filled a backpack with stones, which he carried on his back when he came to see us. He ran from Yokohama to our house, about 18 kilometers. He said he had to reeducate his body. He included me in his practice. My role was to push him in sumo, day after day. At first, we started on flat ground but as he became more and more powerful, we practiced on the steep banks of the Tama River, close to our house. I pushed from top downward and he from bottom upward. I have vivid memories of the day we finished this *keiko*. It was the anniversary of Rakutenkai's founding and I had pushed him for a while when, suddenly, he completely knocked me over, taking all the air out of my lungs. I was stunned, and when I got up, I felt that the world around me had completely changed.

Aoki-sensei was gone and a large plain lay in front of me. I then understood that, for the first time, I could walk alone on this earth. I felt that my body and my mind were released; I was free. This sensation is still at the center of my own *kumite*. I want my partners to feel it after doing *kumite* with me.

This completed the sumo *keiko*, and Aoki-sensei told me that we could officially open it to practitioners.

He then devoted himself to the practice of bojutsu, and especially to the brand-new set of throwing techniques he had discovered during his trip in South America. He saw the movements as if he was watching a film and described them to me, so that I could transcribe them. Then, based on what was written, Egami and I tried the techniques one by one, in front of Aoki-sensei, who was taking photos. Some of them were then taught informally on various occasions. Then, the whole program was definitively fixed and officially presented to the members in 1994, under the name of *soei-kumibo*.

Feeling gratitude

When I presented Tenshingoso for the Doshu exam at the international *gasshuku* in 2004, I remembered my own initiation during the first Daienshu in 1971 and, knowing that this would be the last opportunity, I did it with an immense feeling of gratitude for Aoki-sensei, who was watching me.

Masatoshi IWASE

Mr. Iwase, rather like A. Koyama, is one of the fervent adepts of karate who slowly acculturated to the practices of Rakutenkai while remaining in the suburbs. Their testimony is invaluable in this respect. The initial interview was conducted in May, 2004 through H.F. Ito and the validation of the final text was conducted in May, 2019 by M. Hirano.[1]

Childhood

I was born in 1947 in Isumi, Chiba Prefecture. I have an elder sister. My father was a high school teacher and my mother grew rice and vegetables to feed the family. I was in a baseball club in middle school, and I was a very fast runner, so I had a lot of fun there. Then, I entered Mobara High School and started practicing Wado-ryu school karate once a week. In this *dojo* there were between twenty and thirty people of all kinds who came to practice.

Karate on the roof of Hosei University

When I entered Hosei University in 1967, I immediately looked for a karate club among those offered by the various schools on campus. This is how, on the warm recommendation of an older student, I joined the Giwakai club.

Ishikawa-san, who lived in Yokohama, was going to learn karate with Aoki-san at the Tokyu Dojo. When he entered Hosei University, he created the Giwakai karate club. Being three years younger than Ishikawa-san, I came two years after the club was founded. This club was still so new that we didn't have a *dojo*, so we practiced on the roof of a building with nothing but a rough concrete floor. When we practiced the sliding steps of karate on this floor, our feet got shredded. Ishikawa-san continued to lead the club during my first two years, and despite the bleeding feet and other tough conditions, I really enjoyed that time.

---

[1] **Credits:** *Interview:*   H.F. Ito, P. Quettier. *Transcription:* M. Minagawa. *Editing:* M. Hirano, P. Quettier. *Translation:* P. Quettier. *Proofreading:* L. Seaman.

When Ishikawa-san ran the club, we only practiced karate. However, during my third year in college [1968-69], Matsuhashi-san and Aoki-sensei were invited to teach, and they introduced the practice of shintaido. We were doing the Tenshingoso *kata*, which I believe had just been created. The typical approach to the practice consisted of a long session of usagi-tobi, thirty to forty minutes or even an entire hour, on concrete of course. When we were completely exhausted, we were told that we had released our tensions and the core practice could begin. There was often not much time left.

When I joined the Hosei karate club, I was in the same academic year as Minagawa-san. Since I knew he had practiced judo in Nirasaki High School, I thought he might be interested, so I offered to do karate with him and took him to the roof. At that time, I was the only member and I needed someone to practice with. At first, I thought he wouldn't stay more than a week, but he kept going.

The difficult introduction of shintaido into Giwakai karate

The introduction of Tenshingoso was viewed very negatively. Tenshingoso seemed to belong to a world so different from that of karate. For the members of the club, the goal of the practice was to become physically stronger, and for that, Tenshingoso did not seem very useful to them: "How can one become strong by practicing Tenshingoso?" I thought so, too, and Matsuhashi-san's explanations did nothing to help. We had practiced karate for two years and we were unable to make the connection between Tenshingoso and techniques like *tsuki* and *keri*. To the question "How can Tenshingoso be martial?" we never got a really satisfying answer.

We also practiced Eiko. We were running in the *dojo* on the roof. Tenshingoso and Eiko were introduced around the same time, soon followed by *toitsu-kihon waza*. All this came gradually, alternating with the usual practices based on *tsuki* and *keri*. But karate club members were still very reluctant to open their hands and raise their arms to do Eiko, always wondering, "How martial is it?"

Attendance at Rakutenkai

In my fourth year, I became the club captain. It was at this time that some people from the club had the opportunity to participate in a shintaido seminar in which they were able to practice mutual cuts as well as different uses of the hands in relation to Tenshingoso. Some then began to understand what it meant and what it could be used for. In this way, and by deepening our understanding with Matsuhashi-san, shintaido gradually began to make sense in our practice of karate.

I also went to a karate workshop at Niigata University. At that time, with people like Toshima-san from Tokyo Women's College of Physical Education, Takeo Hokari-san from Niigata University, and others from Ritsumeikan, we had plans to create something like a university union. This is certainly why I was invited to the Niigata workshop.

I also remember taking part in a *gasshuku* at Kujukuri in 1971, towards the end of my last year of university. We learned to cut each other. We were many, but by cutting again and again we ended up forming a whole. I definitely felt that sense of unity. There were several dozens of us, but gradually we became one. It was completely unknown in the world of karate. I said to myself: "Ah, here is shintaido!"

I started to have this kind of experience by participating in Nogeyama practices with practitioners from the Women's College of Physical Education in Tokyo or those from Gakushuin University, such as Tsuchiya Chieko-san, and by following the teaching of Okada-sensei. Aoki-sensei lived near Nogeyama Park. I met Okada-san, Ito-san, Takeo-san and also Gan-san, Okada-san's younger brother. I remember that the practice in Nogeyama Park lasted until two o'clock in the morning. We started at ten o'clock in the evening and after that we shared a potluck meal, each bringing something, then everyone slept side by side in Okada-sensei's prayer room. It was around 1970, before Kujukuri. Minagawa and Hando were also there. It was great. There was nothing like this idea of unification in karate. The idea was rather that everyone should assert themselves. For my part, I was very favorably impressed by this idea of unification.

I remember Ishide Tadashi, the younger brother of Aoki-sensei's wife, and how his personality changed dramatically over the practices. He was still a beginner when we first met in a *gasshuku*, and I had considerably more *keiko* experience than he did. But when I met him for the second time, his techniques and his personality were radically different. I felt like I was meeting a completely different person. His *waza*, and especially the cutting techniques, were extremely strong. His personality had also become very bright. It was the first time I had witnessed such a drastic change in someone. I imagine it was an effect of the techniques of shintaido, but I remain amazed at such a change in such a short time.

Afterwards, I heard that he married Kayoko and went to Hokkaido. I had only met him twice in fact; during a *gasshuku* and then another later. So, when I went to Hokkaido for work, I tried to drive to his mink farm in Kushiro. But the road trip turned out to be more difficult than expected and I didn't have enough time off to continue; so, I had to turn around at Tomakomai.

At one time, we had the idea of creating a shintaido club at Keio University. Since I lived in Hiyoshi, where the Keio campus was, I went there alone and talked to people around me. Masatake Egami-san was a student at Keio, but he was doing Aikido. I met him later during a shintaido workshop I attended at Asama. Ultimately, I don't know what happened to this Keio club because I stopped going there after graduating from university and going into business.

I haven't seen Minagawa-san since I left college, nor Hando-san. I know, however, that the latter joined the Nagano Prefectural Police Department and was assigned to riot police, but he seems to have changed jobs since. I don't remember having any further contact with my college friends after I graduated.

Professional and family life, and reunion with shintaido in Mobara

Subsequently, I stayed away from shintaido for a very long time. And then, strangely, our paths crossed again. After moving to Mobara in March, 1992, I heard that the shintaido headquarters would be set up there in September. I contacted Wendy, the shintaido teacher in charge of Mobara, and left my phone number. Sometime later, she tried to contact me and then, as the phone number she had written down was not the correct one, she came directly to my house. It was my wife who received her, and that is how she became interested in shintaido herself, to the point of starting to practice in Mobara. Fate is curious, isn't it?

I would never have imagined that after fifteen years of absence, I would have reconnected with shintaido; even if the project to set up the headquarters in Mobara ultimately did not work.

I keep very strongly in me this memory of unification that came through the practice of shintaido. I still remember a Kujukuri *keiko* where we were a hundred participants, and how after this very intense practice, each of these hundred people communicated freely with all the others. After practice, once back at the hotel, everyone was talking to everyone in a happy crowd. I think that kind of feeling is really amazing.

I don't know if these things still happen in shintaido, but if the techniques haven't changed, I imagine it must still be the case. I have never had such an experience of arriving in a group of strangers and then, after practice, talking with these same people frankly and with an open heart. I have not found this in any workplace or in any other sport. It is characteristic of shintaido, of the shintaido techniques, and that is why I remain faithful to it. Even though this sensibility is difficult to experience in the real world with society as it is, it seems to me that we have entered an era where everyone is looking for something like this.

Having started with karate even before entering university, I came to shintaido through successive shocks and overcoming successive challenges. When I first met my wife, I only talked about shintaido. Of course, as the years passed, I calmed down, but I kept this kind of awareness and the hope that the world was going in such a direction.

I have read the books written by Aoki-sensei. What he writes is certainly true and wonderful, but I think it is better to feel it directly with your own body and in your life experience.

Gan-Iwao OKADA

We met Gan Okada once in 1981 when he was preparing to leave Tokyo to settle in his hometown. The initial interview took place in September, 2004 through H.F. Ito at the management premises of the nursing home that Gan established and ran. Following this, he took us on a tour of various pilot facilities for different populations, of which he was rightfully very proud. The validation interview took place in November, 2019 through M. Hirano when Mr. Okada had just retired.[1]

The childhood years

I was born on September 4th, 1947 – two years after the war – in Hazu, Aichi Prefecture, between Toyohashi and Nagoya. I am the last of a family of five children, of which my brother Mitsuru is the third boy. Japan was just beginning to rebuild itself, and poverty was the common lot. Nobody owned a car, telephone, or television; in any case, not ordinary families. Today, every house has a bathroom, but back then we all went to public baths. There were two in my town, and our house was surrounded by rice fields.

My father was an engineer in the construction of thermal power stations. He worked in Tokyo and only came back during the O-Bon holidays[2] and New Year. He was constantly on the move here and there across the country to monitor the construction of power plants until their completion. To avoid too frequent trips, he stayed on the spot: in Hokkaido, Kyushu, or Nagoya. My mother followed him to take care of him, because he was unable to fend for himself, and I, still a baby, accompanied her. My other four brothers were old enough to fend for themselves, so they were on their own most of the time.

I lived in Hokkaido and in Kamaishi in the Tohoku region, for one year each time. My mother was constantly going back and forth between the places where my father lived and the house

---

[1] **Credits:** *Interview*: H.F. Ito, P. Quettier. *Transcription*: M. Minagawa. *Editing*: M. Hirano, P. Quettier. *Translation*: P. Quettier. *Proofreading*: L. Seaman, L. Ordeman.
[2] Buddhist festival honoring the return of ancestors' spirits, generally held in August.

where her other four children lived. Of course, even if they knew how to fend for themselves, my brothers needed her regularly. Mother was a wonderful woman. I remember making frequent long train journeys with her, sometimes at night. And then I reached school age and stayed home in the countryside to go to the local primary school with the other children. My mother continued to shuttle between our father and us.

We hardly ever saw our father, to the point where I wondered who he was. He sometimes surprised us with a visit, leaving me with memories that were rather frightening, or at the very least, impressive. He was like that. He drank too much, too, and one day when I was in middle school, he had a stroke, a hemorrhage, which left him paralyzed. Unable to work, he returned home. He could not speak and almost always stayed in bed. It lasted three years and then he died of stomach cancer.

With his death, we lost our only financial resource. Fortunately, my older brother was already self-employed and working in Tokyo, and he was able to send us some money. We had been well-off when my father was alive, but we became poor afterwards. I was able to get into public high school, but we didn't have enough money for me to go to university. It was worse for my brother Mitsuru, who was already enrolled in a private and therefore expensive high school. The Japanese educational system made it difficult to switch schools, so he had to interrupt his schooling.

Rakutenkai

Leading his life in his own way, Mitsuru began practicing karate with Aoki-san at the Tokyu Dojo. As for me, after graduating from high school, I found a job in a bread-making company in the city of Kariya. I worked there for about three years. I was worried about my future and thought that for someone young there would be more opportunities in a big city. I told my brother Mitsuru about my idea, and around 1967 he invited me to visit him in Tokyo.

That's how I started hanging out with Rakutenkai, at Aoki-san's, where I met members like Matsuhashi-san and Jugoro-san, Fugaku-san's [H.F. Ito's] younger brother, and how I started to practice karate. I then went to live in Yokohama. At that time, Matsuhashi-san was someone important. I remember he took great care of me. He took me to Chinatown, here and there. He was a great support to me. Over time, different things happened between the main members of Rakutenkai, and one day Matsuhashi-san left. Apparently, he disagreed with the politics of the practice. Personally, I found the circumstances of his departure shocking.

After joining Rakutenkai, I held various part-time jobs. The Rakutenkai meeting place served as my residence, and to eat I worked as a cleaning man or salesman in a bedding store. I also worked for the Chinese restaurant of Cho-san where my brother Mitsuru worked. At that time, the center of our lives was practice, and practicing was more important to us than eating. As soon as an idea came to Aoki-san, we got together and practiced right away. This made any regular job impossible to hold. That's why we preferred a part-time job so we could work when we wanted to. But in the end, it wasn't very satisfying. So, I passed my taxi driving test, and I became a taxi driver.

The main members of that era were Aoki-san, Kato-san, Matsuhashi-san, Fugaku-san, and my older brother Mitsuru. They kept talking about *keiko* and I was very much involved in this atmosphere. I had the opportunity to study tea ceremony through sessions offered by Shimma Kayoko-san, the daughter of a wood merchant from Yokohama. I also practiced with Saito-san, but I preferred Shimma-san, maybe because she was such a pretty girl.

At that time, Rakutenkai revolved around Aoki-san. The practice had gradually become organized and structured. Eventually, Aoki-san, aided by Fugaku-san, decided to offer the practice outside Rakutenkai, and they opened an office in Shinjuku, Tokyo, in 1970 under the name Sogo-budo Renmei. This office was located on the second floor of a building in Shinjuku 2-chome. Fugaku-san was the manager, and he hired me as his assistant.

It is in this context that Fugaku-san published a large book entitled "Karate-do for Professionals," a compilation of various documents on karate produced by Aoki-san. I went to sell it to various universities and libraries, such as the National Library. I also went to many places to promote shintaido, however little. Then Minagawa-kun joined us. He worked well, better than me anyway. But I still managed to get one or two big orders. We were invited to the annual meeting of the "Nihon Seinen-dan Kyokai."[Japan Youth Association], where we did a demonstration in front of five hundred people, and to the charity association "Ayumi no Hako" [donations for walking[1]].

Practice was central to my life. After the practice, we talked about a lot of different things concerning the *keiko*: Aoki-san explained and everyone discussed. Everyone was pure. In the end, that purity is what drew me in.

I had no desire to get strong or jump high. In reality, I was getting strong and jumping very high, especially in *moro-geri*, but it was a result, not a goal. What mattered to me above all was that the mental or spiritual in me be made clean and pure by *keiko*. This search for purity still lives with me. It is the heart of my life.

Rakutenkai and Christianity

The Bible was another pillar of the practice that founded shintaido. I studied a lot about spirituality by reading the Bible and listening to Aoki-san speak. He had studied a lot, Dogen for example, and ancient Japanese Buddhism, and his teaching was always

---

[1] Ayumi no Hako is a Japanese public benefit association established to promote social welfare through cultural activities such as cinema and theater and to contribute to the development of social sector enterprises. Recognized as a pioneer in fundraising by artists, it was dissolved in May, 2017. The literal meaning of its name is "Box for the Walk" and comes from the box into which donations were initially collected; the idea being that the funds deposited in this box would allow disabled children to walk.

very rich. But as far as I know, the Bible was the backbone of Rakutenkai. The spirit of the Bible and the spirit of Rakutenkai met. After practice, we read the Bible, and this allowed us to understand what we had felt. And so, we went on: reading the Bible, practicing, and realizing what Aoki-sensei taught us.

We read the New Testament, rather than the Old, and we went to many churches here and there. A church was also set up within Rakutenkai itself. We read the Bible, we went to practice, and we re-read the Bible. The days went by like that. This is how shintaido and Rakutenkai were inscribed in me, and the intense memories of these moments remain with me today.

I was baptized by my brother, Mitsuru Okada, who had become a pastor. This was not done at Kawasaki Church but on Kenzaki Beach on the Miura Peninsula. I seem to remember that Toshima Shigeko and Egami-kun were also baptized that day, along with three other girls from Tokyo Women's University of Physical Education. Some people used to go to Kawasaki Bible School in the evenings, but not me for some reason. Anyway, it seems to me that what is at the heart of my activity today was forged at that time.

The Nihon-juku community

In 1973, I went to the United States of America with Aoki-san and Fugaku-san. At the invitation of researchers in psychology, we traveled here and there to participate in summer universities. After that, Aoki-san encouraged me to travel. I was wondering where to go and how, but he gave me a lot of information about various communities: "Go see this one," "Watch out for this one because there may be drugs," etc. So, we separated at a bus stop in Los Angeles, and I went to visit some of these communities, among those that seemed to me the safest, including many Protestant communities.

Rakutenkai was a community. We lived together, with a shared living space, shared food, and a common purse, and Aoki-san often spoke to us about community. The idea of living in a community had been floating around in my head for a while. After coming back from the United States in 1973, I went to see some Japanese communities to learn how they functioned, including those in Nara and Iwate, and I was able to get a pretty good idea of the Japanese way of community living.

I dreamed of living in a community but without too many ideas on how it could take shape. At first, I talked to Masatake Egami, Masashi Minagawa, Tadashi Ishide, and Takeo Hokari for the men, and Shigeko Toshima, Hideko Handa, Kayo Hirata, and Michie Hashimoto for the women. I had named this community the "Nihon-juku"[1] without asking anyone. And then, I rented a small apartment in Yoyogi, and I proposed to those of our generation who were interested to meet there, and possibly, to live there.

Since we needed money to live, I discussed with Aoki-san about different ways to earn it. He told me about raising mink for fur, which he had, no doubt, heard about during his travels abroad. He said that there were very few mink farmers in Japan, and we could go and see how it was on the ground. I left with Ishide Tadashi to visit farms in Hokkaido. I quickly understood that it was not a job for me, but Tadashi decided to go for it. He returned once to Tokyo before returning to Hokkaido to start a mink farm there. Kayoko Shimma, who was a member of Nihon-juku, agreed and said, "I'm going to Hokkaido." As far as I was concerned, I could not conceive of my life without the practice. Raising mink in Hokkaido might allow me to earn a living, but certainly at the cost of sacrificing the practice, and it did not suit me. What would be the point of Nihon-juku without the practice?

In the end, although we talked a lot about what a common life would be like, the means to put it together and building a common spiritual life, it turned out that all the members had their own way

---

[1] Historically, a *juku* was a traditional school of the Edo period, often founded by an illustrious personage with the intention of forming a ruling elite. *Nihon* means Japan.

of living and their own aspirations that led towards disparate activities. Eventually I was the only one left, and I realized the Nihon-juku would never work. I then began to think seriously about what my own way of life should be.

Finding my purpose

At one point I was interested in the theater. Being an actor was part of Aoki-san's plans, and it seemed like a good idea to me. He had met Mitsuya Miyauchi, from the Swedish theater, somewhere in Tokyo in an underground theater. He said he was looking for someone to act in a play that had jumping scenes, and Aoki-san immediately thought of me; I don't know with what idea in mind. That is how I ended up doing theater in the Shinjuku district in Tokyo and Sumitomo in Osaka. I had a few lines to say, but my role was mostly to do a sort of shintaido-looking martial arts, with jumps and kicks. In the end, since there were many avant-garde theater troupes like this and the competition was tough, I didn't get paid. But it didn't matter. Looking back on it today, I see it as a good experience.

After the Nihon-juku stopped, I wondered: "Now what?" I did a retreat in a temple, but it didn't work out. I then thought that I wanted to somehow realize what I had learned from shintaido. I wasn't sure how much I really knew about it, but it was definitely something important. I wanted to do it with a companion who really understands me, and I was thinking of a person for that. To put it bluntly, I loved Hirata-san. But she went to Brazil. There she became a teacher in a rehabilitation school for the disabled. After studying for a while in Japan, she applied for a job abroad and left. I asked her before she left for Brazil, but she didn't agree. I think she had already decided to leave. Looking back, I wonder if Aoki-san intended to start a shintaido club there?

So, I had to do something on my own. I had to stand up, determine my way of life, and understand why I existed in this world. I wanted to do something for the good of others, to be useful to people, and I wanted to clarify my existence. I didn't think I could do that in Tokyo. So, I traveled around Japan again, looking for a place where I could live and accomplish something myself. I traveled to Koshiki Island in Kyushu and Iwate Prefecture, where I volunteered at an institution for disabled children. I had a sensational mind-to-mind meeting there with a mentally handicapped boy, and I finally understood: "That's it, I want to create a center where I can work for these children; I will find my *raison d'être* in that."

Becoming a social entrepreneur

I came back to Hazu, the region of my hometown, at the age of about thirty-one, in 1977 or 1978. After searching everywhere, I was happy to return to where I was born. Since I had a driver's license, I started by working for a local taxi company. For three years, I worked simultaneously as a driver and as a volunteer in a reception center for disabled children. Subsequently, the parents of the children, who appreciated my activities, asked the town hall of the city of Hazu to hire me. After that, those parents and I joined forces to create a small facility to care for ten children. I was assigned there as an employee of the city, which managed the facility. Ten years later, in 1989, I reached the limit of what I could do with this establishment.

The establishment we had created was a day center, because I did not have enough energy to manage a boarding school on my own. Over time, there had been more and more requests from people wishing to benefit from the services of the establishment. But the capacities at the time were insufficient, and the administration also had to deal with an increase in labor costs, so criticism began to be heard.

The amount of my annual salary was around four to five million yen, which seemed to many people like a lot for only ten children, so we expanded slightly, but we reached our absolute maximum capacity at twelve or thirteen children, and the requests kept pouring in.

It was to meet these two expectations – cushioning the cost of my salary while welcoming more children – that I asked to speak to the officials of the town hall and argued for the need to create a suitable structure. It was to be a welfare society, independent of the functioning of the city. I threatened to leave my post at the town hall because I had reached the limit of the bearable. I negotiated a lot in order to bring in excellent employees who already had the necessary technical knowledge. I fought hard, even bordering on conflict at times, but the results were worth it.

If your establishment is public, you must follow the political choices of elected officials, which can be very disabling. My desire for independence was motivated by two reasons: I wanted to be useful to people and I wanted to be able to work on something that resembled the purity of shintaido. So, I prepared myself and founded a welfare society. I had no money, but I spared no effort. And it was the parents who provided the funds, so that we could be independent. The facility where we are today[1] is an extension of this independent establishment. This was only possible with the support of the parents. The name of the establishment is "Tomokuni Sangyo-jo" and it has been operating for about seven years now.

Japanese society will become increasingly old. Today, one in five people is over sixty-five. I am part of the baby boom generation, and when we get older, in ten years, one in four people will be over sixty-five. As the number of elderly people requiring care increases, more care centers or retirement homes will be needed. There was nothing like that in my area until [our] facility was opened in 1996. Nurses and various caregivers work there, and it is home to about 100 residents.

---

[1] The interview took place in a room of the main facility that Gan Okada managed.

Construction began on another site in October, which will allow us to further increase our capacity. It is a smaller establishment, with about sixty-three residents. There are also other facilities, large and small; some for people with intellectual disabilities and others for the elderly. Basically, the elderly are accepted from the age of sixty-five. There are also small apartments for disabled children who have finished their studies and live together in groups of four while working, and a house where eight slightly senile elderly people live together.

From my three-year volunteer commitment, then to my job for the town hall for ten years, and until now, I see that the backbone of my action is the basic philosophy of social well-being that I learned from Aoki-sensei: an absolute reverence for the existence of others and an unconditional respect for life.

When I speak to the managers and staff who work with me, I explain to them how this establishment began, what has happened since, and how we have come to what it is today. What I do is simple: I just want to be useful to people.

Back to the keiko of Rakutenkai

In the end, the most interesting and impressive *keiko* remains for me Tenshingoso. I never liked other techniques and especially those that use weapons. I even hated them, although I practiced them. In the end, the main thing remains Tenshingoso! We always end up coming back to Tenshingoso. Each movement is marvelous and contains Eiko, towards the sky — very strong. I didn't really understand this movement at first, but the more I practiced it, the more I understood that it was a story of purity, even if I can't really find the words to explain it clearly.

This is still true today. When I feel confused, I can pull myself together just by thinking about this or that movement: open up, then rise to the sky. At first, I only cut the space, but finally, I really felt this feeling of cutting the universe. I go up, then I become small again. Tenshingoso is complete and coherent. Without "UN,"

I simply cannot go to "AH." These five movements are logically linked; it is a single Eiko, a continuum, in a large Tenshingoso. No more "this" or "that" — it's all connected.

I think the ability to return to a zero state is crucial; it is the most important. Make yourself small, really. If I am not able to mentally approach the zero state — even if there is a physical form, in the end the mental experience is essential, right? — then Eiko becomes a completely different thing; zero is fundamental. Even though in real life it is very difficult to obtain this "state of being zero," it is very important to strive for it when looking for a new direction to give to our actions. When I am in this situation, I always try to begin by entering mentally into this state of zero, however difficult that may be.

Feedback on the biographical interview

I realized today that I have never told anyone my life story. Your visit today has given me a very good opportunity. I am really happy. Something that I had forgotten in myself resurfaced, and remembering it, I said to myself: "That was it!" There may be imperfect things in my life, my decades of life. Thinking about it, I always wonder what was good and what was not; it's hard to say. But you came to see me and I spoke to you in person, and this allowed me to consider what I had done up till now: "Ah, I lived like that!" It made me feel like what I did wasn't too bad after all. I think I will continue to go in this direction.

If I have one regret, it's not being able to do *keiko*. When I think about it, I'm really sorry and even a little guilty. I don't like martial *keiko*, and I hate fighting. There are times when you have to fight, but basically, I don't like that very much. It can be said that fighting is necessary for human beings to grow. Yet I will always avoid fighting, it's my bad habit.

Kayo HIRATA

The initial interview was held in the spring of 2005, through H.F. Ito, at Kayo Hirata's home in Shikoku, in the presence of a former practitioner from the Keio University group, who then transcribed the recording. Kayo Hirata had spent a large part of her life in South America, in particular in Brazil, had returned to Japan only so that her children could attend Japanese schools, and soon went back to Brazil to work for educational humanitarian organizations. She left no contact information, and neither we nor any of the members of the Tokyo Women's University of Physical Education group could reach her to validate her text. However, considering the value of her testimony, we took it upon ourselves to include her biography in this work.[1]

Childhood in Kagawa

I was born on April 5th, 1950, in Kotohira, Kagawa Prefecture. My parents ran an *udon*[2] restaurant named "Sarasaya." The house looked very old, possibly dating back to the Edo period. I am not the first daughter of my parents, but my elder sister died of an illness at the age of one year, so I grew up as an eldest daughter. I have a brother who is four years younger than me and works at the Kotohira Chamber of Commerce. The restaurant was taken over by a cousin. My parents weren't very strict, and as I was growing up, they never told me "Do this!" or "Do that!" They never told me to study, but I didn't need any encouragement to do so. Even for the choice of high school or university, I only informed them after the fact.

I never came into conflict with people; I was too busy with myself. Since my early youth I have always wanted to do a lot of things. I didn't care if other people were there, even friends. Whatever the other person might feel, like anger, if I didn't notice it, it didn't turn into conflict. And if the other person smiled at me, it was fine. I was really overwhelmed minding my own business, without a moment to look around or take an interest in others. It

---

[1] **Credits:** *Interview:* H.F. Ito, P. Quettier. *Transcription:* Mrs Miho. *Editing:* M. Hirano. *Translation:* P. Quettier. *Proofreading:* L. Seaman, L Ordeman.

[2] Thick noodles made from wheat, most often served in a bowl of broth with various garnishes and accompaniments. *Udon* is a specialty of this region.

was always, "I want to do this and also that." I don't remember what my brother was doing at that time. I don't remember what other people were doing at that time. It was "everything for me," and I was very selfish. I don't remember playing with my younger brother either.

Entering university and discovery of the keiko of Rakutenkai

When I entered college, Toshima-san told me about people who were doing an interesting practice. When I was in my first year, there was a demonstration of martial practices at Hosei University, by Aoki-sensei and Jugoro-san. Toshima-san asked me to go together, and I said yes, but I fell asleep and woke up after the meeting time. I still went to the place of the demonstration, as I had promised. I arrived just as the demonstration was ending. I have a picture where Aoki-sensei is standing and Jugoro-san is lying on the ground. I arrived at this precise moment, and it was my first contact with shintaido. I don't remember practicing that day, but Shigeko Toshima told me later that I learned Eiko there. She later saw me practicing Eiko near the university dormitory and saying "Ah, that feels good." And that's how I started doing shintaido.

Afterwards, I don't remember the details very well, but I started a club with Toshima-san. Michie-chan and Hideko-san then joined us. I think I had the opportunity to tell them about this club because we were in the same class and our student numbers followed each other. Before I realized it, the four of us were doing things together. After a while, Shigeko-san and I were spending more time in *keiko* with Aoki-sensei than in class. Michie-chan and Hideko-san were doing well in class and taking notes, especially Hideko, who was very serious. I hardly attended the lessons. Quite soon, I also went to Yokohama. I would go to college at night to train, then I would go to Yokohama and train again. After a while I only attended college for club activities. I passed my tests and got my course credits by studying the notes that Hideko had taken. It was fun. In the beginning, there were two university dormitories, one inside the university and the other outside. Michie and I were in the inside one and Hideko was on the outside. Then, after a year, everyone left the college dorm. We were very different from each other. I have only fond memories of those times.

Rakutenkai was also very interesting; every day was new. Rakutenkai members like Ito-sensei and Jugoro-san, but also Gan-san, Minagawa-san, Egami-san and Takeo-kun, were fantastic and so serious. As for their studies, I don't know, but they thought about life, they lived it with great seriousness, and they were extremely lively. After the *keiko*, they were always talking about the *keiko*. I liked going there because all those things that everyone was talking about – painting, theatre, music, the Bible, etc. – were really interesting.

This didn't mean that the practice of the university club was not interesting, but what was happening at Rakutenkai was even more interesting, and so new. These people attracted me because I was the type who wanted to know everything. It may be a matter of fate, but I think I probably went to Tokyo to meet the Rakutenkai members and do just what I did there. I was able to get a teacher's license thanks to the university, and it was a good thing for my life, but the most important thing was that I went there to meet Rakutenkai. The probability was only one out of tens of thousands, but I had this chance, and I took it.

Today, I think that everything I learned at that time has been useful for my work. I deal with children with disabilities, and people ask me: "How do you know this?" or "How do you do that?" They are expecting an explanation, but I am unable to describe things theoretically. What I can do naturally is not natural for other people; they need rational explanations. Well! For shintaido practitioners these things are obvious, normal.

Things like this happen so often when working with children. I just think that I was carefully trained in Rakutenkai, in shintaido.

This may be due to having been baptized, but I feel that I have been carefully trained and have only benefited from it.

The turning point of baptism

In my third year of university, I nevertheless went through a difficult period. One day, while walking up the stairs at a train station, Takeo-san said to me point-blank, "When I talk to you, sometimes you tire me!" These words depressed me terribly because I practiced precisely to improve my relationships with people. I could have understood if I had been aware of a problem, but when he said it like that, in just an ordinary situation, it left me distraught and full of questions, like: "What makes me tire people?" or "If he told me such a thing when there was no particular problem, it must be something more fundamental, and is there anything I can do about it?" But no matter how hard I thought, I couldn't find an answer. It touched the very structure of my existence.

At that time, I was reading the Bible. So, since I couldn't find an answer within myself, I concluded that if God existed and if God had made me, then the God who had made me was bad... and under those conditions, how could I hope to heal myself? In the end, believing that God existed, I got baptized saying: "I give you all of me, fix me please." I wanted to be baptized, to be reborn. What Takeo-kun told me was the symptom of the problem. And since I couldn't remedy the problem myself, I told myself that the burden was on whoever had made it. After the baptism, I felt very good and even happy, more than I would have thought.

Then it became easier for me to get along with people. One day I said to Aoki-sensei, "I can't trust people." He replied, "You are stupid. There is only God in whom you must believe. Humans, you just have to love them." I told myself that it was true that if I believed in a person, then I could be, or feel, betrayed and hurt, but if I simply loved that person, it was then a one-sided process, and it became impossible to be betrayed. I still remember those words from Aoki-sensei. I am more physical and athletic than intellectual. I can't really understand things on a mental level if I don't first understand them in my body.

It was words like those of Takeo-san and Aoki-sensei that made me feel a certain defect in my body. At that time, Aoki-sensei constantly said vigorous or direct things like this without hesitation. Really! One day he casually said, "I would like to die for someone I don't know at all." I listened to this, and I said to myself "Yes!" Looking back on it recently, I thought that was a great statement. This kind of thing sticks in my mind.

At one point, I was advised to be altruistic to improve my practice, like, "You can really improve your movements by becoming altruistic." But I had a very strong ego, which I could never completely get rid of. I thought, "Oh, I don't like it, I'm tired, and my legs hurt." I was very sorry for not being able to reach the goal. The stronger the ego, the harder it is to be altruistic. "If I was a baby, I could do this easily," I thought. Whatever I did, my ego remained unrooted.

It was from this moment, however, that I began to understand that beneath the surface of what is visible there is a whole world of invisible things. It has made my life a lot easier. What is visible does not represent the totality of what exists. Doesn't that make a difference?

I may have been strong before I entered college, but when I encountered things that upset me, my worry and pain occupied my mind one hundred percent and I couldn't think of anything else. I was stuck and it was very painful. Now, after having experienced Rakutenkai, I manage to see myself as I am. This would certainly not have been possible without the painful practice of shintaido. Thanks to shintaido, I discovered what to do with my huge ego.

What I learned from Rakutenkai

All of these things are related to my current job. I met God by meeting shintaido, and thanks to that my life became easier. Then

I found what I should do there. This is why shintaido itself remains such a fond memory for me.

Since my childhood, I have always wanted to become a teacher. Now I work with handicapped children; I am doing exactly what I wanted to do. I couldn't do it without shintaido or Rakutenkai. My feeling is that, rather than me, it is shintaido that is at work in my work.

I have incredible memories of training from that time. It was so fun and challenging at the same time! I would never have been able to change without these practices with the Rakutenkai people. I must say that I arrived at the right time. No need to be in the center, it was enough to take advantage of what had been prepared, to flow into the group. It is as if rails had been laid and by following the old ones, we were put on these rails, which we just had to follow. I have only benefited from the good sides of things, through the love of our *sempai*. I only have fond memories of those great times.

The teachers thought so much about what they had to do. And we just had to do what they had already done, focus on ourselves and do what we had to for ourselves. We did not have to think about the organization, but about ourselves, only about ourselves and our lives. I learned a lot from the teachers. They always talked about what to do in different situations, to make things work best: "If we are in such a place, it is necessary to do such a thing at such a time, etc." Or they would ask: "Rather than having a banal conversation, what place should we choose so that the conversation becomes more pleasant or more exciting? Should we move or do something else to make the meeting more productive?" etc. When I was with them, they always talked like that, and every day was like that. The *sensei* was constantly taking notes in his notebook and the *sempai* were studying diligently. It was all very fresh, very new to me, and I listened to their conversations eagerly. I probably didn't understand a tenth of what was being said, but I thought I understood, and I though "Yes, I can do it!"

Rakutenkai was a formidable group. The motto was something like: "Through life we seek freedom, we gain this freedom, and through it we become light." I thought that was amazing. It was not enough to grasp the truth. You had to become the light of the world. The path usually ends in enlightenment. But once free, you had to give something back to the world. It was great!

Teaching and support for children with disabilities

I first became a physical education teacher. I started at Tamamo College near my home. In this college, the class for disabled children was in a separate place. It was then that an older teacher asked me, probably because I was young, "How about teaching physical education outside of class?" So, in my free time, I went to the class for disabled children. And I found that very enjoyable. These students were more fun than normal students. That's why I asked the principal to let me take care of the class for disabled children. This principal was a wonderful person. He asked me, "Do you know anything about special education?" I understood that "special" did not mean "elite," and I answered yes. He then said to me: "Do you really want to take care of this class?" and I said, "Yes, I do." At the end of the year, he called me again and said, "If you really want to take care of children with disabilities, you have to go and do some training, because it's rare that I get this kind of interest from young people." And he added: "As a young woman, you may stop working once you get married, so getting a license like this may prove useless, but you must have a lucky star. So, enjoy it!" That's how I went to train at Yokohama College for a year.

This college happened to be close to Aoki-sensei's house. Again, a matter of destiny, certainly. So, I spent a year in this middle school in Yokohama in order to obtain a license to teach a class of handicapped children. It was a very intense year. Rakutenkai and the *dojo* were close. But I was working, and I felt different. A year later, when I returned home, the principal asked me where I wanted to go to work. I said, "Wherever no teacher wants to go." That's how I taught for three years at the Lion Gakuen school in Busshozan.

I feel good with these children. It goes well with ordinary children, but I feel better with handicapped children. I am relaxed with them. It is presumptuous to say, but I can understand these children, or rather, they and I understand each other. I really like autistic children. I was asked how I could understand them, but I could only answer that I was just doing what I had learned in shintaido. It is natural and intuitive for me to know that it is better to do one thing for this child, and then it is good to do another thing. I see that for some improvement to occur in the condition of this child, it is good to do such and such a thing. All this I did not learn in school. It is therefore obvious that it comes from the sensations that I experienced or the movements that I learned in the shintaido *keiko*.

Starting from myself, inside, I share various subjects with others. Then, coming back to myself, I reflect. As I have time to digest what I reflect on, I manage to take advantage of it and anchor it. I understand and admire the autistic world. For example, a child with severe autism went to get the attendance book but did not return. When I looked for him, I found him asleep. When it is hot, he often goes to sleep in cool places. I would like to be as natural as he is. I am, in a way, "jealous" of him.

I remember a girl who couldn't go to school. I went to see her parents, and as soon as I met them, I felt that it was going to be fine. It is possible that if someone other than me had gone to see her parents, her father would not have sent her to school. But he told me a lot about his daughter, and then he encouraged her to go to school. Since then, she grew up and graduated, but I always kept in touch with her.

A young girl once asked me: "How do you understand what a child thinks?" I replied, "You just have to look at his or her face or observe what he or she is doing." But I could see that the girl did-n't understand me.

I think Aoki-sensei and the other Rakutenkai teachers taught me that. We did a lot of practice, for example, to avoid getting cut from behind. These things seemed natural to us. Besides, if the teacher wanted a cup of tea, one had to be prepared without him even asking for it.

In a workshop in Asama, we trained to listen to the sound of a bell that Aoki-sensei rang to prepare our bodies for the exercise. He was ringing it as he walked away to one end of the *dojo* and we, in line at the other end, had to detect the number of times we had heard this sound, really very distant and very weak. In the end, each of us got a different result from the others. We were told, "You can't hear it because you keep a lot of useless things inside of you. You can't hear it even though you should be able to." And with practice, we ended up being able to hear even very faint sounds. I remember things like that.

I'm not sure I fully understood all of this at the time. But when it comes to children with disabilities, I'm very good at it. Everyone has one's own area of expertise.

The sensei

It is possible that at first I entered Rakutenkai for Aoki-sensei; he was so attractive. When I encountered a difficulty, I often thought to myself, "What would Aoki-sensei think in such a situa-tion? What would he do?" But I really liked all the members of Rakutenkai. I liked these people. I certainly arrived at the best time. If I had been more involved in Rakutenkai, I think a lot of other things would have happened. But that was not the case. I came from outside, I had certain experiences, I expressed my opinion, I walked in the footsteps of the *sempai*, and at the right time, I left. It is possible that those who were more involved in

Rakutenkai suffered. But the three of us[1] were not involved, not inside, and we only had to think about ourselves. This is how I was able to think about my life.

When I look back, I remember how much I loved Aoki-sensei. His very existence, the fact that such a person is alive is incredible, unforgettable. He told me a lot of things at that time. I remember him well, while we were going up to Nogeyama, telling me about the incredible philosophy of Rakutenkai. I have great respect for people who do these kinds of fantastic things. I have no bad image.

I remember one day Suzuki-sensei got mad at me. He taught young people very well and therefore took care of the students during the internships. One morning everyone, including Hideko-san and Michie-chan, went to the *dojo*, to meet our *sensei* there. But I continued to sleep because I was too sleepy. So, Suzuki-sensei came to wake me up. But I continued to sleep. Eventually, he literally kicked me out of bed. I have kept a memory of it that is both terrible and joyful.

Travel and emigration to South America

I went to America and Mexico when I was twenty-six or twenty-seven. In San Francisco, Ito-sensei told me: "There are three ways to get to Mexico. The first is by airplane; it is the safest. The second is the main line bus; it is safe and preferable if you can afford it. And the third is the ordinary bus, taken by the workers; it's the roughest way, but if you make it to your destination safe and sound, you'll be able to live in Mexico without any problem." Presented like this, I obviously could only choose the ordinary bus. And that's how I got to Mexico. I had only brought a dictionary, but in Tijuana I met a worker's wife with her children, who took care of me. She explained to me what to do with my passport at the border and bought me a *taco* in a cafeteria. I still remember

---

[1] Kayo Hirata, Hideko Handa, Michie Hashimoto.

those times spent with her. A good person is a good person, whatever the country.

Having made this trip made me want to live abroad. Once back in Japan, I applied as a Japanese school teacher. Although this was a first application, I was accepted. It seems that the administration had decided to admit a person from Kagawa Prefecture that year. Then I was sent to Brazil, when I would have preferred Spanish-speaking Mexico. Then, after some time working with Japanese people there, I resigned my position to live my life completely among Brazilians. In the end, I stayed there for twelve years, from 1979 to 1991. I got married there and had three children.

Return to Japan for the education of my children

I returned to Japan at the insistence of my husband. He thought Brazil was so inflationary that our three children couldn't go to college. So, we had to go elsewhere to allow them to study. That's how we came back to Japan, where I could easily find work.

While I was still in Brazil, a friend had already mentioned me to the school board. This is how I was able to start working as soon as I returned to Japan in April, 1991. This contract ended after a few months, because I was only a substitute, assigned by the school board. But the commission immediately assigned me to a new job and so on. This allowed me to work at many schools and gain rare experience. I currently work for Chubu Child and Family Services Facility, the largest in Kagawa. I also worked for a similar facility in Takamatsu. I teach in elementary, middle, and high school. I have been working continuously since my return from Brazil and will continue to do so tirelessly. That's why I told my children, "When you're older, your mother will be a senior volunteer." I would like to go to Paraguay or Uruguay as a Japanese teacher. As my youngest is seventeen, that will be soon.

My children are my treasure. I have nothing else, no money, no house, really nothing. But I have three good children of whom I am proud. My eldest daughter had to suffer from bullying. Arriving from Brazil in the fourth year of primary school, she did not speak Japanese. She could not imagine fighting with the other children, saying that they must have their reasons or that she herself had bad traits. She now works in the service of the elderly. She spoke to me about her work as a nurse's aide with great pleasure: such a grandfather was like that, such a grandmother had done this, etc. But there are many disgusting and dirty aspects in caring for the elderly, too, right? Since she didn't talk about it, I thought she didn't care. But, after about six months, I asked her the question anyway. So, she told me about a recent case of food poisoning with diarrhea and vomiting! I thought she was doing an amazing job. But, if I hadn't asked her, she would have continued to talk only about pleasant things: the grandfathers and grandmothers who are so cute, or those who, because of dementia, forget everything and sing nursery rhymes. One day she took a picture of a good grandma with a cell phone, which was so cute! She says she is really good for this job as a caregiver.

My second child wants to go as a youth volunteer to Canada. She wanted to go straight away, but I asked her to first get a qualification, in order to live in good working conditions. That's what she's doing right now. She's a nice child. I send her money for her everyday life, but she saves it to send some of it to a Cambodian child and to go as a work volunteer. She's a great kid.

The youngest wants to study law. He wants to help others by assisting them on a legal level. They are really three good children.

When they were born, I thought that I no longer had the right to die of my own will. Alone, it would have been unimportant to die anywhere, anytime, but not anymore. I also thought that if I had to die to save my children, I should accept it even if I didn't like it. I immediately felt capable of carrying the burden of a family.

Hideko HANDA-HOKARI

We knew Hideko Hokari well, having been received by her and her husband many times in the past. The initial interview was held in the spring of 2004, through H.F. Ito. In 2019, informed of the resumption of work on the texts by her husband, Kazuo Hokari, she asked to receive hers by email. We therefore sent it to her, not without some apprehension that she might ask for changes that would degrade the original spontaneity of the text. To our great relief, she returned it to us in May, 2019, approved without any significant changes.[1]

Childhood in a mountain village, athletics, and studies

I was born in 1950 in Matsushiro, a small town in Nagano Prefecture. My maiden name is Handa. My father is the third son among four boys. His three brothers died in the war. When it broke out, my father was a student at the University of Science in Tokyo, where he was involved in research in a telecommunications laboratory. After the war, his father, a farmer, asked him to return to Nagano to take over the family farm's rice production and silkworm breeding. This is how my father gave up his research and left university just a few months before graduating. He married and had three daughters, of whom I am the youngest. My mother, also from Matsushiro, is my father's cousin.

When I was a little girl, I loved playing in nature, running in the hills and mountains. I became agile and fast there. I also helped my parents in the fields when there was extra work planting rice or raising silkworms. As we were in the countryside, I picked delicious wild herbs in the spring and mushrooms in the fall or caught insects to play with. My parents took great care of the eldest child at the beginning and of the youngest, so cute, at the end; leaving me, between one and the other, very free. This is how I grew up unhindered in this beautiful natural setting.

For primary school and middle school, I went to the small village school. In middle school and high school, I was part of an

---

[1] **Credits:** *Interview*: H.F. Ito, P. Quettier. *Transcription*: M. Minagawa. *Editing*: M. Hirano. *Translation*: P. Quettier. *Proofreading*: L. Ordeman, L. Seaman.

athletics club because I ran very fast. Then I entered a high school in Nagano, far from my home. All the students at this school were very good, and I conceived, for the first time, a feeling of inferiority. I was also part of the athletics club there, doing my best. It was in 1969, when I entered the Women's University of Physical Education in Tokyo, that I was finally freed from my inferiority complex. For the first six months, I was part of the folk-dance club, where we danced with male students from another university. But I soon realized that the motivation for most of the girls in the club was to find a boyfriend. I was not there for that, and I spent a few months wondering what I was doing there.

The university's Sogo-budo club

At the end of the summer holidays of the first academic year[1], a classmate, Shigeko Toshima, invited me to join a Sogo-budo club she was creating. I immediately bought into the idea, soon joined by two others, Michie-chan and Kayo-chan, and the activity started as a small club. Not being an official club, we could not access the university gymnasium. So, we met after class to practice in the courtyard of the university or in a small *dojo* that we reserved nearby. I had reservations because I found certain practices painful. However, I felt something intriguing in this practice.

Rakutenkai

Shortly after the beginning of the practices at the university, Shigeko-san took me to Rakutenkai, and I met there Aoki-sensei, as well as other members of the group. Rather than the practice itself, I was more strongly drawn to the ideals of the Rakutenkai members, the atmosphere they created, and their tremendous energy. Toshima-san also took me to practice at the Tokyu Dojo with

---

[1] In Japan, the academic year runs from April 1 to March 31 of the next year (the first semester runs from April 1 to September 30 and the second from October 1 to March 31).

Matsuhashi-san, who I also thought was great. I was really very impressed by these people.

One day, I can't remember exactly when, I was invited to participate in a *gasshuku* at the Niigata University Karate Club. In a small meeting at a cafe before the workshop, I met Takeo-san. He was fasting for several days and did not consume anything while everyone else was eating and drinking. Again, I was surprised to meet a person with such mental strength. Then, once the *gasshuku* started, we only did *kaikyaku-sho*. After an hour, I had more than enough and left the *dojo* to go for a walk by the sea. Then, as I looked out to sea, wondering what I was doing there, a boat appeared on the horizon, grew in size and then disappeared. Seeing this, I realized how tiny a human being was, how tiny I was, and how tiny my disorder was. I then felt better and went back to practice. I went to the end of the *gasshuku*, as demanding and painful as the *keiko* were, and I resolved to continue to practice after the *gasshuku*. Without this experience, I would have fled shintaido. But I continued to hate suffering.

The most surprising thing I encountered in Rakutenkai was Christianity. In my childhood, by tradition inherited from my grandparents, I had grown up in a Buddhist environment, close to the ancestors and the Buddha. I had had no contact with Christianity, and I was greatly surprised to discover it within the framework of Rakutenkai. At the same time, these were people who took everything so seriously. These are probably the two reasons why I wanted to persevere. And of course, what Aoki-sensei said was always so new and attractive that I was enthusiastic about it.

I thus participated in Rakutenkai until my fourth year of university, and then I entered active life. In 1973, after working for nearly a year in Tokyo, I quit my job and determined to return to Nagano. To say goodbye to Rakutenkai, I went to Ipponmatsu Elementary School where they were having their *gasshuku*. Aoki-sensei invited me to participate, and I accepted, telling myself that it would be for the last time. I don't remember the content of the course, but I have vivid memories of a great *kumite* with Aoki-sensei. I had the impression of rediscovering shintaido, as this *kumite* gave me access to extraordinary perceptions.

Family life

In October, 1974, I married Shiko-san[1], whom I had met in Rakutenkai. Before that, I went back to my parents in Nagano. I had lived selfishly, thinking only of myself all these years, and I felt the need to strengthen the filial ties before leaving my parents permanently to live in Tokyo with Shiko-san. Once married, I worked for about six months as a part-time PE teacher in middle-school and high-school. Shiko-san was living in Aoki-sensei's house at that time, and we stayed there for a while before moving to Kawasaki. Our room was right across [a breezeway] from Aoki-sensei's. He would open his window and say, "Hideko, I'm hungry!" It was more than I could bear. In the end, we only stayed there for a month, but it felt like an eternity, and I welcomed our move to Kawasaki with relief.

After our marriage, we continued our shintaido life. Our older daughter was born in 1975, and the younger was born in 1978. We went to the Sendagaya gymnasium *keiko* every week with our children.

In 1978 and 1979, meetings of shintaido leaders were held in our house in Azamino. Aoki-sensei often came there with the other supervisors. And then, in December, 1979, Shiko-san was seriously injured in a traffic accident. He remained hospitalized for three months, and when he was released in March, 1980, we visited Fugaku-san[2] in the United States to spend his convalescence there. This year was also the year of the first international shintaido event in San Francisco.

---

[1] Nickname of Kazuo Hokari.
[2] Nickname of Haruyoshi Ito.

Shintaido at the center of my life

Before this international *gasshuku*, I traveled by myself to the United States for a month, and after that we went to Mexico with Shiko-san. These moments were a real turning point in my life.

I took a Greyhound bus to the East Coast, carrying in my bag many *onigiri*[1] made for me by Fugaku-sensei. On the second day, they were a bit sour, but I ate them anyway and didn't get sick!

I also visited Yosemite Mountain with Fugaku-sensei and Minagawa-san. I remember beautiful scenery and such delicious water. Ultimately, this trip — my first abroad — was the biggest turning point in my shintaido life. I was inspired by the lifestyle of American members and felt a strong urge to "do something." Thus, immediately after my return to Japan, in 1980, I created a shintaido group at my home in Azamino.

This period, between 1980 and 1987 was extraordinary, the most active shintaido of my life. In addition to my Azamino group, I taught quite a few other groups: about twenty agents from a life insurance company from 1984 to 1985, mothers from a kindergarten for two years, and three male high school students at an improvised *dojo*, on the banks of the Tama River, for a year.

When the Azamino group was created, I invited Michael-sensei, who was then living in Japan, to teach for a year. We were initially challenged [by the local jurisdiction] about the free use of a room in the primary school for the practices because students were being charged tuition. So, we brought in a teacher from outside the group in order to be able to officially justify the expenses. I then gradually took over the class. I led the *keiko* for eight years. Every year, we did a workshop, during which the children of the members practiced with us. Aoki-sensei was invited there to teach and give evaluations. We also organized a few *gasshuku*. The number of regular practitioners was about ten people, out of about thirty

---

[1] Rice ball pressed and surrounded by a sheet of nori seaweed.

registered. When I stopped leading the group, Ushirokoji-san took over. The people in this group have remained friends to this day.

In April of 1985, the first publication of Aoki-sensei's book, *The Body is a Message of the Universe*, was celebrated at the Tobu Hotel in Tokyo. The following year, in January, 1986, we celebrated the opening of the Myogadani *dojo*[1]. There was a great ceremony bringing together one hundred and thirty people. At the time, Aoki-sensei was in contact with influential businessmen, such as Inamori-san of the Kyocera company. Many of them, as well as university professors, were there. This is how I ended up doing *wakame-taiso* with [Maseru] Ibuka-san, one of the founders of Sony Corp.

The years 1986 and 1987 were incredible. I first joined the faculty of shintaido Kyokai in 1986 to lead the practices of the Yomiuri cultural center. In August, 1986, the whole family took part in the American Shintaido Ten *gasshuku*. The following year, in 1987, I was invited by Fugaku-sensei to teach in England and France. I remember a practice on a huge property in the South of France. In 1987, I was invited to teach at the American national *gasshuku*, held on an island near the Boston airport.

Distancing from shintaido

The fourth international *gasshuku* took place in 1988 in Japan. Then, in December of that same year, I informed Aoki-sensei that I was resigning from shintaido. Shiko-san had, for his part, resigned at the time of the international *gasshuku*. For some time, he felt that everything was over and had resolved to step down, but he had waited until then to officially transfer his

---

[1] Since the beginning of the organization, the practices were held in various municipal or private halls and the headquarters had its offices in an independent place. This *dojo* in Myogadani brought together for the first time the practices and the central administration of the shintaido school. This initiative did not survive the drying up of financial support following the bursting of the financial bubble in 1991.

responsibilities as director of the International Shintaido Federation to Funakawa-san.

Until 1987, the world of shintaido, the Aoki world, was everything to me. And then I ended up wanting something else. There was a time when my body moved quite naturally under the direction of Aoki-sensei's *gorei*, his mind, or his *kiai*. But once out of this world, his influence no longer had an effect, as if he was playing alone with his own mind. I then began, around 1988, to see things from the outside, from the point of view of people who did not practice shintaido.

From the moment that shintaido was no longer enough for me, I began to feel a real urgency to know all these good things that existed outside. It's like I was waking up from some kind of possession. I had been involved for almost twenty years, and now I wanted to explore everything that was not shintaido. That's why I had to distance myself completely.

I then threw myself into many new things, on a voluntary or professional basis. And in doing so, I was able to realize how deeply the bases of my thought and my values testified to my shintaido experience. My dearest friends are the members of Azamino or Michie-chan groups. At the end of the day, I think shintaido is really great.

Looking back

When I encountered Rakutenkai Christianity, I was fascinated by the existence of a previously unsuspected invisible world. From the perspective of the sciences learned in school education, I had remained insensitive to such things. It wasn't until I joined Rakutenkai that I became interested in the existence of the invisible world of mind and thought.

It is certainly by multiplying the ability to feel through the body that the invisible world opens up. The practice of shintaido gives this increased sensitivity which, in turn, gives access to the perception and exploration of such an invisible world. I realized this much later, after doing many other things. Even today, I continue to feel things through my body more than I see them with my eyes. When I stand in front of a work of art, a statue of the Buddha, or I am in nature, I have an instant feeling of oneness with these things. It goes through the body, regardless of what is seen by the eyes or understood by the brain.

I recently quit my job and am now enjoying a new lifestyle. I'm excited about the new things that are coming.

When I'm doing something, and it occurs to me that maybe I've done enough, my interest suddenly dries up. I feel the need to take a break or end it. Jokingly, Shiko-san said to me, "But how come you don't get bored of married life [laughing]!"

I no longer remember the *keiko* concretely. Simply, experimental *kumite* with Aoki-sensei which allowed him to confirm his hypotheses or find new things. My body reacted naturally to his energy, and it was useful to him without me really understanding what.

I also remember advice Aoki-sensei gave us in difficult times. When we were struggling to create a shintaido group, he told us: "As long as a baby bird stays on the branch, no one knows if it will fall or fly. Only by getting started can you know what you are worth." He was always encouraging with his advice and his *kumite*.

In the early days of Rakutenkai, the boys wanted to become stronger or technically better. But none of that interested me, and I just wanted to move with others and feel the common direction.

When I didn't feel in good shape, I didn't go to Rakutenkai. As a student my first duty was to succeed in my studies. I joined Rakutenkai activities when I felt good. I found a friendly and interesting atmosphere there, but I was above all a student. My parents financed my studies, and I owed it to them to graduate with flying colors. I took my classes seriously and went to Rakutenkai when I felt fit. But now, after several decades, only the memories of Rakutenkai remain clear, and I have forgotten all about the rest of university life.

Michie HASHIMOTO

Since Michie Hashimoto and Hideko Hokari remained close over the years, the initial interview, conducted by H.F. Ito, took place in September, 2004, at H. Hokari's house. Sometime later, after separating from her in-laws, Hashimoto left to work for a Japanese humanitarian organization in South America. In May, 2019, during a hiatus between two of these stays abroad, we met with her to confirm the text of the original interview in Japanese, as edited by M. Hirano.[1]

A childhood in the countryside

I was born on July 8th, 1950, in Atami Village, Koriyama Township, Fukushima Prefecture. It was a village lost in the mountains. My father is of *Buraku* origin[2], and my mother came from Tokyo to live in Fukushima to avoid the bombings during the war. My father is a farmer from Fukushima. My parents bought a wooded area with money borrowed from the government and cleared it. We were very poor, and electricity didn't come to the house until I was five or six years old. Of course, there was also no running water, and you had to fetch it from the river. There were two of us kids; I have a younger brother. Cleaning the lamps was child labor. As we were very poor, we sometimes lacked the money to buy oil. When the electricity came on, I remember that the bulb looked very red to me. I imagine it is because it was low power, in order to save electricity.

I walked twenty minutes on foot to get to school. When I entered primary school, radio sets began to spread. We also had one, but we hardly listened to it because it had been damaged by mice. We didn't subscribe to any newspapers either. Gradually,

---

[1] **Credits:** *Interview*: H.F. Ito, P. Quettier. *Transcription*: M. Minagawa. *Edition*: M. Hirano – *Translation*: P. Quettier – *Proofreading*: L. Ordeman, L. Seaman.

[2] *Burakumin* (部落民) (literally "person from the hamlet") is a term for a socially discriminated and economically marginalized Japanese social minority (Source: Wikipedia and Szczepanski, Kallie. "Japan's Untouchables: The Burakumin." ThoughtCo, Jun. 14th, 2018, thoughtco.com/who-are-the-burakumin-195318).

however, we emerged from deep poverty, and in 1964, the year of the Tokyo Olympics, a television set came to our house.

We were growing poor-quality rice because our land was dry. No one wanted to buy it from us, but we couldn't afford to hire a bulldozer to make the land arable. For that, we would have had to borrow, and we could not, for fear of being unable to repay. When I was in college, I also helped my parents with the farm work. My job was to mow hay for the cows we raised. I was doing this job to help my mother, who was not strong enough. We had to mow a lot of it, dry it, and put it in a silo for winter. There were also corn stalks. As we were poor, we only had a few dairy cows.

The University, shintaido, and the Bible

When I finished high school, my parents offered to arrange a marriage for me. Since I didn't want that, I asked them to give me the wedding money so that I could go to university. A private university is very expensive compared to a state university. To help me get into a private university, my father sold a piece of farmland. This is how I came to study at the Women's Gymnastics University in Tokyo in the spring of 1969. From the second year, I received a scholarship, but I continued to work at part-time jobs to earn money.

In the first year of university, I entered a gymnastics club to do apparatus there. Then, after the summer holidays, in October, Toshima-san came to introduce us to shintaido and lead a class. She also talked about the Bible. Once when I was fifteen, a group of volunteers from the American Friends International charity group came to my village. Their activity consisted of volunteering to build roads in the mountains in return for accommodation with farmers. One of these volunteers gave me a pocket Bible. It was the New Testament written in Japanese and English. I had kept it with me since but never read it.

When I was introduced to shintaido, I was immediately interested. As my father practiced kendo, maybe I was attracted by the martial aspect? Then, when I went to the church in Nogeyama, the presentation and the discussions on the Bible interested me even more. I started going to church in Nogeyama at the same time as shintaido. I didn't participate much in university club practices, preferring Nogeyama instead. Kayo[1] encouraged me, too. I still participated in the club's activities until the end of the academic year, and then I went to Aoki-sensei. Again, I was more interested in the Bible than in shintaido.

At that time, I had a lot of dreams, quite various. For example, I dreamed of a grave on which was inscribed some words from the Bible, words that I did not understand. Aoki-sensei suggested that I write down my dreams even though they didn't make sense. And then one day, I went to the mountains of Tanzawa with Aoki-sensei, and I suddenly felt like I had been there before. In fact, it was in a dream that I saw myself in these mountains, with my school bag on my back. I talked about it to Aoki-sensei, who told me to write down this dream.

Rakutenkai ... without too much keiko

In Rakutenkai, I didn't do a lot of *keiko*. I was more drawn to the Bible or experiences like these dream stories. Among all the members of Rakutenkai, I am probably the one who has done the least amount of *keiko*. The *keiko* seemed very hard to me; I didn't understand it. Even when we were only discussing the *keiko*, I didn't understand anything about it. I preferred anything that had to do with the senses and sensibility, like dreams or the words of the Bible, and all that sort of thing.

Still, one day when I was running in Nogeyama Park, I remember being pulled upwards, like a feeling of being absorbed by the sky, and I was crying. I couldn't stop myself from crying; it was as if someone was inviting me and saying: "Come, those who carry a very heavy load!"

---

[1] Kayo Hirata.

After university, I got married. I did not leave shintaido immediately after my marriage. My shintaido continued in my daily life. I did not physically practice the *kata*, but I felt the spirit of it, what flows inside the shintaido. For me the Bible and shintaido are one and the same thing.

From time to time, while reading the Bible, I thought to myself: "That's it!" I accepted the Bible. When I had problems, I read the Bible. Without moving my body, I felt what flows inside. After I was married, I still had my *bo*, and from time to time I would attend bojutsu *keiko* at the Tokyo Gymnasium in Sendagaya. Though I was hardly going to *keiko* at all, in my head I had not left shintaido.

The difficulties of life and shintaido

I was able to talk about my difficulties with Hideko-san. When I told her about my problems with my children, she gave me a lot of energy; whether that came from shintaido, I'm not sure. While Kayo was living in Brazil in 1974, I often dreamt of her. I was living in Hiroshima then. Around 1982, I went to a *gasshuku* organized by the Azamino group [H. Hokari, p. 281], to which Kayo came with her whole family. On this occasion, I told Aoki-sensei about a dream I had in which Kayo was crawling on the ground, and he replied that it was because I was experiencing a similar condition. It was true that I had come back from Hiroshima because of problems I was having with my parents, and also in my relationship with my husband.

Concerning the Rakutenkai *keiko*, I remember that the hardest practice was bojutsu, but it was interesting: for example, the transmission by telepathy to know what a person located far away thinks. I did this with Ma-chan[1] and Minagawa-san. I believe I was a student at the time. Another exercise — a person stands behind me, she raises an arm, and I guess on which side. I really

[1] Masatake Egami

found this type of *keiko* interesting. Kato-sensei, Shiko-sensei[1], and sometimes Suzuki-sensei, too, had us do this type of *keiko*, after most people had left, in this old house of the Nogeyama church.

I went to the Rakutenkai *keiko* for three years, when I was a student, from October 1969 to 1972. The Nogeyama *keiko* were very interesting, while the practices of the club at the university seemed very hard to me, and especially the *gasshuku*. When we practiced *kata*, Aoki-sensei would ask us to open our bodies, but I couldn't. I especially hated *kaikyaku-zenshin-sho* and *kaikyaku-zenshin-dai*. These jumps hurt my hip joints and femur. It was quite easy for me to dislocate my hips or my knees. No, really, I preferred to open the Bible.

My mother told me that after my marriage, I became harsh and disagreeable. I think it came from the problems I had with my mother-in-law at the time. She had asked me to cut off all relations with my friends. In 1998, I was operated on for cervical cancer. After that, I was able to tell my husband, "I can't take care of you anymore." God gave me the strength.

When I have difficulties in life, I do Tenshingoso, and it gives me courage. Obviously, as I only practiced three years, my *kata* is no longer very correct. But still, doing Tenshingoso gives me confidence. It even influences my family. I believe that my mother considers Aoki-sensei to be a great master, and she continues to give me news of him.

---

[1] Kazuo Hokari

Kenji SATO

Kenji Sato was initially interviewed in the spring of 2005 by H. F. Ito in Mr. Sato's bookstore. Mr. Sato confirmed the text with the help of Mieko Hirano in November of 2019 at the same place and in the presence of Junko Sato, Mr. Sato's wife.[1]

A childhood in the countryside

I was born on August 15th, 1948, in Yamagata Prefecture. My parents were farmers and had five boys, of which I am the second. The eldest stayed in the countryside, and all the others went to work in Tokyo. I also went to Tokyo after finishing junior high school.

Three years after the end of the war, all Japanese were still poor. In our case, even if we were indeed poor, our situation as farmers sheltered us from food deprivation. On the other hand, school books or clothes passed from one child to another and were well worn. But in those days that was the case for everyone. Maybe it's the carelessness of childhood, but I don't remember being affected by it.

Yamagata is a land of extreme cold. Snow covered everything for about four months. When it fell in a storm, you couldn't see a meter away. To go to school or play, we were therefore always in a group, with friends. I believe that this environment forged my patient and supportive character. I remember many of our fights between brothers, because we were very close. Our parents raised us well.

My father quite liked to drink, but I had a lot of respect for him. When I left for Tokyo, I came back home from time to time and told him a bit about my life, telling him one story or another. While drinking *sake*, my father would give me strict advice on how to behave regarding work, like: "You can't do this or that." I

---

[1] **Credits:** Interview: H.F. Ito, P. Quettier. *Transcription*: H. Hokari. *Edition*: M. Hirano. *Translation*: P. Quettier. *Proofreading*: L. Ordeman, L. Seaman.

was respectfully grateful to him for these conversations. He is now deceased, while my mother is still living.

Arrival in Tokyo and meeting with Saito-san

Immediately after finishing junior high school in 1964, I came to Tokyo on a "group job."[1] At first, I lived in a company dormitory. In those days, young junior high-educated workers like me were called "golden eggs."

My first job when I arrived in Tokyo was with a *sembei*[2] manufacturer. There were about thirty employees, and I met Saito-san [p. 152] there. She worked in offices and I in manufacturing. We got to know each other and got on well. Some people don't get close, even when they're in a group. In our case, we surely had affinities.

Saito-sensei was already teaching the tea ceremony and, a few years after getting my job, I started learning it from her.

Tea ceremony classes and Rakutenkai keiko

Saito-sensei was part of Rakutenkai, and she quickly encouraged me to go there. I was in my twenties. Other students of Saito-sensei also participated in Rakutenkai but not for very long. For her part, Saito-sensei incorporated some of the body relaxation methods of Rakutenkai into her tea classes. This is how her students were led to practice Tenshingoso quite intensively.

In my case, I mainly chose to actively participate in Rakutenkai activities because I was looking for something spiritual. Thus,

---

[1] *Shudan Shushoku* (lit. "cohort employment"): During the postwar reconstruction period, the great need for labor for the reconstruction of the economy, combined with the great poverty of certain regions of Japan, led to a program for "group employment" that was organized for young people from these regions who did not wish to pursue higher education or who did not have the means to do so. The departmental authorities organized these cohorts in coordination with the industries concerned.

[2] These are savory biscuits made from rice flour and covered with soy sauce before baking.

while studying the tea ceremony, I was drawn to Rakutenkai of Nogeyama, and from there to Christianity.

At that time, we intensively practiced *usagi tobi* in Nogeyama Park. This practice had a great influence on me. I went there at least once a week. Since I worked all week, I got into the habit of attending Saturday night *keiko* and staying there until Sunday. I loved those Sundays. I did this for several years.

As for the tea ceremony, there are different ways to learn it. Saito-sensei preferred to proceed by *gasshuku* of about three days/two nights. We did exercises there that were pretty unusual, such as, for example, during a *gasshuku* in Enoshima or Kugenuma, we stood upright while holding a carafe full of water at arm's length for an hour. More than interesting, this way of practice was supernatural[1], though I'm not sure if that's the right word. And to think that we were only doing this to prepare a delicious cup of tea for our guests! As far as I am concerned, of course, I feel that this was primarily aimed at increasing my own spirituality.

Saito-sensei's way of teaching was really extraordinary. First, the *gasshuku* format that she liked is not very common in tea circles. Classes are usually held in the teacher's own home. Then, I don't know of any tea school that begins the session with physical exercises or a reading of the Bible! She also had the habit of naming everything — teaspoon, tea box, or whatever. To name is to create and express what you feel there. For example, if a *kakejiku*[2] was hung, she always asked you what you thought of it. I believe that the feeling of the day at that precise moment certainly represents how the person experienced that day. This is why Saito-san's way of teaching tea is not limited by time or place. I happen to sit in front of the kettle and make a cup of tea, and that's only part of the day. Everything is connected. Therefore, I who prepare

---

[1] K. Sato uses the expression *"kami gakari,"* literally meaning "possessed by the gods" or "superhuman."

[2] Calligraphy displayed in a room's place of honor (*tokonoma*), generally together with arranged flowers.

the tea, I am identical to me who does anything. It happens by chance that this is expressed by the word "*keiko*," but we can also say that it is a time that extends. This aspect is the one that is most dear to me. Whatever I find myself doing, I strive never to forget that spirit or step out of that attitude.

What I am today comes from what I practiced during the *keiko* of tea and Rakutenkai. I did not waste my time there, far from it, and my present existence is the direct consequence of these experiences. They give me an advantage, and I feel them at work in the diversity of my daily activities.

In the used book business in which I am engaged, honesty with customers is an essential virtue. One cannot be honest today and not tomorrow; honesty takes consistency and life is long. I have been in this business for about 28 years. Our customers are universities and research institutes. No matter how much time passes, my customers continue to buy their books from Nishida, and it will continue to do so, for reasons of trust and honesty.

I also served for two years, until last May, as director of the Kanagawa Prefecture Antiquarian Book Trade Association. It is an association of 145 antiquarian booksellers. The responsibilities and tasks are multiple: to make decisions, to manage, etc. It is necessary to be sincere and humble, but also bold and sometimes even to speak strongly. My attitude towards my work and the organization are all questioned. People look at everything coldly, with pragmatism. If I do my best, they respond. If I act correctly, I am rewarded.

Today, I also trade in new books, and I have managed to establish many relationships with publishers or agencies. I am capable of all of this because my life has been what it has been.

Study of Christianity, baptism, and shintaido keiko

After leaving the company where I worked with Saito-san, I entered Kawasaki Bible School, run by Pastor Shelhorn, to study Christianity for two years. After all, the people of shintaido were

Christians, and I thought they must have found something there. So, I studied Christianity and was baptized by Okada-san in Kenzaki. This baptism, what a superb ceremony! It really happened in the sea, what an effect!

Shintaido *keiko* was hard because it required us to go beyond our limits. Was it overcoming or transcendence? I must say that this was an aspect of Rakutenkai that I did not appreciate. Even if I was not directly obliged, I was made to feel that it was necessary. There was perhaps a lack of understanding on my part, but I felt there was a kind of extremism of beliefs.

The atmosphere of Rakutenkai was not that sweet. In the end, it was a battle with oneself, and only those who took a step or two forward in this battle gained joy from it. Of course, I can understand that the results obtained by those who have fought hard for themselves or who have exceeded themselves differ from those obtained by those who have simply done things in the ordinary way. It was therefore useful to show ardor. However, I still wondered if they were not demanding too much of certain people. I wonder if that might be why some people left feeling a kind of unease about that vibe. All the members were basically nice, but there was a part of them that was competitive.

Anyway, it is thanks to these life experiences that I got to where I am. I have tea in my life, I have shintaido and Christianity; all these different parts have built who I am now. If I look at my current life, taking into account the financial aspect, my children, my family, and my business, I feel that I have led my life well.

Company management

After my marriage, about 28 years ago, I took over the Nishida second-hand bookstore from my father-in-law. This book store was very old. At that time, I was still working as a very active salesman at Yurindo, a publishing house and bookstore-sales company, and I wondered if I would be able to keep this old bookstore alive. As I read about the store's clientele, I saw that among them was a university with which I had previously worked. Thinking about it, I had the idea of bringing to the Nishida bookstore the know-how I acquired at Yurindo to get more customers. It seemed possible to me, and I set myself the goal of making it what it has become in the space of ten years. I would have preferred seven years, but it took ten. For all of this, I am indebted to the foundations laid by my father-in-law and, of course, to our customers. In ten years, the bookstore has therefore been transformed into a multi-story building, and the number of customers has increased significantly, leading to very high activity. I became so busy that I no longer had time to attend tea ceremony *keiko*.

I didn't live here when I took over from my stepfather. I took the bus home. At that time, I had long hair and tied it with a string for work. I remember that when I got on the bus with this appearance, the passengers looked at me with reproachful eyes. This happened to me more than once. Yes, I often worked until midnight or even until morning. I really didn't have time to practice tea, read the Bible, or do shintaido. I sometimes did Tenshingoso because it was easy to do at home. But the spirit of the tea ceremony or the spirit of Christianity can be practiced within any activity. This truth suits me well. This is how everything I have experienced and accomplished in my life has paid off and made me who I am now.

There are many lifestyles and attitudes. As far as I'm concerned, I don't make a distinction between work and private life; I'm always myself. Surprisingly, this way of doing things does not tire me. Of course, during my two years as president of the Kanagawa Prefecture Antiquarian Book Trade Association, I felt some stress. To achieve my goals, I sometimes had to step back before I could take a step in the direction I wanted, and I must say in the end, I more often happened to step back rather than move forward. I often had to resign myself to keeping my ideas to myself, and that ended up stressing me out.

My current job is entirely up to me. I take full responsibility for it, and in return, if I do things right, I am completely free to do whatever I want. This is the advantage of not being an employee of a company. Obviously, this implies a great responsibility and, as far as I am concerned, I invest all my energy in it, both physically and financially.

Feelings

Among the shintaido *gasshuku*, I well remember those of Asama-sanso — so interesting. I also remember those at Kujukuri, which came a little earlier.

The first-generation Rakutenkai members are individually amazing people. Just as with a company, the founding people are extremely important. There must be charisma, something that attracts people. Aoki-sensei had that, and Saito-sensei, too.

I clearly remember in shintaido *keiko* the sensation or the very clear bodily experience of what is called "God," for lack of another word. At that time the people of Rakutenkai, and therefore myself, were Christians. So, I think it was God in the Christian sense. But I had the feeling of being in the presence of something that was beyond human knowledge.

There is a Zen sect university among my clients. When I go there, I see various people there and, of course, monks. I have no uncomfortable feelings. Everyone designs their business or activity as they see fit. I take things as they are, without waiting for an explanation.

My wife also leads a very active life. She draws and teaches painting. She will organize an exhibit at the end of the month, and one of her works was used for the cover of a book. We think it's more fun to work hard on your own terms than to do work for others. There are different ways of life, but it is certain that it is best to do things in a positive and joyful way.

I inherited from my mother a desire for purity and from my father the sense of never hiding from important things. When I was in elementary school, I remember that the Nikkyoso [National Union of Teachers] was very popular among teachers. One day, when I came home, I repeated what the teacher had told us, and my father replied that he did not agree. The next day, I shared my father's words with my schoolteacher, and that same evening he came to my house on a motorbike and chatted over *sake* with my father. I remember my father saying things when it was necessary. Never shirk when it's important. I think my dad was bold.

After I led the union for two years, the next person who took over made a problem. After carefully considering the issue in the context of the moment, I talked with this person. I explained to him how I considered his position incorrect, and I clearly dissociated myself from it. Some people thought everything was fine, but having managed the union for two years, I knew very well that it was absolutely not going to work. I remember a postcard sent by an employee at the time who said to me, "Sato-san always has an upright heart."

I think it is necessary to always live like this. You have to have the courage to speak up when something's wrong. The word "courage" may be a bit outdated these days, but no matter what business you are running, determination and courage are absolutely necessary. Without them, you won't achieve anything. To make people understand what is important to me, I have to use words. It takes courage and determination to say what is right. Without these, we become irresponsible.

Teaching shintaido to children

I never injured myself doing shintaido, although there were times that a stick hit me when practicing bojutsu or kenjutsu. I still have my *bokuto* and my *bo*. I did various practices, and at Asama I even took exams as well as an assessment, but I never got far.

I should have qualified as an instructor by examination, since I taught fifth and sixth-grade children in primary school [11 and 12 years old]. At the time, I lived in Oguchi[1], and I rented the gymnasium of an elementary school. I taught five or six children there every Sunday morning for about ten years. Children were jumping and running. I wore a hakama, of course. At my wedding, all the children came. It was right at the time of Aoki-sensei's trip to the United States, and my witness was Hokari-san. Today these children are adults, and we have lost touch with each other.

---

[1] A town within the Yokohama metropolitan area.

The Rakutenkai – a martial counterculture

Run comrade,
The old world is behind you!
Graffito, Odeon Theater, Paris
May 15th, 1968

Run, run young people!
Eyes fixed beyond the horizon,
Tomorrow is for you!
H. Aoki, November, 1969

As we have seen, Rakutenkai, a phenomenon of the 1960s, questioned the classic canons of martial arts and embodied spiritual and artistic aspirations in an original form. Concurrently, a global youth culture challenged existing societal norms and values, and found new ways of living and of artistic and spiritual expression. Could Rakutenkai be classified as an expression of this youth movement, which is sometimes called the counterculture?

Situating Rakutenkai in its cultural and social context, this chapter examines its social, intellectual, and emotional affinity with the global counterculture at that time, highlighting some of the sources that motivated the Rakutenkai members, and the ways in which they went about doing their research (what might be called the "Rakutenkai culture."

ABOUT CULTURE

Culture is a complex concept, but in the 1950s American scholars Kroeber and Kluchon[1] collected several different anthropological meanings of the notion up to that time. In essence, they found that culture had variously been defined as:

- "Knowledge, belief, art, law, morals, custom and all other abilities acquired by a [hu]man as a member of a society" (Tylor, 1871);
- "Inherited techniques, artifacts, manufacturing processes, ideas, *mores* and values" (Malinowski, 1931);
- "Traditional means of solving problems (...), responses that were accepted because they got success; the learned solutions of problems" (Forde, 1942);
- "Meanings, values, norms, their interactions and relationships, their more or less coherent groupings, their ways to materialize into characteristic actions or other vehicles in an empirical socio-cultural universe" (Sorokin, 1947).

The term culture thus refers both to the way of living and being of a given society at a given time, but also to the various ways in which members of that society produce accounts of this culture. Thus, when society changes (perhaps under the effect of such major events as wars, famines, or epidemics, or through scientific or technical evolutions and their internal dynamics), its culture also changes, and new forms of cultural expression are born. In addition, producing an account of a culture is in a sense a reflexive

---

[1] Kroeber A.L., Kluckhohn C. (1952), *Culture: a critical review of concepts and definitions*, Cambridge (Mass), Papers of the Peabody Museum of American Archeology and ethnology, Harvard University XLVII.

activity: as well as commenting on and revealing its own culture, it also testifies to itself and to the quality of its perception of its own time.

INDUSTRIALIZATION AND THE AVANT-GARDE

Throughout the Western world, and in Japan, the later 19th century saw rapid industrialization stimulate powerful systemic change in society. As mechanization created a world of iron and steel, so human society and culture themselves changed in many ways, away from a close relationship with Nature towards an industrial, urban modernity. Philosophy and the arts each bore witness to this change in their own way, and this brought the emergence of what became known as the avant-garde, the intellectual and creative movement that sought to explore the meaning of this modernity on the way people live, feel, and express themselves. In doing this, many avant-garde artists and thinkers did more than question the culture upon which they were commenting but, ever more so, they questioned their own vision. Subject and object entered into dialogue, in new ways which were often fruitful but sometimes violent. As awareness grew that the old "natural" certainties (which many people still clung to), were steadily weakening, so the avant-garde went to extremes to break down and even destroy what remained of these certainties. Instead, they sought the purity of the immaterial moment.

The changes wrought by industrialization were only accelerated in the 20th century, not least by two devastating world wars, the second of which was even more murderous, more inhuman, and more global than the first. The Second World War climaxed in August, 1945 by the dropping on Hiroshima and Nagasaki of the atomic bombs created by the Manhattan Project, an unprecedented collaboration of cutting-edge scientists with the American government, and created the conditions for a new systemic change within modernism, as the "culture" of the Western scientific and artistic elite now went global. This change also presaged the automated processing of information, thus becoming a prelude to yet another social revolution: the advent of the digital world.

With the world divided into Western capitalism and Eastern communism after 1945, offering two irreconcilable concepts of modernism (social as well as esthetic) as well as two opposing power blocs, the succeeding 20 years focused on reconstructing the shattered economies of the combatant nations, including Japan, and establishing societies with stable values. The result was the creation of apparently monolithic societies, which as the 1950s went on, were then increasingly questioned, initially in the West by avant-garde artists, thinkers and writers – Abstract Expressionist painters, Existentialist philosophers and Beat Generation writers among others – and then by a revolt of young people who protested against the values of their parents' generation and sought their own ways of living, freed from what they saw as the deadly certainties of the past.

ABOUT THE COUNTERCULTURE

The youth movement of the 1960s, which began with pop music and opposition to consumerism, developed into a full-blown challenge to the values of the previous generation and created a way of life (often called "hippie") and culture all its own. Because it sought to be independent from the established culture and aimed ultimately to replace it, this movement was more than an avant-garde development, and was named (by Theodore Roszak in 1968[1]) a "counterculture".

This counterculture emerged initially in the United States and in Western Europe, especially Britain, France, and Germany. While different countries saw different manifestations, it was a globalist movement, and the key features were common in each country. They included:

[1] Roszak T., *The making of a counter culture*, University of California Press, 1995.

- Vigorous anti-militarism, fueled by the tensions of the Cold War, and by opposition to the anti-colonial wars, most importantly Vietnam. The backdrop to this was the still-fresh trauma of the Second World War and the awareness of the potential for apocalyptic devastation caused by the nuclear arms race.
- The political aspiration to freedom and enjoyment of life beyond the oppression of class, consumerism, and technocracy, in the expectation of redistribution of wealth.
- Artistically and philosophically, as the intellectual and creative revolutions of the interwar period came to maturity, there was a radical re-examination of the very notions and conditions of thought and art at the heart of ordinary life.
- Through the powerful rhythms of rock'n'roll music and adoption of consciousness-altering drugs, whether "psychedelic" (cannabis, mushrooms, LSD) or "hard" (amphetamines, cocaine, opium derivatives), young people sought new ways of directly experiencing the world itself, a new esthetic, and new forms of spirituality, all enhanced by a growing interest in Eastern arts philosophical practices (meditation, yoga, martial arts, etc.)

Counter-cultural idealism

While some members of the "counterculture" engaged politically and engineered classic revolutionary confrontations with the forces of the established order (the events of Paris in May 1968 or Chicago a few months later being major instances), others renounced direct political involvement entirely. Following the initiative of writers and poets such as Kerouac, Ginsberg, and Ferlinghetti and inspired by the European avant-garde, they chose to step outside conventional society; they grouped together by affinity and aspired to build a new way of life, frequently anarchistic or communitarian, according to whatever ideals, romantic, ecstatic, or mystical, inspired them.

French sociologist Edgar Morin became involved in the Californian counterculture, and in his journal of those times[1] he defines, echoing Roszak, the hippie "cultural revolution" of the Beat Generation as:

- The desire, "as in all great revolutions," to "preserve and to achieve an infantile universe of communion and immediacy; hippieism... is an attempt to realize the child's imaginary world in adolescence, in life."

- Neo-Rousseauism: "a counter-current caused by the increasing restrictiveness of modern life. It carries within it the quest for the free and fulfilling life of the body, the repose of the soul, communion with nature, of the primitive way of being in all its forms." Morin referred to this as an eco-movement.

- Radical Christian virtues: "the Sermon on the Mount making a sudden bid for freedom from the strait-jacket of the institutionalized churches. The need for purity and communion, the proclamation of the Beatitudes for the humble in spirit and in possessions, the quest for salvation have been revived and are being experienced in the here and now. This profound reincarnation of evangelical values has led to shame and disgust at a life based on selfishness and self-interest, in other words, at the bourgeois life of white America."

- Hedonistic individualism: "in the new culture hedonism has metamorphosed. The individualism of sensation, enjoyment and exaltation is now opposed to the individualism of property, of acquisition and of possession; consummation is opposed to consumption, ... and the hedonism of *being* (cultural revolution) is opposed to the hedonism of *having* (bourgeois society)."

- Communism, "in its double, total, contradictory, confused, but immensely rich and powerful original nature: as both

---

[1] Morin E., *California Journal,* p.80. (originally *Les États-Unis en révolution,* revue Esprit n°396, Octobre 1970); published in English by Sussex Academic Press 2008.

community-oriented and libertarian. Communism is attempting to establish itself as a way of life rather than a theoretical tool."

- Mysticism, sometimes drug-fueled and often drawing on Eastern philosophies: "the quest for the true world concealed beneath the world that only seems to be real, the quest for the inner secrets of the psyche, the quest for communion with the Being through the ecstatic life and even for Nirvanian obliteration."

He summed up these aspects in the lapidary phrase, "Paradise Now."

JAPAN AND THE COUNTERCULTURE

This revolutionary counterculture mostly was expressed in parts of the United States and western Europe, and did not massively affect Japanese society. Even so, its manifestations there were very real, in response to the concerns of the time. As in many other war-affected countries, Japanese youth actively participated in the denunciation of the militarism of their parents' generation. This moral denunciation was accompanied for some time by a student insurrectionary movement in 1968-69; at the same time, on the artistic level, the performing arts were at the forefront of the avant-garde.

Antimilitarism and politics

The direct traumas of war on the Japanese people – the demands of militarism, the firestorms caused by using incendiary bombs, the loss of loved ones and, finally, the nuclear disasters of Hiroshima and Nagasaki – had been terrible, especially in the big cities. Added to these were the indirect traumas, the psychological after-effects, general insecurity, devaluation of the currency, inflation, poverty, and the terrible privations which followed the surrender.

Japan also had to support the American occupation. This began with a general occupation that lasted six years, after which a security treaty reduced the zones of military occupation; even then, entire regions remained American territories where the Japanese people had very few rights. Incidents, often fatal, occurred between the military and the populace, and justice could not be found[1]. In 1961 Japan and the United States signed a Treaty of Mutual Cooperation and Security. This agreement, although more favorable than the previous one, met with very strong opposition from leftist forces and student youth. There were violent demonstrations, with deaths and many injuries. Protests continued through the decade as the Americans used Japan as a base for the war in Vietnam.

Student protests then began, initially as a reaction to the conditions for study in impoverished conditions (expensive tuition fees, university overcrowding, administrative corruption, embezzlement). Starting out with simple demands and a desire to negotiate, the students gradually became radicalized through their encounters with "deaf" university management and complicit union bodies. They also met with brutal repression — from private paid mafia-like militias, from university administrations, and then from public power itself. All this made the students aware of the determination and extent of the collusion that was — as they saw it — aimed at enslaving them.

---

[1] In her September, 2004 interview, Harue Ishide recounted the death of her grandfather, a man of great quality, Buddhist monk, healer and leader of the local fishing union, intentionally knocked down by a G.I. who was chasing him with his jeep as he quietly rode his bicycle. The U.S. military accepted no responsibility and the family was immediately dissuaded from any action. Even today a large part of the island of Okinawa is occupied by a huge American base. Chalmers Johnson's remark [p. ix] that "the rapes, murders, assaults, bar fights, hit-and-runs from traffic accidents, plane crashes and the incessant noise of artillery practice" paled in comparison to "the damage done to the culture of Okinawa," in the preface to Kensei Yoshida's (2001) *Democracy Betrayed: Okinawa Under U.S. Occupation*, gives an idea of what the populations close to these bases have endured and are still enduring.

In 1968, libertarian and communitarian struggle committees known as the Zenkyoto[1], coordinated the protests throughout all the universities, and the movement continued into 1969. They also saw the sense of energy or effervescence, intellectual openness, and solidarity customary in revolutionary struggles. As one student reports, "We had daily conferences. We listened to top-notch debates, talked about things we'd never heard of before, and saw so many movies. Ironically, we felt good, and began to enjoy college life for the first time. The large number of students who had been isolated in the banalities and the boredom of everyday life now merged in the commune, where all were comrades."[2] In early 1970, however, the movement came to an end, without having managed to broaden its appeal or connect with wider socio-political movements as had happened in France. The revolutionary movement continued for some time, however, particularly in opposition to the building of Narita International Airport which required large tracts of land.

The struggles between students and the authorities were often extremely violent. The students, armed with *geba-bo*, formidable combat sticks [Minagawa, p. 238], engaged in impressive pitched battles not only with police forces (themselves very belligerent), but also between rival ultra-left factions. And there were deaths.

---

[1] "Autonomous, self-organizing committees operating in the form of commissions controlled by the members and revocable at any time. The Zenkyoto were the antithesis of the Zengakuren (majority student union, affiliated with the Japanese Communist Party). The members all participated equally, the initiatives came from the base and were voted on by a show of hands." [Excerpt from " Zenkyoto : les comités de luttes étudiants des années 1960, et l'anarchisme au Japon", Ed Le cri du Dodo, July 2011, https://lecridudodo.blogspot.com/2011/07/zenkioto-les-comites-de-luttes_05.html].

[2] "The students thus began to transform their university into something else: by organizing conferences with outside guests, and showing films. Despite the constant fear of fascist attacks, the occupiers felt that they had finally become themselves, free and proud. It was a cultural revolution, and above all a social revolution, because we understood that through struggle, social relations in daily life could change. The students identified with the barricade, which became the symbol of their new identity." [ibid.].

Artistic counterculture

The performing arts, theater and dance, were directly at the forefront of this radical counterculture. As Japanese-American sociologist Kiyoko Ishikawa observed, "the artistic creation of this period can be characterized by action; not words on the page nor static pictures, but the presence of the body which moves, provokes."[1]

The French avant-garde proved very influential, thanks to the translation into Japanese, from the 1950s, of major authors such as Aragon, Gide, Valéry, Malraux, Sartre, and Camus, but also more challenging figures such as Sade, Lautréamont, Jarry, Breton, Artaud, Bataille, and Genet. Although the Japanese artistic avant-garde was given the American-inspired name of *angura* ("underground," a reference to underground cinema), it was mainly these French authors who inspired creators and performers like Shuji Terayama, Juro Kara and Tatsumi Hijikata. One important influence was the Living Theater which, though based in New York, toured the world extensively through the 1960s and itself was inspired by Antonin Artaud.

Terayama, initially a Surrealist poet, used theater and cinema as total environments in which to make various artistic forms interact: painting, poetry, music, singing, pantomime, etc. He directed films worthy of Buñuel and founded the Tenjo Sajiki troupe — named in reference to Marcel Carné's classic film *Les enfants du paradis*. Ishikawa believed that Carné "experiments and tries to destroy theatrical conventions, to subvert the actor-spectator relationship"[2]. As a reader of Artaud, Terayama tried to destroy

---

[1] Ishikawa K., "La France et la contre-culture du Japon dans la période de haute croissance économique (1960-1970)" in *La modernité française dans l'Asie littéraire (Chine, Corée, Japon)*, Haruhisa Kato (ed.), PUF, 2004, pp. 49-60.
[2] Ibid. p. 53.

the imaginary wall between theatrical performers and audience[1], and concluded, "The system of the theater itself is abolished, because the acting leaves the room and invades reality."

Like Terayama, Juro Kara also took the theater out into the street before setting it up in a tent pitched, officially or otherwise, in the heart of the city. The *Aka-tento* ("Red Tent") thus became the symbol of his Jokyo Gekijo ("Situation Theater") according to Sartre and Debord. His acting was a surreal mix of declamation, pantomime, and antics in which the performance of actors with strong personalities predominated: "The comedian to come will emerge from the tomb of Antonin Artaud with a resentment like Jean Genet, a humor like Arthur Cravan and the obscenity of Asakusa's stripteases."[2]

Living in Japan at the end of the 1970s, I myself had the chance to attend the performances of these two troupes. From Tenjo Sajiki, I recall a striking beauty and an astonishing eclecticism, harmoniously mixing dance, rock music, magic tricks, and surrealist scenes in different parts of a deconstructed room. From the *Aka-tento*, I remember a troupe of formidable actors, in burlesque Kabuki costumes and make-up, with car inner-tubes around their necks, singing, dancing, and screaming more than declaiming incomprehensible texts while crossing watered footbridges and spraying the assembled spectators; everyone screaming and laughing heartily.

---

[1] "In 'Knock', a very controversial and monumental play from the 1970s, 33 actions take place simultaneously in a district of Tokyo for 30 hours, the spectators-walkers unknowingly attacking the peaceful life of the inhabitants." [Ibid.]

[2] Juro K., *Tokkenteki nikutai ron* (1968), Hakusui sha, 1977, p. 39 [quoted by Ishikawa, Ibid. p. 56].

Yasuko Ikeuchi[1] mentions that Tatsumi Hijikata[2], the dancer who initiated the avant-garde form known as butoh, participated in the provocative performances titled Koshimaki Osen ("The hermit in a loincloth") which preceded the *Aka-tento* shows. She also indicates that the performance of *"Hijikata Tatsumi to nihon-jin - nikutai no hanran"* (Hijikata Tasumi and the Japanese: the rebellion of the body), "had a huge impact on the theater of Terayama Shuji and Kara Juro." This piece, like all the butoh that followed, was particularly marked by its exposure of the body. In the absence of text, the dance exhibited there the rawest humanity through the body of the dancer suffering or enjoying in all the dimensions of the stage space. Hijikata's works referred to the writers who had inspired them: Mishima, Genet, Sade or Lautréamont. Hijikata was soon joined by another great name in butoh, the luminous Ono Kazuo.

Hijikata, then little-known, sometimes led dance seminars for the Katei-gakuen school in Yokohama, in which Etsuko Aoki worked[3]. This is how she learned about butoh, was introduced to Ono Kazuo and began to study with him. H.F. Ito mentions[4] that Aoki requested detailed reports of the sessions from his wife, elements of which Ito then found in some "weird" work proposals that Aoki made during Nogeyama practices. Aoki does not specify the means but does mention[5] having studied Ono's research and received many ideas from it. A deep friendship connected the two men until the death of Ono at the age of 103. There are also

---

[1] Ikeuchi Y.(2006), « Performances of Masculinity in Angura Theatre : Suzuki Tadashi on the Actress and Sato Makoto's Abe Sada's Dogs », in *Performance Paradigm – Japan After the 1960s : The Ends of the Avant-Garde*,
https://www.performanceparadigm.net/index.php/journal/article/view/14.

[2] Yoneyama Kunio (1928–1986)

[3] Aoki H., email, Fall, 2004.

[4] Email of 10/15/2019 and interview of 09/19/2019.

[5] 2004, Ibid.

various traces of influence of the practices of the Rakutenkai in those of butoh[1].

Finally, this overview of the Angura scene must mention the names of *Jiyu Butai* ("Free Scene," 1961) then Waseda Shogekijo (small theater of Waseda, 1966) by Tadashi Suzuki, and that from *Engeki Senta* ("Theatre Center", 1968/1971) by Makoto Sato, better known as *Kuro-tento* ("Black Tent"). All these creators provoked the Japanese gaze and brilliantly embodied the rejection of the regimented consumer culture of post-war Japan as well as the aspirations of youth for freedom.

Psychedelism

Although psychedelic drugs use was an important aspect of the counterculture in the West, this was not the case in Japan. If there was any drug use at all in post-war Japan, it involved methamphetamines inherited from the GI's[2]; psychedelia was clearly not a driving force behind this counterculture. This is no doubt due to the rigor of the Japanese administration and its police. In the 1970s, Japanese youth in search of sensations enjoyed inhaling solvents, including the dreaded tri-chloroethylene [Minagawa p. 233].

A MARTIAL COUNTERCULTURE

Counterculture finds its origin, its *raison d'être*, in the "desire for opposition": a dissatisfaction, even frustration, with the existing culture and a desire for something else, something bigger, more beautiful, more exciting.

---

[1] Iwahara C. (2007), « Les destins renouvelés d'un principe de mouvement : du shintaido à la création chorégraphique du buto », in *Japon pluriel 7 : Histoires d'amour, quelques modalités de relation à l'autre au Japon*, Dir. Arnaud Brotons & Christian Galan, Transactions of the seventh colloquium of the French Society of Japanese Studies Éditions Philippe Picquier, p. 59-68.

[2] Wada K., « The history and current state of drug abuse in Japan », Annals of the New York Academy of Sciences : *Addiction Reviews*, 1216(1), pp.62-72, https://doi.org/10.1111/j.1749-6632.2010.05914.x .

For Japanese people, the pressure to conform is quite strong. It is not good to be the "protruding nail" (someone who stands out by their critical nature or oddity, thereby endangering the smooth surface or harmony of the whole society) or to bring shame on your family through inappropriate behavior or language. This characteristic can generate great frustrations and anxieties that may lead to desperate solutions: disappearance from society (*jouhatsu*), withdrawal into oneself (*hikikomori*) or even suicide. More positively, it is also at the heart of what the Japanese call *ikigai* ("reason for living"), a continual reflection in your innermost being, on the place that one occupies regarding your aptitudes and aspirations, the expectations of the world and the possibilities offered by your situation. And when you have found the way to your *ikigai*, you invest in it without restraint.

The biographies of Rakutenkai members reveal how many had suffered from the war: directly in some cases and indirectly in others. The post-war shortages accentuated, if possible, the pressure to conform. The expression of any kind of opposition could therefore only be expressed within an "acceptable" framework. This led some members of the Rakutenkai to engage in the study of law or karate. Or others – beginning with the founders - to convert to Christianity. While the hippies in the West were, according to Morin, making a return to early Christianity, these Japanese young people were entering it for the first time, thereby breaking, latently if not openly, with the socio-Darwinism of their own culture. They may not yet have been aware of it, but they had begun a process of transformation that would lead them to the counterculture.

In this process, they would explore most, if not all, of the aspects of the counterculture that Morin had identified [p. 306]:

- The childlike universe of communion and immediacy.
- The free and fulfilling life of the body, of the repose of the soul, communion with nature, and the primitive in all its forms.

- The Gospel virtues of purity and communion, the proclamation of the beatitudes for poverty (in spirit and in goods), the quest for salvation.
- The individualism of sensation, enjoyment and exaltation, a celebration of *being* rather than *having*.
- The communist way of life in its original dual meaning: both communitarian and libertarian.
- The mystical search for the true world concealed beneath the world that only seems to be real, the search for the inner secrets of the psyche, and for communion with Being through the ecstatic life and even ego-obliteration in Nirvana.

Readers of these lines, after reading the autobiographies of the Rakutenkai members, will surely appreciate the extent to which it really was a genuine counter-cultural community.

From the aspirations of the founders of Rakutenkai, aspirations in which the members recognized themselves and to which they added their own, this community was constituted in just these terms. From it emerged, first, practices and then original techniques in the fields of martial arts, the arts, and the spiritual realm. Although the contributions of these different fields were appreciated very differently by each member, the overall view gradually reveals itself as one reads their stories. Out of necessity, I must now "flatten" this 3D image to produce a linear picture.

Karate as engine of transformation: to live is to burn!

Just as rock music and psychedelic drugs had been true accelerators of change in the West, in Japan karate proved an equally powerful effector of transformation. It achieved this effect through the force of its dynamics, the total investment that it requires, the intense cognitive activity that it creates and the effects of group cohesion that it arouses.

It was karate, under the enlightened direction of Egami, that gave Aoki the means to realize his potential, first for himself and

then as a means of action and transformation of his young emulators.

It was karate that allowed the younger Japanese practitioners,
like their *sempai*, to go straight to the sources of stimulation, satisfaction, training, and mystical knowledge which their counter-
parts from the West found when, disillusioned with "artificial par-
adises", they turned to the East.

From the early 20th century when the notion of the uncon-
scious was first explored, the Western avant-garde arts — Surre-
alism and jazz in particular — had sought a state in which the conscious mind would no longer be an obstacle, whether by stressing
the body to exhaustion, or through automatic writing, improvisa-
tion, and of course alcohol or drugs. Karate provided its own
route to the same states of being.

Egami had already managed to make his karate practice more
intense, by lowering the stance to ensure a longer, more powerful
strike and by lengthening sequences of continuous practice. In his
book *The heart of karate-do* he explains how to practice a *kata* in
such a manner as to free the body from stress and the mind from
intentions, so that the body can act on its own. He says:

> "...after 10 or 20 repetitions [they will] become exhausted, for there is a
> limit. Continuing to practice, they will become even more exhausted, to the
> point of not being able to stand up, their breath will come in gasps, and their
> vision will blur. Out of sheer exhaustion they may wish for unconsciousness.
> But they should not stop. Continuing in this state, they will become like
> automatons, and will be unable to concentrate any power in their
> movements. To put it simply, they will not know what they are doing..." [p.
> 106].

At this point, he concludes that their movements will have become "smooth and natural" without the distraction of a "useless
mind." But he does not stop there, advising the student to continue through various states of consciousness or unconsciousness,
and become able to react to the lightest stimuli or reach a state in
which, as the body is active and awakened so the mind becomes

increasingly calm and able to perceive the situation as "from out-side" (a state valued by the Japanese poet and *Noh* actor Zeami Motokiyo as one of the highest states of consciousness for his art). We can thus imagine the situations in which he engaged Aoki as together they sought to find the primary meaning of the move-ments of the *kata*, as described by the practitioners of the time.

According to K. Ito [p. 100] and Hanaki [p. 159], when Aoki took charge of club practices, he not only implemented the same principles, but intensified them still further. He did this especially with the development of jumps intended to strengthen the lower body. From the jump called *usagi-tobi* (literally "rabbit jump"), he developed two new jumps, each intended to amplify a particular characteristic: *kaikyaku-zenshin*, which dramatically increased the effect of opening the body, and *renzoku-soritobi*, which in-creased the effect of an explosion of energy.

Development of the usagi-tobi karate jump into
a bilateral opening jump or slide, kaikyaku-zenshin (left, top and bottom),
and a longitudinal opening jump, sori-tobi (right)

He also insisted on the practice of simultaneous karate jump kicks – both feet together – at truly amazing heights (some vin-tage photos show jumps that could possibly have broken Olympic records).

Typical vertical jumping exercises for shotokai karate: mae morogeri (left)
and yoko morogeri (right)

In any case, and for several years, the jumping sessions that traditionally began the practices gradually lengthened until they occupied most of the time available. Thus, the Rakutenkai members, unlike Egami and the early practitioners of Shotokai karate who had never lost sight of their martial objective, cultivated states of trance that could be reached "beyond the limits," as being desirable in themselves, states of exploration of a reality of a religious order, in a shamanic or pure artistic way.

"Life, Burn" was the title of a text of visionary exhortation written by Aoki for the students of Chuo University karate club[1]. In it he advocated they should seek what Edgar Morin called "oppose consummation to consumption" or even "to search for the real world hidden under the apparently real world, search for the inner secrets of the psyche, and search for communion with Being through ecstatic life and on the verge of ego-obliteration in Nirvana."[2]

---

[1] See Appendix 2.
[2] Morin E. (1970), p. 531.

The "zero point": research of essences and "avant-garde"

Aoki, for his part, while involved in Egami's project of "cleansing" and recording the karate *kata*, kept well in view the production objective of their work. As an artist himself, he was also keen to produce new *kata* that would embody his own discoveries. As we have seen, Egami had regretted that over-rationalization of karate had weighed down its forms. To escape this, he had suggested modes of practice to wear out the practitioner and make it possible to abandon any superfluous tension or intention and to access natural movements as well as states of distanced consciousness.

Aoki continued his mentor's approach and was aware of the phenomenological and artistic advances that had accompanied the Western industrial revolution. His increased insistence on going beyond the limits that he demanded of the members of the karate clubs and his own *dojo* – those who would come to constitute the Rakutenkai – probably originated in these avant-garde Western approaches.

In Section 6 of his book [1992] he makes a vibrant plea for a "stripping of all spiritual pretensions", exhorting the practitioner to seek the "zero point" of intentions by practicing as "a machine or a robot," so that "the movement of the sword is self-explanatory" or "*tsuki* is forward movement of the fist from the hip." This condition of self-obliteration allowed the body to resonate and the technique to be performed in such a way as to allow the essential reality to emerge in the moment.

In 1911 the philosopher Edmund Husserl, founder of phenomenology, freed himself from accusations of relativism or psychologism by proposing a method of "purifying" subjective experience in order to extract its essence. This method, which he called phenomenological reduction or eidetic reduction, consisted in mentally varying the content of the experience by removing its different elements, or aspects, one at a time, while enquiring if the resulting essence remained unaffected. If one felt that the essence remained intact, then the element that had been removed could be considered as accessory rather than essential. It went on until an ultimate variation removed all meaning from the phenomenon. The essential aspect had thus been identified, and the object or idea could be reorganized or redefined, starting from this "purified" essence.

Aoki referred to the painter Paul Gauguin[1], who had developed a not-dissimilar approach to rendering three dimensions on the two-dimensional canvas, rather than Husserl, but his approach was very similar to Husserl's eidetic reduction. Extending the vision of his mentor, this search for the "zero point," by reducing one by one the accessory elements of the *kata*, offered him and his working group the means to develop new *kata*, the way and the goal of the new discipline.

The quest for superpowers

Edgar Morin described one of the key aspirations of the counterculture as being the prolongation of childlike dreams. At the time, he assumed that these dreams of "communion and immediacy" were the kind featured in the heroes of tales and legends reinterpreted in Disney cartoons. But there is another mythic universe, still childlike but perhaps more masculine, to be found in the comics of the counterculture: that of ordinary people transformed into superheroes. Ken Kesey, for example, counter-cultural leader of the group known as the Merry Pranksters[2] and author of *One Flew Over the Cuckoo's Nest*, liked to show up at acid-test parties in a Captain Flag costume[3]. This kind of American superhero figure, even if fantastic, is well suited to the extension of

---

[1] On page 40, Aoki (1992) quotes from memory Gauguin's definition of painting as "...a two-dimensional world of methodically systemized color."

[2] Wolfe, Tom (1968), *The Electric Kool-Aid Acid Test*, Farrar Straus & Giroux Publishers.

[3] The Blue Ribbon Comics superhero who was later taken over as the modern "Captain America" in the Marvel Comics superhero galaxy.

the infantile universe into adult life: people feel it just "might be possible."[1]

Such aspirations for superpowers can be traced in the accounts given by some of the members of the Rakutenkai. There is, however, a major difference. It was not fantasies that they sought but tangible, experiential realities: the ability to hypnotize or control from a distance, to capture or transmit distant thoughts, to acquire inexhaustible strength, to anticipate events, and so on. Their accounts of practices, in the *dojo* or in ordinary life, testify to an active search for such capacities.

The search for such superpowers is inherent in certain forms of Buddhism. In ancient Japan, the fortune of Buddhist sects and their temples depended largely on the ability of their monks to stop epidemics, anticipate calamities, or favorably change the course of wars. Tantric Mikkyo Buddhism [2] represented this "magical" Japanese Buddhism, oriented particularly towards the arts of protection. In a more down-to-earth, perhaps less magical way, Mikkyo practices had, and still have, a reputation for helping to develop extraordinary human abilities[3]. Protection, wealth, or extraordinary powers were considered by Vajrayana Buddhism

---

[1] These same aspirations are extended today in the notion of augmented human – by digital technologies associated with activities – or, even more profoundly, in transhumanism – by technologies integrated into the body itself – which are widely fantasized today.

[2] Set of tantric (non-sexual) practices with magical connotations from *Vajrayana* Buddhism and hybridized with the shamanic practices of the regions he traveled through (Tibet, China). Imported to Japan at the beginning of the 9th century by the monk Kukai (Kobo-Daishi) in Shingon Buddhism and by the monk Saicho (Dengyo Daishi), then by his disciples Ennin (Jikaku Daishi) and Enchin (Chisho Daishi), in Tendai Buddhism. There were also hybridizations with the animist practices of the Japanese *yama-bushi*, the shugendo. For a historical overview of the introduction of these different forms of Buddhism in Japan, read the first part of the book by John Stevens, *Marathon Monks of Mount Hiei*, 2013.

[3] Thus, the young monk Kukai had practiced the rite of Kokuzo gumonji-ho which would be expected to give him an infallible memory: Bowring R. (2005), *The Religious Traditions of Japan 500-1600*, Cambridge University Press, p.135.

(which was represented in Japan by the Mikkyo) as "salvific expedients,"[1] steps on the way to enlightenment.

The pragmatic samurai had noticed this possibility of acquiring extraordinary abilities and this prospect of awakening, and study of the Mikkyo was part of the technical arsenal of many martial arts schools as offering many additional means of survival and action. It is thus not surprising that Egami and Aoki describe having practiced them, and that Aoki undertook an in-depth study.

The ability most often mentioned by members of the Rakutenkai, male and female alike, is telepathy. The purpose of this acquisition is to anticipate an opponent's intentions. And some men — including those claiming to be initially uninterested in the prospect of becoming stronger than other people — also recall with great feelings of satisfaction such exceptional practices such as holding a heavy stick or sword at arm's length nonstop for hours, while standing or while running.

In support of this research, several evoke the way in which ordinary (naturally weak) people could perform truly extraordinary acts once placed in dramatically critical circumstances. On the strength of such examples, they could work towards this kind of achievement by studying Mikkyo practices and by putting themselves in a critical situation in the *dojo*.

As with the Vajrayana "salvific expedients," it was important that the practitioner's intentions were compassionate. The ability to anticipate an attack in order to "nip it in the bud" was thus developed into the ability to anticipate a person's "need" in order to respond to it even before they consciously feel this need. A magnificent example of the results of this training is found in the extraordinary way Kayo Hirata [p. 273] put her great powers of perception at the service of the children with disabilities whom she was called upon to accompany.

---

[1] In Sanskrit *upaya*, in Japanese *hoben* 方便.

Christianity: the power of love

Love is at the heart of Christianity. It is also recognized as essential by many other religions, but Christianity uniquely presents it in terms of the love of a parent for his children, of a child for his parent, of a child for his brother or sister. In a word, Christian love is filial and, in principle, unconditional.

Systems theory teaches us that one of the key characteristics of a system is to have boundaries. Even if openings are arranged across those boundaries, there is an inside and an outside; on one side there is the same, the "Like-me," and on the other side there is the "Other." Thus, it would be "normal" and "natural" for the feelings experienced within the family system to be different from those prevailing outside, and for the feelings experienced between members of the same social group – village, tribe, ethnic group, country – to be different from those experienced for others.

By redefining God, the "Absolute Other," as "Father," and his messenger Jesus as "Brother," Christianity broke with the terrible (moralistic, even vengeful) or enigmatic (nameless) image of the divine. God is love, the same kind of love that most of us have experienced as a child and a brother, sister, parent, or grandparent. This radical redefinition, linking the two extremities of the relational arc between "Little-Me" and the "Great-Other," shatters the borders of the interlocking identification systems by which we define ourselves.

When Hiroyuki and Etsuko Aoki founded the community that was Rakutenkai, they undertook to breathe this Christian love into the "pagan" world of Japanese martial arts. The story of Rakutenkai is that of an inculturation by which, for a time, this graft of love and its traces were embodied in the lives of its members and in the cultural objects it produced.

We know from K. Hokari [1989], that Aoki only persevered in the path of karate — in a rather brutal university club, which he had chosen by default — on the admonition of his director of conscience to make it his "mission", in the Christian sense of his task to transform. This is how he not only stayed in this club but became its captain, a year ahead of what was the club's custom[1]. How was that possible? Without prejudging the power of transformation of individuals by Christianity or of karate, or perhaps even in support of them, the operation resembles a Jesuit practice known as inculturation.

Jesuit inculturation, the Japanese way

The Catholic Order of Jesuits, who had been active missionaries in India, China in the Early Modern period, and Japan until they were driven out of the country in the early 17th century, made inculturation the subject of a long theological debate among the Catholic authorities. This concerned the question of whether the Christian rites could be adapted to the "target" cultures. These debates eventually led to the following definition, given by the Jesuit Pedro Arupe in 1977:

> Inculturation is the incarnation of the Christian life and message in a concrete cultural area, so that not only is this experience expressed with the specific elements of the culture in question (it would then only be a superficial adaptation), but also that this same experience is transformed into a principle of inspiration, both norm and force of unification, which transforms and recreates this culture, thus being at the origin of a new creation.[2]

By adopting the principle of inculturation, some Jesuits, like Matteo Ricci, became true Chinese mandarins, while others, like Roberto de Nobili, became Indian sadhus or, like Éric de Rosny, Nganga exorcists in Africa[3]. The success of the inculturation enterprise lies in abandoning, or at least voluntarily letting go of,

---

[1] Following a Mafia compromise, the entire fourth-year promotion had to resign [see H.F. Ito p. 114].

[2] Arrupe P. (1978), Lettre sur l'inculturation (May 14, 1978), in *Écrits pour évangéliser*, pp. 169-170.

[3] De Rosny É. (1981), *Les yeux de ma chèvre*, Ed. Plon, http://dx.doi.org/doi:10.1522/030617955.

one's own culture. Normally, principles would be worth little if they can be easily abandoned; on the other hand, powerful essential principles, such as those of Christianity for Christians, should be capable of spontaneous reaction and reformulation to generate new ideas and practices in the very terms of their host culture.

It is unlikely that Aoki's spiritual director, who was an American evangelist, was particularly fond of Jesuit subtleties. Even so, Aoki also had the field of reference of Japanese continual improvement and learning culture and its ability to assimilate and go beyond whatever cultural object it gives itself.

For in Japanese culture, inculturation is a cardinal principle. It is this that allows foreign customs to be, first, adopted and then to undergo a "Japanese-style" transformation, while leaving the basis of Japanese culture itself unaltered. This inculturation is based on the ability to "annihilate one's ego," a skill considered vital to accessing the true seat of consciousness in Hinduism, Buddhism and Taoism[1]. Certain everyday circumstances – recognizing a mistake, learning, exploring a problem, listening to an expression of pain, etc. – also require the annihilation of the ego to give access to a receptive mental state. Japanese children are familiar from an early age with this state of being, which is at the heart of their ability to learn and to exist in society. Martial arts have codified the learning operation in the sequence *shu, ha, ri*. The first stage of learning, *shu*, which means "to enter the mold," designates this annihilation of the ego that makes it possible to approach learning not as the accumulation of knowledge to oneself (a plus as we might think of it in the West), but as a reduction of oneself, a minus, aiming to fit oneself into an existing form of knowledge. Thus, beyond the knowledge and skills to which it

---

[1] It is likely that the practice of Hinduism, Buddhism, or Taoism, all paths urging to seek emptiness, can promote the acquisition of this skill. To reach or approach non-ego is to experience another consciousness, unspeakable and pure, considered the true seat of consciousness.

provides access, inculturation constitutes an exceptional key to continuous learning, problem solving and innovation.

Aoki's missionary project was to convert karate to Christianity, and inculturation was a means and end to accomplish it.

In praise of weakness

Aoki had lost his mother, a brother, and a sister in the fire-bombings, leaving him just his father and a sister. His biography describes him as fragile and solitary, subject to being teased by his comrades. Presumably he did indeed suffer from discrimination and perhaps even harassment[1], which reinforced the solitary-romantic side of his character.

In the end, it seems that these cumulative sufferings made him a somewhat desperate pre-adolescent, who owed his salvation only to the "encounter with Christ." I use this expression because he converted to a form of American evangelism which today we would call radical, where one "meets Christ," "accepts him," and "is saved;" there is a before and an after. In his case, according to K. Hokari, this encounter took place at the reading of the 2nd Epistle of St Paul to the Corinthians (11:30): "If I must boast, I will boast of the things that show my weakness."

We can only conjecture about this Japanese teenager who accidentally comes across an epistle of St Paul. Be that as it may, it was this meeting and this community that gave him the ideal, the support and the hope that he lacked and encouraged him to live and develop.

This praise of the sense of weakness at the moment of his conversion confirms what has been mentioned on inculturation and learning, because this is precisely the feeling when observing that one "knows" nothing or "is" nothing and which leads to, or realizes, the voluntary annihilation of the self; an annihilation which

---

[1] Japanese society is rarely kind in dealing with difference or weakness, and children's society even less so.

in turn opens one up to otherness and novelty. Weakness is liberating. For the transformation to occur, however, it is necessary to accept the feeling, which is rather unpleasant, and not to try to escape the despair. You have to "stand in the weakness," cherish the sense of it and return to it when necessary.

If weakness is a pathway to holiness, then karate could be redefined as a Christian practice. Annihilation leading to emptiness of the self is a canonical virtue of karate. To be convinced of this, we should recall the high esteem in which Funakoshi, the founder of modern karate, held the Buddhist Heart Sutra[1], a much-loved treatise on "emptiness." The quest for omnipotence, whether divine omnipotence in Christianity or personal in karate, finds its root in a feeling of omni-*im*potence.

It is nevertheless very difficult to maintain a feeling of weakness over time, as the practice of karate increases each day a little more the strengths and the skill of the subject. It was therefore necessary to create conditions for "ordinary" access to this feeling of weakness. We have seen that Egami's karate promotes beyond-the-limit practices with the aim of freeing the body from tensions and the mind from intentions; tensions and intentions being seen as so many obstacles to a natural, free, and fluid performance of movements. We have also seen that when Aoki took over the direction of the teachings, this intensity of the practices grew considerably. I hypothesize that Aoki's insistence on cultivating the beyond-the-limit practices is explained by the desire to experience, for himself and his emulators, concretely in the movement

---

[1] Funakoshi appears holding a copy of the Heart Sutra – a treatise on emptiness – in his official photograph. He means by this without ambiguity the Buddhist meaning he intends to give to the term *kara* (empty) of the name of the discipline and, from there, his spiritual ambition: "annihilation of the self" rather than simple "emptiness of the hand".

of the body, still and again, the desperation of weakness and the liberating power of its acceptance[1].

Love and punches

The notion of efficiency is very concrete in the context of karate: a *tsuki* is truly effective if the partner cannot parry it. Thus the "young people" were frequently encouraged, sometimes *ad nauseam*, to test their *tsuki* by attacking their *sempai*, who parried the attack with a rather painful impact sweep (*gedan barai*). The pain made them want to become stronger until one day they might break through and finally reach the belly of the *sempai*.

Many factors contribute to making a *tsuki* effective. It must begin at the right time — if possible in a slight break in the partner's concentration — the imminence of its departure must be undetectable and it must be fast and powerful. Each of these notions by itself could be the subject of a long treatise. Anyway, eventually the members of the Rakutenkai were able to reach the belly of their *sempai*.

The explanation given by H.F. Ito [p. 118] is edifying but also paradoxical: purity and love. The purer the state of mind, the emptier it is of tension, intention, desire and so on, and the more sensitive one becomes to the slightest variation in the condition of the partner. Thus "emptiness of the mind," a privative concept, is sublimated into "purity of the heart," a positive concept. The purer the condition of the attacker, the more the moment of the attack results from a natural reaction of the body to a tiny opening in the concentration of the partner; without intention, it is undetectable.

Purity, which is personal, is however not enough to "commit" the relationship. By adding to it the sincere projection of a pure

---

[1] This argument was later explicitly developed during talks given by Aoki on the theme of the union of 0 and 1. We find such injunctions to the annihilation of the will, to the point of renouncing God himself, in Meister Eckhart, a 12th-century theologian of whom Aoki was a reader, and Angelus Silesius, a 15th-century mystical poet.

feeling of love for the partner, we direct it without adding tension. Love is a flow of feeling without beginning or end. The adage that "in karate, there is no advantage"[1] is then fully satisfied. By constantly cultivating a pure feeling of love for fellow karate practitioners, colleagues as well as *sempai*, we give ourselves the means to deliver them an undetectable *tsuki* that is as powerful as the love we feel for them. Christian "magic" can be even more effective.

Thus, by Aoki's example and because the notions he proposed found their justification in the concrete situations of their martial practices, the members of the Rakutenkai followed him. As far as he took them, this demand for efficiency was always "the proof of concept" of his teachings and it has remained a constant in their relationship.

The original community

These simple "salvific expedients" were not in themselves enough to bring about the effects of major change and innovation that the Rakutenkai produced. They also required a favorable environment. This is where the role of Etsuko Aoki [p. 48] was crucial. She offered the place and, with her husband, the living model of an open, generous, tolerant, and joyful Christian family.

When we look at the stories, we find that the theme of the "last train" often recurs: the interactions, driven by the *sensei*, were such that the student missed the moment for leaving to take the last train, whether one from the nearest station or one from the station that would allow them to catch the last connection to get home. From this arose two phenomena: leaving the family home and sleeping in a different home. In the case of Egami's

---

[1] "*Karate-ni sente nashi*". This adage attributed to Funakoshi, but certainly older, means that of two partners, the one who mentally initiates the interaction has the advantage. Whatever the actual configuration of the situation afterwards, she or he will keep this advantage. This adage is therefore an incentive to "always be ready," to "stay aware," "prepare in advance," etc.

"Wednesday evening talks" [H.F. Ito, p. 115], missing the last train encouraged emancipation by forcing people to make other arrangements to sleep. One had to manage by walking home, if possible, or by sharing a room with a friend, solutions that did not contribute directly to engaging the student with the *sempai*'s life.

In the Aoki house in Nogeyama, on the other hand, one was invited to sleep there and, very often, to share a potluck meal. To accept such an invitation and to accept it repeatedly, was to enter *de facto* into the role of child of the house or, in martial culture, of *uchi-deshi*[1]. By creating the conditions for this situation and freely offering their hospitality, the Aoki couple created both a filial relationship with the "young people" and a fraternal relationship between them. We can also analyze this symbolic act as a desire to demonstrate Christian love. They pledged that their very daily life would become an example to follow: a heavy responsibility.

---

[1] *Uchi-deshi*,(internal or domestic disciple). Most students of a martial arts master were *soto-deshi* or external disciples, who were taught for a fee, and who otherwise lived their own lives. The *uchi-deshi*, on the other hand, were attached to the master's household and continually exposed to his influence. The term domestic is appropriate as they often played just such a role, effectively earning their keep. Much could be said about the various forms that the role of *uchi-deshi* took in martial arts. Many stories or legends exist of famous disciples of famous masters. However, the practice died out due to the significant means it required – if only in terms of space in a house – but also for lack of candidates in a society where martial skills had lost their social value.

Typical scene of a Rakutenkai communal meal

The Japanese are trained in communal life from a very early age. Standards of behavior are widely shared, to the point that there really is a Japanese "common sense," a way of being together, the fruit of more than two centuries of confinement, which suffers only minor variations from one part of Japan to another. The younger students reacted as well-bred Japanese and entered the mold of Aoki's atypical environment.

We have seen [p. 55] that Aoki had also instituted the systematic study of the works, novels, or testimonies of model authors of the Christian tradition. This practice followed a tradition of reading advice, common in the martial arts – the *sempai* advising the student on a reading likely to support his or her practice – but in a more elaborate form. These literary circles could very often be immediately resonated with an ad hoc practice on the heights of Nogeyama, followed by a common meal, which was also a time for debriefing and a few hours of collective rest, crammed into the same room.

In the end, between the *keiko* enculturated in the Christian way – karate but also tea ceremony – the study of great Christian authors or of holy scriptures, and the experience of an original community of Christian fraternity, few of Nogeyama's visitors resisted conversion[1]. After a few years, and especially after the creation of Eiko — the symbolic fulfillment of both martial and Christian dreams — and the arrival of the new generation, the Nogeyama community had become the Nogeyama church. Baptisms were celebrated and Sundays were days of worship and joyful sharing, much appreciated by all.

The intensity of these relationships was the result of the complete, honest engagement of each member, disciples as well as *sensei*, with the others. No-one was in any doubt about the nobility of their ambitions, the purity of their intentions or the mutual sharing of their discoveries. However, anyone who did have doubts about any aspect did what good disciples were taught to do: namely to keep quiet, to investigate the matter further, and ultimately, if the doubts remained unresolved, to leave the group. As a result, the group became what today we might call a religious cult, or more simply, a cult. At that time, the potential dangers of this phenomenon were poorly understood, though it became increasingly common as many new forms of communal living emerged throughout the various so-called "developed" nations.

Nevertheless, the Rakutenkai community, unlike some other cults, was always subject to the test of reality, and once its mission was complete, it disbanded. Although the "older" members did try to extend the life of the "family" through various communal enterprises, the prosaic reality of transmitting martial skills required the formation of a formal martial arts school, while the egotistical realities of the visual arts meant that Aoki needed to turn inward, severing his own ties to the community. Both needs militated against the continuation of the communal and immediate environment that they had created.

---

[1] Those who resisted were also separated by the greatest distance geographically, staying only very briefly in Nogeyama.

Aoki actively tried to disrupt any developments that might have led towards the establishment of a true sect: he stopped the religious services, thus both disturbing the communal life of the cult and suggesting its pure and simple disturbance, or rather transforming it for everyone, in the generally accepted practice of *keiko*. Minagawa described what happened during a workshop on the theme "Going out into the world," during which the last official religious service of the Rakutenkai was held: "Aoki-sensei invited us to make our practice a celebration. From that time, shintaido keiko itself became our cult." After this, Aoki did not strongly encourage the attempt to establish a community among the younger members of the second generation, and finally no such community came about.

This workshop thus began the closure of that enchanted moment of the extraordinary Rakutenkai community that had existed, like so many others at the time, somewhat outside the norms of Japanese society. The effective closure then happened for each member – including for Aoki himself – at his or her own speed, in accordance with their family obligations, their professional or social opportunities and their own understanding of what had happened during those years. Some lingered a while longer and certain tensions and frustrations or conflicts that appear in the stories reflect this. We, whether as researchers or as citizens living in an era as different from the 1960s as the 1960s were to society between the wars, cannot properly judge some of the stresses and choices made at this time.

A space for living for some, a space of healing for others, this Rakutenkai community was above all, and will remain forever, the place of emergence of new *kata*.

From martial art to fine art

Art was always deeply important to Aoki, and he ensured that it was an integral part of the outlook of the Rakutenkai members.

We should attempt to understand what art meant to the members of the Rakutenkai, and particularly regarding the distinction they made between Japanese arts and Western arts. This will allow us to grasp their intentions, to understand their actions, and to contextualize their productions.[1].

There are two important notions to distinguish in matters of the arts: artifice (that which is not natural but is made) and utility.

Art has been defined as "the set of means and conscious processes by which man tends to a certain end, seeks to achieve a certain result[2]," or as "the product of technology to modify nature with the aim of adaptation to human use." The craftsman's art thus involves artifices (technologies, processes) to create other artifices (artefacts) that are useful to ensure our survival and our life. In this sense, art is the competitive advantage that our hands and our brains give us over other living species.

Then, and only then, can the question of beauty arise. Here Japanese culture differs profoundly from Western cultures: every artifice should be inspired by the beauty of nature. Or perhaps we should say, every artifice should embody accuracy, economy of means, balance etc., of which the beauty of nature is the sign. The sense of beauty that seizes us when observing nature thus becomes the yardstick by which we measure accuracy, economy of means, balance, etc. of our artworks.

A Japanese landscape gardener was once asked what is important in his work. His answer was simple: observe nature and be inspired by it. Does a bonsai look anything but natural? If we carefully observe the trees exposed to the harsh climate of the

---

[1] I use the plural because, to me, their group resembles that of the Surrealists: a set of creative personalities gathered around a strong personality. It must be remembered that the number of Shotokai karate practitioners who eventually followed the direction of Aoki could be counted in their thousands. Those who joined the Rakutenkai were therefore not "just anyone", but individuals with specific aptitudes, aspirations and artistic sensibility.

[2] The ideas here are taken from definitions of the Centre National de Ressources Textuelles et Lexicales (https://www.cnrtl.fr/definition/art).

mountains, we see they all look like bonsai, sometimes only slightly larger. So once, when quietly contemplating a Japanese garden of a Kyoto temple, I suddenly found myself transformed into a giant contemplating a peaceful wild valley and its pine forest. As I found myself thinking, "The sense of beauty seizes me ... at the same time ... as something else."

The West has a very different approach. In the Judeo-Christian culture, God created the natural world, but the natural world is not God; humans, conceived in the image of God but not God, inherited the natural world and dwell in it; however, they are not exactly part of the natural world nor are they bound by it. Thus, as humanity in the West freed themselves from the yoke of nature thanks to the slow, cumulative, and irresistible rise of science and technology, art ceased to be utilitarian and instead became pure, less concerned with nature but more with the relationship between humanity itself and an abstract idea of beauty and Art, one that showed humanity in all its "divine" glory.

Artworks of the martial counterculture

In love with every kind of beauty, converted to Christianity and nourished by the great works of this humanist Western art, Aoki aspired to be the man who would elevate the martial arts – an eminently utilitarian artform – to the rank of truly fine art. Great martial arts masters had in the past undeniably achieved what he called "a world of non-attachment and complete freedom,"[1] like some great Western artists. His intention was that the martial notion itself should be transcended. He dreamed of creating a new Art, for which the martial aspects would be – like sound in music or color in painting – a component, but one which would equally contain beauty and spirituality: it would not be just another martial art but a true martial Art.

---

[1] Aoki H., 1992, p. 38

For this, the essential components were not simply *kata* but humanity itself; one might say that new *kata* had to emerge from the human clay itself. The three great forms developed at the time of the Rakutenkai demonstrate this in different aspects.

The first, Tenshingoso, was essentially utilitarian. It was a concentrated martial arts encyclopedia, the product of Aoki's collaboration with Egami, his karate masterpiece. Although in his book, Aoki modestly uses the word "we" regarding the development of Tenshingoso, he was undeniably the author of this modern *kata*, though "perched on the shoulders of the giants" of the martial tradition.

For the second form, Eiko-no-ken, Aoki had rigorously created the contours and conditions for it[1] but had "almost given up hope of seeing this form born in [his] lifetime, expecting that it would take a hundred years or more for it to appear." The group was nevertheless actively working on it. The "creation myth" of Eiko, based on the testimonies of certain participants, and on Aoki's own testimony[2], shows that the form was indeed the fruit of the aspirations and inspirations of the whole group; those members who were present of course, but also all those who had contributed to making such a moment happen. Thus, the description given by Aoki in his book begins by using "I" for the presentation of the expectations and conditions, then continues to "we" though this is no longer simple modesty: he is describing their discussions and their shared developments of the Eiko phenomenon as an instituted and transmissible *kata*. We note in passing that these developments, but especially the name they gave to the *kata* – "Sword of Glory" then simply "Glory" – bear witness to the assumption that this new practice had a religious orientation.

---

[1] Ibid. pp. 47-51.

[2] "Tenshingoso was born from my idea and perhaps I could say that it was my discovery. But this form, which suddenly appeared from afar, was like a divine apparition." ibid. p. 50.

The third form, Hikari-to-tawamureru ("playing with light" – photo 9), is not specifically mentioned in the biographies nor presented by Aoki as having had a particular moment of creation[1]. Although it has a name and can be taught, we do not really have a *kata* that would symbolize it with certainty. It emerged and re-emerged as the culmination of practices, of any practice, pushed to their ultimate point and then beyond. The inherently poetic and genuinely exuberant bodily movements of Hikari-to-tawamureru no longer respond to a voluntary, mental control but to the direct expression, via a body totally free of tension, of the practitioner's internal state, visions, and feelings. It is a trance that testifies without restraint – some would say without shame – to the most complete freedom of the actor.

Presentation of Hikari-to-tawamureru (first named such on this occasion) during the Daienshu gasshuku at Asama-sanso (1971)

This work with spontaneous expression truly marks the counter-cultural affiliation of the Rakutenkai. Through it, the practice of Rakutenkai meets that of butoh. It also marks a point beyond

---

[1] It comprises the subject of chapter 3 of Aoki's work (1992), a chapter evocatively entitled: "What shintaido has conceived : Hikari to Tawamureru", pp. 52-54.

which very few martial artists wished to venture, even though the total freedom of movement, the awareness, and the hypersensitivity of Hikari-to-tawamureru perhaps make it the ultimate survival *kata* in a hyper-hostile environment such as a battlefield.

There is no doubt that according to the classic martial canons, the techniques of Hikari-to-tawamureru, Eiko or even Tenshin-goso would have been precious secrets, esoteric. The fact that they have been brought to the light of day is an additional sign of Rakutenkai belonging to the counterculture, a catharsis opening up modernity to the post-modern era, known as the "information age." As the adage goes, "Anyone can access it, but who can access it?"

THE END OF RAKUTENKAI

The counterculture of the 1960s was a short-lived phenomenon, which collapsed in the mid-1970s as worldwide economic conditions changed, making the withdrawal from mainstream society less easy and idealistic communes harder to maintain. Nevertheless, some communities and ideas survived and continued to develop, importantly contributing to many aspects of the modern world including the spread of liberal, individualist values, the environmental movement, the feminist revolution and even the digital revolution.

As we have seen, the Rakutenkai community did not withstand the test of reality and broke up after five years or so, once its mission had been accomplished. Whatever efforts the "elder brothers" made to prolong the "family" in common enterprises, the prosaic realities of martial transmission or fundamentally ego-based reality of Art subverted the space of communion and immediacy that they had established. While it lasted, this counterculture community of the 1960s had nevertheless been a real living place for some, a resource for those who were more distant, and a crucible of new *kata*.

Appendices

Appendix 1 – University karate clubs

University clubs

In Japan, as in Anglo-Saxon countries, the time of university studies is used for the moral and social training of new generations, through various practice clubs. The initiative of these clubs, their financing, and their operation are left to the students in total self-management. Clubs can be free or registered with the university administration. In this case, supervision of activities, particularly from the point of view of moral responsibility, is entrusted to a volunteer teacher (called *Bucho*) who has the confidence of the club's senior practitioners.

Depending on its means, the university makes premises available. It can even subsidize the activities of the most prestigious clubs (baseball for example) to augment the school image. Over the years, all kinds of activities come to be offered (sports, dances, arts, theatre, language practices, martial arts, etc.). Very early in the school year, the senior practitioners of the various clubs' staff booths and perform demonstrations to attract new recruits. Some clubs call on external expertise, most often remunerated, and daily supervision is provided by fourth-year students. Depending on the activities, methods of organization and teaching are established according to a strict hierarchy of responsibilities, determined by seniority and appointment. These assumptions of responsibility are an integral part of the moral and social formation of students.

MARTIAL ARTS CLUBS

Martial arts clubs place their practices under the authority of an external person (*Shihan* or master) delegated by an official school. Schools are fond of this university anchoring. Students find themselves in this pivotal period of their existence when their bodies have acquired sufficient maturity to support without damage the significant efforts of practices and where the mind is sufficiently receptive to novelties to accomplish in a very short time a deep inculturation into the world of *budo*. These few years thus play an initiatory role; an immersion in the values and social practices of classical Japanese culture as "coded" in the forms of these traditional folk arts.

Martial arts schools thus come at the right time to bring traditional knowledge and companionship to the processes of individuation and identification at work in these student groups. Relationships created in this setting last a lifetime. More prosaically, it is common that a personal history mentioning a second dan, or even a third, issued by a reputable school of martial arts, influences the chance of being hired during a job search in large Japanese companies, who are looking for new recruits who are disciplined and level-headed. Alumni who wish to do so often play a coaching role for the club.

THE KARATE CLUBS IN FUNAKOSHI'S TIME

The cornerstone of a martial arts school, the headquarters *dojo* [*honbu-dojo*], is the founder's official place to teach. The practice also takes place in external *dojo*, private or institutional, which are affiliated with the central *dojo* and maintain close ties with it.

The Gichin Funakoshi *dojo* was inaugurated in 1936. Funakoshi named it Shotokan after his pen name "Shoto" (*kan* meaning house or meeting place). The association of practitioners, which was already well developed at the time, took the name of Shotokai (*kai*: group or association)[1].

Like Jigoro Kano, the founder of judo, Funakoshi was an educational professional[2] and saw the educational mission of his art as paramount. The external *dojo* of the Shotokai were university clubs, and their development was so important that Funakoshi chose to devote himself to them, entrusting the teaching at the Shotokan to his son Gigo Funakoshi.

After the 1945 defeat, with many of the instructors killed in action and its *dojo* destroyed, the Shotokan/Shotokai, slowly rebuilt itself. When he returned to karate, Shigeru Egami was entrusted with the management of the university *dojo*. Gichin Funakoshi, already elderly, was to take over the management of a new kind of club, a company club, for the Tokyo transport company Tokyu. His sudden death in April, 1957 prevented him from doing so, and this club was also entrusted to Shigeru Egami.

UNIVERSITY CLUB ROLE TERMINOLOGY

- **Bucho** 部長: University professor appointed as guarantor of the club in relation to the university;
- **Shihan** 師範: Master / **Shihan-dai** 師範代: Master-Assistant or Second-Master, if applicable;
- **Kantoku** 監督: Member of the alumni association more specifically responsible for supervising club practices;

---

[1] Subsequently, various splits occurred, until finally the term "Shotokai" designated only the group of practitioners gathered around Shigeru Egami.

[2] Jigoro Kano had held a position equivalent to that of an academy inspector and Gichin Funakoshi was a teacher.

- **Shusho** 主将 or **Captain**: Fourth-year member designated to lead practices. Most of the other fourth-year students generally do not practice much because they are focusing on graduation and preparing for entry into the workforce;
- **Fukusho** 副将 or **Sub-Captain**, as needed, for example if the group practices in two distant sites, as was the case in Niigata;
- **Manager** マネージャー: Supports the administration of the club (accounts, room reservations, relationship with the administration, etc.);
- **OB Kai**: Association of former students of the club, made up of current fourth-year students and former students (OB meaning Old Boys). Most often, the former Captains constitute the Management Committee of the club.

Appendix 2 – Life, Burn

This article was originally written for the junior members of the Chuo University Karate Club shortly after the author graduated. It marks the beginning of the creative process which led to shintaido.

I

To express "something invisible" which exists absolutely, without flowing with the passage of time, nor being invaded by the changes of the world, through *kata* ("forms") which should be developed and reformed as time goes on. This is a mission or a destiny with which every "art" is charged. Its mission is not to create something new or to build up a plausible system by replacing what has been handed down from generation to generation, but to catch sight of something which has always existed somewhere from earliest times without ever being seen by our two eyes, and to express this something with our own body. Its mission is to express through the body's forms or movements some sort of "perceived world" which visits us with time, while satisfying the limited conditions special to *budo* ("martial arts"). We can say that this is the pursuit of human life, nothing less than the pursuit of truth. We call the art "avant garde" which takes these as its goals.

To every young man who will follow the path of *budo* in order to fulfill this cruel and at the same time blessed duty, I can't help crying: "Be a man of true avant-garde *budo*." What we have to establish should be a *budo* of new and unknown technique, forms or expressions which must add much more light to the world of *budo* rather than extinguishing its flame. In a strict sense, it is, therefore, not a creation but "an embodiment of secretly hidden cosmic breath."

II

In order to break new ground and create a much better *budo* we must overcome many, many obstacles. A time may come when we must discard all that we have mastered or when we will be repudiated even by our friends. The tradition of our club (which is a stepping stone our predecessors have made for us) may become completely useless. More than that, who can deny that we may have to fight with that "tradition" in the future? More dangerous for us are the fixed ideas and the temptations within ourselves which would make us look back.

But stick to it! Study, devise, and practice with unremitting efforts! Young men, tomorrow is for you.

The world of soul is larger than any exercise hall or any organization. It is boundless. If we depended only on decaying tradition without seeking after the center from which springs our fountain of life, our predecessors' words: "Karate is still immature. Who in the world will complete it?" would vanish unanswered.

III

I wish that our brilliant future "karate" might not occupy merely a part of the world, but that, as an infinitely expanding cosmos, it might contain the whole world in it. (It is uncertain that the term "karate" will still be used at such a time). "Karate" would then be no longer *budo* as a means of expression, but an art concerned with the problem of Being.

I am now extremely anxious to express with my body what I have secretly felt, that is, what is thought nearly impossible to express with the body, while asking for a reverberating encounter with an ever-unperceived realm.

                                                        Hiroyuki Aoki

Appendix 3 – Additional biographical records

Indispensable to the historical precision and the coherence of this work, is mention of all the members of Rakutenkai whose direct biographies do not appear in this volume. They played no less a role and, as such, are quoted in the autobiographies of the Rakutenkai members who provided their life stories directly. They therefore deserve to be, at least, named and presented. So, in addition to the autobiographical accounts appearing in the second part of this work, we include in this appendix short biographical sketches of the members who did not respond favorably to our requests for interviews or who, after having consented to the first interview, did not want their autobiographical stories to be transcribed in the final work. They are presented in alphabetical order.

Eiichi Ho

Eiichi Ho's interview was conducted in the spring of 2005 in Japanese, collected with the help of H.F. Ito, and in French. After transcription and translation, the autobiography, written in French, suffered from some shortcomings, and a meeting was organized in 2019 to complete it. The interview was very cordial, and the resulting document was sent a few days later. In return, Mr. Ho sent a request for the withdrawal of his text, alleging "faulty memory."

Eiichi Ho was born in January, 1944 in Hokkaido, where he lived until the age of fifteen. His family then moved to Yokohama, where his father founded a real estate agency.

He started karate at Tokyu Dojo when he was in high school. Later, upon entering Chuo University, he did not join the Chuo karate club and remained attached to the Tokyu *dojo*.

Very athletic, he often served as a sparring partner for Tomonori Kato and, especially for Hiroyuki Aoki. He trained intensely and was thus led to participate in the *gasshuku* of other clubs, as well as in the various *keiko* of Rakutenkai, tea ceremony and studying the Bible.

In 1971, he left Rakutenkai by going on a trip. He went to Europe where he joined Marc Bassis, founder of French shintaido, with whom he participated in a few *gasshuku* before distancing himself; possibly due to an authoritarian drift of the group. For a year, he shared the life of different neo-rural communities in France, teaching karate there, then joined the Red Buddha theater group he met in Avignon. He participated with the troupe in the inauguration of the Sylvia Montfort Theater and then, in 1973, traveled with it throughout France and then to the United Kingdom, Italy, and the United States. In 1977, he returned to Japan and was hired as an interpreter in the Algeria oil fields.

Ho eventually returned to Japan to take over the management of his family's real estate agency.

Harue Ishide

Harue Ishide was born in November, 1941 in Kanda, Tokyo. Because of the war, the members of her family took refuge with her maternal grandfather in Chigasaki, where they remained until 1948. Her father, the manager of a small furniture factory in Kanda, had lost everything during the fire bombings of Tokyo, and the restart was difficult.

Entering high school, H. Ishide chose to continue her studies in evening classes while working part-time during the day. She was passionate about music and literature and read a lot. Four years younger than her sister Etsuko, the future wife of Hiroyuki Aoki, she also became interested in Christianity and converted around the same time.

When the father of the family died in the early 1960s, her mother, helped by Etsuko, took over the management of the family business, set it up again and made it prosper.

After the founding of Rakutenkai, H. Ishide became a member, attracted by its religious and artistic aspects. She married H.F. Ito in 1970 and they lived for a few years in the Nogeyama house.

In 1971, she took over direction of the artistic axis of the school and forged links with many "free" artists of the day in theater, jazz, performance, etc. Later, assisted by one of the members of the second generation, Gan-Iwao Okada, she organized an avant-garde festival on the beaches of Kujukuri, the Ningen to Uchu no Matsuri (Festival of Humanity and the Universe), where many artists from the underground scene performed.

She then radically changed direction, reconnecting with her initial religious aspirations, and joined the church in Kawasaki and then, like Nishiyama [p. 356], she distanced herself from Aoki's too-syncretic approach. Very pious, she remained faithful to the Kawasaki church until her death in the spring of 2019.

Kayoko (SHIMMA) ISHIDE

Kayoko Ishide's interview was held in the spring of 2005, at the same time as that of her husband Tadashi Ishide. When in 2019 we requested an interview to confirm the transcription of her interview and that of her husband, who had had died in the meantime, Ms. Ishide did not consent to receive us and refused publication. We therefore produce this short biographical sketch from various sources.

We don't know Kayoko Shimma's date of birth. She was the youngest daughter in a family of five children. Her father was an architect and owned a lumber business. Having built several churches, he had become acquainted with ministers of worship who influenced his and his wife's eventual conversion to Christianity. His young daughter Kayoko was thus very early acculturated to Christianity and received baptism while in high school.

At working age, she entered as a boarding school mistress for Kyogoin, a Christian school for delinquent children where she met Etsuko Aoki. She took part in Mrs. Aoki's tea ceremony [*sado*] and was soon invited, as a Christian, to attend Sunday services in Nogeyama. There she also attended *sado* lessons that Mrs. Aoki's gave to the members of the future Rakutenkai.

When Etsuko Aoki was no longer able to provide *sado* practices, she passed the responsibility on to her students, Y. Sato, and K. Shimma. Each then became tea-ceremony teachers themselves, opening regular *keiko* in their own homes. Kayoko's were held in a dedicated tea room in her parents' large house and were quite popular.

Kayoko showed no interest in the martial *keiko* of the members of Rakutenkai but enjoyed their company and especially the teachings of H. Aoki. He invited her as moral support for the group[1] and to be head of the tea ceremony. During one *gasshuku*, she held a dedicated tea room in which participants who wished could come and enjoy a moment out of time, as only the tea ceremony can provide[2]. Moreover, capable of very beautiful calligraphy, she transcribed the texts written by H. Aoki and those of the organizers of the collective events in order that they be mimeographed, thus contributing a little more to the already very high cultural value of the activities of the group.

In 1974, she married Tadashi Ishide and accompanied him in his attempt to establish a branch of Nihon-juku in Hokkaido and then in his worship ministry in Yokohama, ministry that she took over on the death of her husband and until her own retirement in 2020.

Tadashi ISHIDE

Tadashi Ishide's interview was conducted by H.F. Ito and Masashi Minagawa, at the same time as that of his wife, Kayoko Ishide. Sometime later we learned of the sudden death of T. Ishide. We nevertheless transcribed and edited the interview and then asked permission for publication from his wife, who did not allow it. We therefore produce this short biographical sketch from various sources.

Tadashi Ishide was the younger brother of Etsuko Ishide-Aoki. We have no precise indication of his date of birth but estimate it by cross-reference to be around 1946. He met Hiroyuki Aoki when Aoki was starting to court his elder sister and when he himself was in middle school. Later, having failed his entrance to university and feeling somewhat disillusioned, he became a taxi driver and began to lead a carefree life.

---

[1] He invited her, for example, to attend the course of the Tokyu Dojo as a spectator, because he appreciated the effect that her presence had on the practitioners, without it being possible to discern whether it was the spectacle of this affable young person valiantly seated in *seiza* throughout the *keiko* or her "telepathic" abilities as a tea master, or her empathy as a Christian in prayer, that had the most effect on these young people full of vigor.

[2] A bit like the eve-of-battle ceremonies attended by Japanese generals in medieval times.

After his sister's marriage, he was invited by his new brother-in-law to join the *keiko* of the Tokyu Dojo. Showing little taste for karate or even for the effort, he nevertheless persevered in the *keiko*; perhaps by simple attraction to the charisma of Hiroyuki Aoki. Later, he was invited to join the *keiko* of Rakutenkai and to stay in the family house of Nogeyama. This is how, from one *keiko* to another, his attraction to the powerful and warm world of Rakutenkai increased, and he soon became a full member.

The Ishide parents had been very devoutly affiliated with the rigorous Buddhist Nichiren sect. By discovering, through his sister and his brother-in-law, a tolerant and non-fatalistic approach[1] to Christianity, he became interested in the practice and soon became one of the most fervent among those attached to the Christian dimension of Rakutenkai. In 1972, he was baptized by Mitsuru Okada, who had just become the official pastor of the group.

When the second generation, to which he belonged, conceived the project of founding the Nihon-juku, he traveled to Hokkaido to explore the possibility of setting up a mink farm there. Kayoko Shimma, a tea student of Etsuko Aoki, was the only one willing to accompany him. They got married, and went to Hokkaido to learn the trade by working on a farm.

They stayed there for five years but did not set up a breeding farm there nor a branch of the Nihon-juku, whose project had meanwhile been abandoned by the other members. On his return to Tokyo, T. Ishide reconnected with the Kawasaki church, reinvested in religious activity, and undertook theological studies to become a pastor. Then, faithful to the spirit of Rakutenkai, he founded a small parish community in Yokohama and undertook its pastoral ministry until his death on July 2007.

---

[1] In essence, weakness or disability seen, not as a consequence of past lives – i.e. *karma* – but as an invitation to the expression of divine glory – i.e. salvation.

Shigeko (TOSHIMA) ITO

Shigeko Toshima-Ito's interview was conducted in September, 2004. Contacted in 2019 to review the text before editing, Ms. Ito declined the proposal, clearly unwilling to stir up what she considered unhappy memories. This biographical sketch is a brief summary from various sources.

Shigeko Toshima began practicing karate at the Tokyu Dojo at the age of sixteen. She began attending Rakutenkai *keiko* after the basic forms of Eiko and Tenshingoso were created.

At eighteen, she entered the Tokyo Joshi Taiiku Daigaku [Tokyo Women's University of Physical Education] and, after a year, she opened a sogo-budo club there with some fellow students. She led the *keiko* of the group, playing the role of *shihan-dai*, while Hirata Kayo [p. 265] held the position of captain. S. Toshima-Ito was so invested in Rakutenkai that she missed the opportunity to take the exams necessary to obtain her university diploma.

She passed the Sogo-budo Remmei instructor's exam when it was first established in 1971.

She participated in the production of the book "Karate-do Kata for Professionals" as a photographer during the Heiho Kenkyukai *gasshuku* on the beaches of Kujukuri. It was she who undertook the laborious task of developing the film that captured the numerous sequences of *kata*, doing so in a makeshift photo lab installed on the first floor of the Nogeyama house. She remained in support of official *keiko*, first of Sogo-budo Remmei and then of Shintaido Kyokai, even as her interest had begun to wane. Towards the end of the 1970s, she actively assisted Yoshitaka Ito in his efforts to transform Shintaido Kyokai into a professional organization of international stature. She took part in the first international *gasshuku*, in San Francisco in 1980, and distanced herself upon her return.

She is married to Yoshitaka Ito, and she works as a teacher of flower arrangement.

Yoshitaka ITO

Yoshitaka Ito's interview was conducted in September, 2004. Contacted in 2019 to review the text before editing, Mr. Ito declined the offer, clearly unwilling to stir up what he considered unhappy memories. This biographical sketch is a brief summary from various sources.

Yoshitaka Ito was born in Hiroshima in 1945, two days after the nuclear attack and three weeks before the Japanese surrender that marked the end of World War II. He stayed in Hiroshima until he was 18. Passionate about mathematics, he chose to go to Tokyo to do his graduate studies at the University of Yokohama and to study karate, like his elder brother Haruyoshi, but at the Tokyu Dojo.

The *keiko* of the Tokyu Dojo was led by H. Aoki, assisted by T. Kato. The *dojo* was open from 12:00 p.m. to 9:00 p.m. Yoshitaka stayed there whether there was a *keiko* or not, alone or with a teacher. Soon he followed Aoki to other karate clubs like Chuo and Gakushuin. He thus reached very quickly the fifth dan. A year after beginning to practice he joined the Nogeyama group, which would become the first generation of Rakutenkai.

In Nogeyama, Mr. Ito learned about the Bible, became a Christian, and attended Bible school for two years. Practicing day and night to improve his abilities, praying, studying the tea ceremony, and living with the Rakutenkai community seemed enough for his happiness.

In 1970, he was hired by IBM and his practice became more episodic. Soon, IBM sent him to Germany for a stay of several years which allowed him to practice with the newly created shintaido group in England. In 1978, back in Japan, he resigned from IBM and took over the management of Shintaido Kyokai, following Masatake Egami and Masashi Minagawa.

Very serious in business, he rationalized the administration and designed a four-year course aimed at training instructors, both Japanese and foreign, to a comprehensive and in-depth knowledge of the shintaido culture inherited from Rakutenkai.

His ambition was to make Japanese shintaido a worldwide organization. To do this, he had to simultaneously control the inspirations and aspirations, sometimes a little erratic, of the founder of
the discipline and deal with the ambitions of other well-meaning
members of Rakutenkai, such as his own brother and Kazuo Hokari, who aimed to establish the shintaido school as an international federation[1]. This was obviously too much for one man, and
in 1981 he resigned and then distanced himself from shintaido
organizations.

He married Shigeko Toshima and began a new career as a
coach and trainer for Japanese companies of international scope.
Taking advantage of his international experience and his many
talents, he made sure to support the adaptation of their execu-
tives to foreign social realities, to the customs of international
business, and to global ecological issues.

Chieko (TSUCHIYA) KATO

*Chieko Kato received us for the initial interview in 2004. We met her again in 2019 to confirm
the text before publication. Much had occurred in the meantime, including, in 2012, the death
of her husband, Tomonori Kato [p. 92]. Together, we made some minor corrections to his
autobiographical text and obtained her permission to publish. Shortly after this meeting,
however, Mrs. Kato asked us to withdraw her own text. This biographical sketch is a brief
summary from various sources.*

Chieko Tsuchiya was born on July 2nd, 1947, in Tokyo, Suginami Ward. She did her high-school studies at the secondary school
of Gakushuin University and then continued her university studies at this same institution.

At thirteen, she met Shigeru Egami and started karate the following year. Since Gakushuin's middle school was for girls only,
its karate club was all girls. The Gakushuin University club, meanwhile, was mixed but, in fact, almost exclusively male. She joined

---

[1] He envisioned an international organization as a branch of the Japanese organization,
while they envisioned the Japanese organization as a branch of an international
federation. Conflict was hard to avoid.

it nevertheless a few months after the start of her first university year.

Choosing to study Japanese literature, she specialized in the works of Basho, the great poet of haiku.

By then, when she was in her third year, the night classes at the club began to be visited by advanced teachers and practitioners from Tokyu Dojo, primarily Hiroyuki Aoki, Yoshitaka Ito, and Yoshitake Matsuhashi. After some time, she was invited to participate in the regular classes of the Tokyu Dojo and of Chuo University. She also participated in Rakutenkai *keiko*, on the banks of the Tama River and during retreats on Kujukuri Beach in Chiba.

At the same time, she opened a karate club in Suginami, near her home, and she also taught at Gakushuin middle and high schools. After completing her studies, she worked for three years as a legal research assistant for Gakushuin University and took the opportunity to found a bojutsu club there.

In 1973, at age 25, she started a family with Tomonori Kato, former second master of the Tokyu Dojo and responsible for the *keiko* of the Sogo-budo Remmei. Together they had two sons and a daughter. She maintained regular participation in regular *keiko* until the birth of her daughter and participated in a few workshops. Around 1978, she opened classes for children in her own house, equipped with a small *dojo*. At the very beginning of the 1980s, she stopped attending official shintaido practices.

At the age of thirty-six, in 1983, she embarked upon three years of acupuncture training and has been practicing this profession ever since. In 1989, Mr. Ogawa, the former technical director of the Gakushuin karate club, introduced her to Noriaki Inoue, founder of shin-ei-taido. She became passionate about the discipline, which she practiced until the death of the master in 1994.

Having maintained her ties with the alumni of the Gakushuin club, she is a member of Yutenkai, an association continuing the work of Shigeru Egami. As such she dedicates to teaching, especially to children.

Toshikatsu NISHIYAMA

Toshikatsu Nishiyama immediately refused to meet with us for an interview. However, as he was an important member of Rakutenkai, this simple biographical sketch has been composed, from elements of interviews with people who knew him well, Yoshitake Matsuhashi and H.F. Ito.

Toshikatsu Nishiyama began studies in the Department of Engineering at Chuo University in 1961 and joined the karate club around the same time. He and Yoshitake Matsuhashi were very close. They undertook together the responsibilities for management of the club – Matsuhashi as second captain and Nishiyama as treasurer – and they evolved together towards involvement with Rakutenkai.

On December 1st, 1966, he was part of the group of practitioners who discovered Eiko. He attended Kawasaki Bible School with the original group. As such, he was very close to Tomonori Kato and H. Ishide. He regularly helped Etsuko Aoki organize community life.

After obtaining his engineering degree, he entered the service of a telecommunications company and put the means that this regular job gave him — a quality car in particular — at the service of the very young organization Sogo-budo Remmei, directed by H.F. Ito.

Also at this time, his two younger brothers, Michio and Haruyoshi, opened a bojutsu club, a branch of the Sogo-budo Remmei, in Nagoya.

Following the division of the Sogo-budo Remmei into different axes of development, Nishiyama's preference was for the religious dimension. This affinity grew to the point that he underwent theological training and was ordained pastor of a branch of the Kawasaki congregation in Osaka.

Around 1975, he left Rakutenkai for good.

Mitsuru OKADA

Mitsuru Okada was part of the second wave of interviews, conducted in September, 2004 with the help of H.F. Ito. In 2019, he was very enthusiastic when we contacted him to submit his autobiography, but he gave us no further sign once it was received. We concluded that he no longer wished to follow up. We therefore provide this short biographical sketch from various sources.

Mitsuru Okada was born on June 18th, 1941, in Hazu City, Aichi Prefecture, the third child of five boys[1]. His father fell seriously ill as Mitsuru was entering high school. The conditions at the time were such that he had to give up his studies in order to contribute to the household income and take care of his father.

It was around the same time that he began practicing Shotokan karate. Later, he was recommended to go to Tokyo to study with the best specialists, which he did in 1959.

This is how he entered the Tokyu Dojo, two years after it opened, and began to practice assiduously under the direction of various instructors, including Hiroyuki Aoki. After some time, he was invited to join an experimental training group, bringing together the most diligent among the practitioners who followed Aoki, including Y. Ito, K. Ito, E. Ho and Nakaike. He was also invited to join the retreats of nearby university clubs, such as Chuo and Gakushuin. One day, he accompanied T. Kato to the *keiko* at Nogeyama, where he quickly became a regular visitor.

In 1963, sometime after he started visiting Nogeyama, he set out to finish his high school course in four years of night school. In 1966, he was one of eight regulars who participated in the *keiko* from which Eiko emerged.

Following this *keiko*, he converted to Christianity and there too became very earnest. To make his schedule freely flexible, he worked as a taxi driver. At that time, he also engaged in theological training in order to qualify as a pastor, capable of officiating

---

[1] Further information on the Okada family can be found in the autobiography of Gan Okada, youngest of the siblings.

for the church of Nogeyama. In 1975 he began studying acupuncture, like Tomonori Kato, and graduated in 1978.

Thereafter, he accompanied the Japanese organization's various evolutions that came after Rakutenkai, under different names, even directing the organization for a time.

Takashige ONOZATO

We became aware of the person of Takashige Onozato very late in the project, as his activity is mentioned by H.F. Ito and Y. Matsuhashi, and we though important to include his presentation.

Takashige Onozato is known as the earliest disciple of Hiroyuki Aoki in karate. He resided in the Nogeyama house, where we assume that he rented one of the numerous rooms.

H.F. Ito mentions Onozato as the person who suggested to him the possibility of visiting Aoki in Nogeyama on Sundays. It is difficult to imagine that Onozato took the initiative alone.

A Rakutenkai participant in whose life Mr. Onozato seems to have played a very big role is undoubtedly Yoshitake Matsuhashi. Matsuhashi remembered:

> Onozato-*sempai* took good care of me. I don't know why, but he took me under his wing. He often invited me out to eat; even if nobody believed me when I spoke about it, because he was known to be so frugal. His mother ran a small restaurant where I felt at home. I was in my first year when he was in his fourth. The fourth-years are like parents and role models to the first-years, so much so that the good and bad habits of the fourth-years are often reflected in those of the first-years [p. 130].

Onozato was the eighth participant in the legendary founding *keiko* of December 1st, 1966. It seems that he walked away immediately afterwards. Onozato died of kidney failure sometime after hiring Matsuhashi in his building materials business and making him his successor

Afterword

Jean-François Dégremont,
Professor (Université Paris 8)

In the French martial arts clubs of the 1970s, a cult of heroes, simplistic references to Japanese society, and destructive practices for the body gave students some largely outdated models of behavior in the face of the modern world. When, after having abandoned Shotokan karate, I myself began to practice shintaido around 1974-75, in the classes given by Robert Bréant at the Maison des Jeunes et de la Culture in La Celle Saint-Cloud, little was said about the collective experience of the Rakutenkai. Instead, Robert favored a discourse centered on the "founder," Master Aoki. At that time, the cult of leaders was a common practice in French society, which was partly strongly marked by neo-Stalinist practices and partly still under the influence of the great leaders of the Second World War.

Many years later, thanks to the essential contributions of Master H.F Ito, who often visited France and thanks to the organization of an "empty centered" structure of French shintaido set up by Alain Chevet and Pierre Quettier, a culture of collective creation emerged. The work of Rakutenkai was cited as an example, but only empirically and through the evocation of memories.

Reading this book was therefore, for me, an opportunity to structure this knowledge, to establish it historically, and to understand how Rakutenkai was the crucible of shintaido.

Pierre Quettier's analysis and the links he establishes between the creation of Rakutenkai and the idealistic youth movements that marked the years 1960-70 all over the world give a deep and scientifically based coherence to this astonishing human adventure. The life stories and analysis offered in this book also open up many exciting avenues of research. Let's examine some of them.

PERSONAL STORIES AND HISTORY

History is defined as, "the knowledge and the narrative of past events, of facts relating to the evolution of Humanity (or of a social group, of a human activity), which are worthy or deemed worthy of memory"[1]. This discipline has three sources: mute sources (material relics), written sources, and oral sources of which the accounts of witnesses constitute the main part[2].

This means that wherever possible a historian should collect direct testimony. As such, she or he is subject to the same biases as ethnologists or sociologists. Each individual, when asked to recount their life, or a segment of their life, will indeed transform a set of latent and disparate memories into a coherent narrative – but this is done according to multiple contexts.

The first of these contexts is, in part, internal to the individual: his or her current physical and psychological condition, the opinion she or he has of his past, of him- or herself, of people, his or her physical and psychological evolution since the events related, his or her daily or exceptional experiences, readings, arguments,

---

[1] Bonnechere, P., (2008), « 1. L'histoire : définition et finalité » In : *Profession historien*, Presses de l'Université de Montréal.
https://doi.org/10.4000/books.pum.446.
[2] Bonnechere, P., (2008), « 2. Les sources de l'histoire », *ibid.*

fights, etc. All these things mean that each time one recounts one's life, one makes choices about which facts to tell and which to pass over in silence, but also choices about how to tell those facts and about their interpretation.

The second context, external to the individual, concerns the reception of his or her speech: the moment of the testimony   and the recipient of the story (the relationship to this person, their reactions during the telling, etc.).

Oral historians, aware of these issues, set up various methods for transitioning from narratives to History. Among these devices, which we find in the work of Pierre Quettier, are the search for the multiplicity of stories, the confrontation with the factual elements of the existing literature as well as with the material record (photographic and cinematographic in this case). Modern ethnologists and sociologists, like Pierre Quettier, also insist on the control of the distancing of the author of the analysis.

History inevitably includes an element of subjectivity within its essence: who decides that events or facts are "worthy of memory"? One often sees, perhaps turning up in flea-markets or in bookstores deep in the countryside, local histories of villages that scrupulously record extraordinary details: for example, the names of scores of inhabitants who participated in making floral bouquets for a celebration that took place in the village on August 15th, 1926. This may seem of negligible value for anyone interested in the evolution of nations or societies on a global scale. But, for the villagers themselves and their descendants, the history of nation-states is very remote, while the history of their village is an important part of their identity. And indeed sometimes, this very local detail can form a vital building block for "great" History.

It is noteworthy in that some of the members of Rakutenkai were already aware at the time that their actions were part of histories that went beyond their modest existences: the history of martial arts, the history of the reconstruction of Japan after the Second World War, the history of youth protest movements between 1960 and 1975. I was therefore very interested in the analysis proposed by Pierre Quettier, who uses all the stories to show how this story of Rakutenkai both stems from history and participates in the construction of history. I think that, in the future, the considerable increase in the corpus of autobiographies, which stems from the increase in the proportion of the population capable of writing their stories, and the generalization of digital devices facilitating their storage and publication, will profoundly transform the way history is constructed, and many new avenues of research will thus open up.

TO SAY OR NOT TO SAY? MECHANISM OF CHOICE

To assemble this book, Pierre Quettier collected life stories in 2004 and consolidated them in 2018. These stories would have been different if they had been collected at other times. Indeed, in 2018, a significant portion of the members who had testified in 2004 did not want the story they had told 15 years earlier to be published now.

Knowing why each person judges that his life story has become inappropriate a few years later is not very important, because this reason is constantly changing: just like the story itself, the evaluation of the story is constantly changing. However, one cannot help but ask the question.

As the published accounts show, the experiences lived within the Rakutenkai were extremely varied: artistic, martial, or mystical, but also physical or mental, romantic or friendly, individual or collective. The same is obviously true for members who did not wish their story to be published. Telling or remaining silent, both positions are equally possible.

I assume that accepting to be in the publication has the main purpose of testifying so that the astonishing collective adventure of the Rakutenkai is known and transmitted to future generations, so that the collective creative genius which was expressed then leaves a historical trace, and to participate in an academic attempt to describe a phenomenon that is particularly difficult to describe. But accepting publication also means accepting that one's story is in a way "frozen" in the work and perhaps allowing oneself to be locked up in this frozen story — even though, as many stories describe, the Rakutenkai adventure and shintaido continue to influence the lives of each of the members.

Not to accept being part of the publication was to remain silent, the absolute right of everyone to keep their secret garden closed. The intensity of the individual and collective experiences lived by the members of the Rakutenkai certainly filled the secret gardens! Not to accept being in the publication was to refuse to be locked into one's opinion of the moment – the moment when the story was told – and thus to embody the absolute right to change one's mind about one's own history and the history of the group without having to justify himself. Not agreeing to be part of the publication, was finally to express a doubt that affects many artists: how useful is it to describe how a work was born, if doing so highlights the imperfection of the creative group and the environment in which this group evolved? Many artists consider the work to be sufficient, in the perfection of its beauty, and feel that talking about it does not add much, especially if it emphasizes the pains of its birth.

There will undoubtedly be new testimonies one day that will tell us more about this study and the reasons that led some to testify and others to remain silent.

THE EMERGENCE AND DISAPPEARANCE OF THE GROUP

On reading these life stories, the reader is initially both dismayed and dazzled by how difficult it is to maintain a distanced posture in the face of their intensity.

Dismayed by the repeated observation that the negative feelings, the deviations, the internal contradictions of each one, the interpersonal confrontations, make it seem very difficult to extract oneself from the detritus of daily life, and that one too often finds oneself surviving when one would so much like to live.

Dazzled by the creative power of the group's dynamics and by the quality of its production in the field of martial arts, by the immensity of the feelings that the participants say they have felt, by the plenitude which many of them say they have reached, by the very clear way in which the stories show that while each member built themself thanks to the group, she or he also built the group and participated in its creativity. Also dazzled by the quality of the life paths of most members of the group after Rakutenkai.

As we can see from reading the biographies of great artists, the context of creation is sometimes very dark, sometimes even full of mediocrity and negative feelings. Is it necessary for this context to be made public? It does not affect the quality of the works produced. However, from the point of view of the historian of art and creativity, it is essential because it makes it possible to describe how the work emerged and to build a knowledge of the mechanisms of creation.

If the conditions and circumstances of the creation of the Rakutenkai emerge clearly from these life stories, the reasons and the circumstances of its dissolution are less clear. Did the contradiction between words and deeds kill the group? Is the answer to be found in autobiographies? If not there, then where? This dissymmetry between the relative clarity of the reasons for the emergence of a social group and the complexity of explaining its disappearance is very frequent and would justify additional studies.

EXISTENTIAL QUESTIONING

This work exposes the way in which the founders of the group answered their own existential questioning and then proposed their answers, first to a small group, then in a socially and geographically expanded form.

It also shows, through the biographies, how each member of the group acquired and used what she or he received from the founders to answer their own existential questioning.

An interesting aspect of the system put in place by the founders is that it leaves the possibilities of appropriation very open. Master Aoki, aware of the immense variety of potential contributions of the training and personal development system he has developed, can consider that his contribution is concentrated in this system itself, and not in its implementation, which creates a responsibility of the teacher vis-à-vis the students. From this point of view, no one owes anything to anyone and everyone retains the freedom and responsibility for the use they make of the device and what they get out of it.

This way of building an educational system and implementing it raises many questions regarding the teacher-learner relationship and the posture of the learner. Thus, the question of the involvement of the learner is treated in several autobiographies and deserves further exploration. Is it necessary to learn? If so, how to make this learning appear and develop? If not, what are the factors of knowledge transfer or construction by the learner of the extension of his or her skills?

Master Aoki began by creating a community of practice, which gradually transformed into an epistemic community that operated alongside a community of learning. This evolution is classic and has been observed in many social groups. Comparative studies would certainly make it possible to deepen the mechanisms of this evolution in order, possibly, to extract methods for the collective construction of innovation and teaching systems.

WALKING FURTHER ON THE PATH

As we have seen, the avenues for research are many and varied. It will take time to engage with them and navigate them. And, as always in research, the results obtained are accompanied by new questions and the appearance of new avenues. Each step taken is a joy, since the fog of the world is revealed and fills the desire to know. But the task is infinite and, after having savored this book, one can only invite everyone to continue walking, in their own way and according to their preferences, on the long path of knowledge.

Glossary

Age-oroshi (上げ下ろし): The practice of holding either a *bo*, or sometimes a *bokuto*, in front of you at arm's length, raising it to the vertical (*age*) and then lowering it horizontally (*oroshi*) several hundred times, the "canonical" number being one thousand. This practice is a meditative version of Eiko.

AH-UN (阿吽): Two fundamental expressions present in both Tenshingoso and Eiko. As a practice, it takes the name of Tenso. Also mentioned, as "Yin and Yang", in Appendix II of S. Egami's book [1976, p. 122].

Asama-sanso (浅間山荘): Mount Asama is a volcano in Nagano Prefecture, a two-hour train ride from Tokyo. Sanso means "mountain lodge". Asama-sanso has facilities for large groups and was chosen as the venue for the national *gasshuku* of the Shintaido Sogo-budo Remmei, named "Daienshu" (大演習), starting in 1971.

Bo (棒): A stick approximately six feet in length (about 1.80m).

Bokuto (木刀): A thick, straight wooden sword, specially designed for shintaido practice.

Budo (武道): From "*bu*" (武), war or warrior, and "*do*" (道), way, refers to the ethics, the code of honor, of samurai warriors. The term *bujutsu* (武術), from *bu* (武) and *jutsu* (術), technique, designates the different fighting arts practiced to perfection by every good samurai. In the middle of the 19th century, when the samurai lost their social utility and their caste privileges, *bujutsu* nevertheless continued to be practiced by amateurs in special schools. These schools also conveyed the ethical principles of *budo*, so they replaced the suffix "*jutsu*" in their name with that of "*do*," thus marking the tradition of excellence of their predecessors. Jujutsu became judo, aikijutsu became aikibudo and then aikido, kenjutsu became kendo, etc. After that, the term *budo* came to designate all these arts, and also their common ethic. The practitioner of a *budo* is called a *budoka* (武道家).

Chan (ちゃん): See "San."

Chi-no-kata (地の型): Although its name contains the word *kata*, this practice is a *kumite*. The use of *kata* marks its essential and formal character and formal character; it consists of parrying a single *tsuki* attack with a low sweeping block (*gedan-barai* [下段払い]). The attacker has a formal advantage – ready in attacking position - while the receiver is open in a neutral position. The purpose of this *kata* is to put the receiver in a position to anticipate the attack based on subtle signals in order to "catch the wave" of the partner's intention. Chi-no-kata (*tsuki* at belly level, received with *gedan-barai* or sometimes *ude-uke* [腕受け]) goes together with Ten-no-kata (*tsuki* to the face, received with *ude-uke*).

Daienshu (大演習): Literally means "great maneuvers." Name given to the annual *gasshuku* of the Sogo-budo Remmei.

De-o-toru (出を取る): Ability to perceive weak or even very weak signals from an opponent, making it possible anticipate an attack in karate. The term literally means the ability to sense the earliest movement, or even the "pre-move-ment" of the attacker. Some practitioners refer to this as a kind of "telepathy."

Dojo (道場): Training hall or field. More generally it refers to the notion of "place" or "field" (*jo*) which represents both a physical and relational space. Something is "happening" there. Ritually, a *keikonin* (see below) acknowledges the *dojo* space by bowing before entering and before leaving.

Egami-sensei (江上先生): Master Egami, successor of Master Funakoshi as the leader of Shotokai, which he would make an independent branch of karate.

Eian-ro (永安楼): Chinese restaurant in Yokohama. The owner, M. Cho (張さん), was an alumnus of the Chuo Karate Club and a strong supporter of Rakutenkai (often feeding or employing its members and encouraging Master Aoki in various ways).

Eiko (栄光 - glory): Absolute extension of being towards the infinite. This foundational movement was first discovered during the practice of December 1st, 1966, when the partic-ipants were apparently seized with an intense inspiration that made them point their swords, with all their being, to infinity. The remarkable character of this extension, imme-diately recognized by H. Aoki, was that it did not vary at all, no matter which direction the swords were pointing. Later, he formalized this principle of action in a movement (a *kata*) of cutting with the sword, pointing vertically to infinity, and then gradually descending, still pointing, towards the hori-zon to infinity. The absolute commitment of the original in-spiration was then sought for an extended period, an hour or sometimes several hours. Even more fundamental than Tenshingoso, Eiko is considered to stand at the core of shin-taido.

First-year (一年生): Refers to a student doing his or her first year in a university club. The role of the first-year in a university martial arts club is to practice enough to destroy the ego, to be attentive to what is expected, and to conform to the models of excellence that the elders (*sempai*) represent.

Fourth-year (四年生): Refers to a student completing his or her fourth year in a university club. At this point, most students stop participating in club activities in order to focus on graduation and to prepare for entry into the workforce.

Funakoshi-sensei (船越義珍先生): Master Gichin Funakoshi, founder of modern karate-do.

Gasshuku (合宿): Residential workshop.

Gedan-barai (下段払い): Blocking movement by sweeping the arm downwards.

Giwakai (義和会): Hosei University Karate Club

Gorei (号令): The word *gorei* means, strictly speaking, "to set the tempo of the collective action" (by counting out loud) and more broadly "to order the start or stop of the action" or "to decide on the nature of the action", and even more broadly, "to direct the action of a group of people (including oneself) in personal development." This notion, common to all martial arts, has taken on a broader meaning in the artistic dynamic impelled by H. Aoki, inspired by orchestral conducting.

Goreijutsu (号令術): The way of doing *gorei*. The early Rakutenkai members learned *goreijutsu* in their bodies, by experiencing Aoki-sensei's way of leading the class. Martial arts are a group of fighting techniques, originally for samurai, but always contained a component of what it takes to be a good samurai lord, a good leader of people. The learning of martial arts also became a kind of leadership training. The Rakutenkai members aspired to bring this unique approach to other people through the way they practiced and taught and acted toward each other and in the world. This *goreijutsu* also applied to *gasshuku* management, and thus to management in all kinds of settings

Goreisha (号令者): Person giving the *gorei.*

Hanmi-handachi (半身半立ち): Knee-walking position, with the front knee elevated and the back knee on the floor or ground. Also refers to the technique using that position for movement, by "walking" from one knee to the other. Among other advantages, this posture and movement allows the practitioner to go directly into action from the *seiza* position. It is also practiced to strengthen the *koshi.*

Harai (払い): Suffix indicating a sweeping movement. Most often used as *kiri-harai*, to cut by pulling (the sword's edge sliding from the base to the tip) as opposed to *komi.* Also also used to denote a *tsuki* block with a sweep of the arm, *gedan-barai* (where the "h" sound becomes a "b" sound by the rules of Japanese pronunciation). ###

Heiho (兵法/平法): In Japanese, the expressions "method of war" and "method of peace" are both pronounced *heiho.* By playing on this homophony, Inoue-sensei and after him Egami-sensei taught that their respective martial arts were methods - or "ways" - of moving from one form of *heiho* to another; from "war" to "peace."

Heiho Kenkyukai (平法研究会): Peace Research Association. In the late 1960s, projects to develop Shotokai karate by members of Rakutenkai working together with S. Egami, were symbolically grouped under the name of Heiho Kenkyukai, in reference to the martial quest pursued by N. Inoue, S. Egami, and H. Aoki.

Hikari (光): Abbreviation of Hikari-to-tawamureru (光と戯れる – playing with light). A practice consisting of free-form movements, first appearing while H. Aoki was receiving the continuous attack of his students. After exhausting all their energy, attackers were encouraged to continue and keep, by an effort of pure will, an active contact with the "target" who was being attacked. What emerged in that space between the attacker and the receiver was a phenomenon of great freedom, later called "playing with light." This practice is emblematic of the inherent artistry of shintaido.

Honbu 本部): The headquarters, in this case of the shintaido organization, founded in 1970. In biographies, the term is used either to describe the practice itself (at the rented *honbu-dojo* gymnasium in Sendagaya or during retreats of several days' duration in the countryside), or the administrative offices located in Shinjuku.

Iaido (居合道): Practices that combine various ways of drawing the sword from the scabbard, attacking, and then returning the sword to the scabbard.

Ichigo ichie (一期一会): Means "One life, one chance." It is a principle of the tea ceremony, inviting the participants to "seize the moment." Since the time of Rakutenkai, this concept has been incorporated, into the culture of shintaido to signify the need to "be present when things are happening." In the biographies of Rakutenkai members, the aphorism also echoes the sense of competition between them (i.e., "I was there" or "I missed it").

Inoue-sensei (井上先生): Master Noriaki (鑑昭) Inoue. Mentor of Master Egami (江上) in Shinwa-taido (親和体道). Master Inoue changed his first name several times during his life: Kitamatsumaru (1902), Yoichiro (1903), Yoichiro (1909), Yoshiharu (1920), Seisho (1940), Hoken (1948), Teruyoshi (1971), and finally Noriaki (1973).

Irimi (入り身): Various ways to enter the partner's space

Jiyu-kumite (自由組手): Partner work with free-form attack and free-form receiving.

Junbi-taiso (準備体操): Warm-ups.

Kaiho-kei (開放系): Practices in opening and extension, particularly emblematic of early shintaido. See also "Yoki-kei."

Kaikyaku-zenshin (開脚前進): Jumping practices that open the pelvis laterally. The *kaikyaku-zenshin-dai* (開脚前進大) form requires half bending of the knees and the *kaikyaku-zenshin-sho* (開脚前進小) form requires full knee bends (squatting).

Kangeiko (寒稽古): See "*Keiko.*"

Kata (型): Sequence of movements. Also means "form" or "style" as expressed in the word *katachi* (形). In Japanese martial arts, a *kata* constitutes a formal series of movements, a work of art like a composition, often attached to the name of its creator.

Keiko (稽古): Practice or training. From *kei* (稽) "to think, reflect" and *ko* (古) "ancient things," typically used in the practice of traditional arts. The term implies the idea of learning by reproducing classical works. The term *kangeiko* (in this position in the word, "k" becomes "g" in Japanese pronunciation) refers to a practice during the coldest time of the winter. It is often an outdoor workshop.

Keikogi (稽古着): The uniform used in *keiko*.

Keikonin (稽古人): Person who practices *keiko*.

Keri (蹴り): Various kicking movements. Also in compound words (with the pronunciation of "g" instead of "k") such as *mae-geri* (forward kick [前蹴り]), *yoko-geri* (side kick [横蹴り]), or *moro-geri* (jumping kick with both feet simultaneously [双蹴り]).

Kibadachi (騎馬立ち): Literally "horse-riding stance," in which the feet are parallel at about twice the width of the pelvis. In this technique, the center of gravity of the body is lowered to improve balance.

Kihon-waza (基本技): Basic techniques.

Kiri (斬り): A prefix used to identify cutting movements

Koan (公案): Literally "riddle." The mode of teaching by enigma, forcing the apprentice to "reconstruct" the knowledge by oneself, typical of the Japanese tradition. The *koan*, nonsense at the ordinary level of understanding, requires a change of point of view, and therefore of point of reference, in order to make sense. This change of viewpoint is precisely the object of the enigma. In the tradition of Zen Buddhism, the *koan* is a verbal enigma, and the answer can be in words, gestures, or nothing at all. The term is sometimes used in martial arts to describe expressions that do not have an ordinary martial interpretation.

Kohai (後輩): Someone who is "junior" in age or experience or both. See "*Sempai*" (先輩).

Kokutsu-dachi, Kokutsu (後屈立ち, 後屈): Stance with weight shifted to the back foot.

Kokyu (呼吸): Breathing out or exhaling. Qualifying the *kokyu* of a person is a way of describing in general the expression of that individual's energy, concentration, or focus, in relation to the "particular" way of breathing, and especially exhaling, in action. *Kokyu* could be expressed "calm," "deep," "dense," or "long," while "excited" *kokyu* would be more accurately expressed as "high," "shallow," or "short," indicating a deficiency or a lack of concentration or expression. The underlying practical concept is that by controlling our breathing during action, we can naturally improve the general quality of our concentration or expression.

Komi (込み): A suffix indicating movement by pushing in (as opposed to *harai* [see above]). The term is most often encountered as *kiri-komi*, cutting while pushing (the edge of the sword sliding across the opponent's body from the point to the base).

Koshi (腰): Refers to the hips and lower back. Region of the body where movements should originate. Many practices are aimed at strengthening the *koshi*, and practitioners are reminded to open their *koshi*. By extension, the term is used in a metaphorical sense in various expressions of strength or endurance (the English equivalent for a person would be "Put your heart into it!")

Kumite, kumitachi, kumibo (組手、 組太刀, 組み棒): Partner exercises done with hands only or with sword or *bo*.

Kun (くん、君): Suffix used after the person's name, usually for young men. See "San."

Mae-geri (前蹴り): Front kick

Makiwara (巻き藁): A pole with a straw cover on the top, formerly used for training and hardening the fists.

Moro-geri (双蹴り): *Keri* (jump) with both feet, forward or to the sides.

Mudra (印/ 位): Special positions of the hands and fingers used for different types of meditation. The Japanese term for "*mudra*" is "印" (pronounced "In"), but Master Aoki initiated the idea of "full-body *mudra*" (位 ["I"] rather than "印") for meditation poses.

Nihon-juku (日本塾): Literally "Japanese School", a name adopted by some members of the second generation of Rakutenkai and initiated in 1970. The term "*juku*" means a traditional local private school or community, and many have been opened throughout Japanese history. *Nihon*, or

Nippon, is the Japanese term for Japan. The second-generation Rakutenkai members may have selected this name because of their strong desire to create a shintaido learning community that would foreshadow the communities of shintaido to come, spread over different countries.

Nogeyama (野毛山): Neighborhood of Yokohama where Master Aoki's house was located. In the biographies, the term can mean, "the Aoki house" or "the meeting place of Rakutenkai" or the "Rakutenkai crib," or "the park near the Aoki house" where most of the practices took place, or even "the church of Nogeyama," referring to the room that was set aside for worship activities after M. Okada became pastor.

OB-kai: Old Boys' Association (of graduates who were formerly members of a university club).

Oizuki (追い突き): Chasing *tsuki* (See "Tsuki").

Oku-san (奥さん): Literally "wife," often used to refer respectfully to Mrs. Aoki.

Rakutenkai (楽天会): Rakutenkai is the original community whose research and action led to the creation of shintaido.

Renzoku (連続): Generally used to qualify a movement that is being repeated continuously (for example: *renzoku-tsuki* or *renzoku-keri*). For Rakutenkai, the term was more specifically used for the "arched jump" (*sori-tobi* [反り跳び]), a sort of forward-moving version of the lateral opening jump. *Renzoku-soritobi* was later renamed "shintaido-jump."

San (さん): Suffix title meaning "sir" or "madam". In Japan, the title depends on the relationship between the speaker and the person being addressed or discussed. San is the most common term for adults. The suffix "chan" [ちゃん] can be used for children and the suffix "kun" for youths. By extension, the shifted use of the title conveys a special relationship with the person being spoken to: "chan" affectionately for an adult friend or "san" for a young person treated as an adult.

Second-year (二年生): In martial arts, refers especially to the person who is in his or her second year in a university martial arts club. The second-year student occupies a very specific position within the group, simultaneously learning from the more experienced students and teaching the less experienced students. Much of the second-year's responsibilities involve being a "learning model" (showing how to learn) for first-year students (first-years).

Seiza (正座): Low-kneeling posture with the feet and legs tucked under, commonly used in traditional Japanese rooms (on tatami). Also used in meditation, in which case the expression "do *seiza*" can mean "meditate").

Sempai (先輩): In a learning process, this term refers to the senior or elder person in the relationship (e.g., "our *sempai* took care of us"). Also sometimes used as a suffix title (e.g.: Onozato-sempai took care of me). See also *kohai*.

Sensei (先生): Suffix added to a proper name or used alone to designate, with respect, a teacher, master in his or her discipline, "the one who was there before me, who is the guarantor of the knowledge and experience of techniques or knowhow." By extension, the term is also used to designate any person on whose knowledge one relies, for example the mayor of a town.

Shihan (師範): Master instructor of a *dojo.*

Shihan-dai (師範代): Assistant instructor of a *dojo.*

Shinai (竹刀): A substitute for a sword used in kendo, consisting of four bamboo blades connected by leather bands.

Shin-ei-taido (親英体道) : See Shinwa-taido.

Shintaido Kyokai (新体道協会) : The name by which Japanese shintaido has long been known.

Shinwa-taido (親和体道) : Refers to the discipline developed by Master Inoue. He later renamed it shin-ei-taido.

Shoko (証光) : A standing (rather than running) practice of Eiko consisting of holding the sword out at arm's length and maintaining that position for quite a long time (an hour most often). According to H.F. Ito [2016], this practice predates Eiko, as a secret practice of the imperial family transmitted by N. Inoue.

Shotokai (松涛会) : An association of karate instructors at the time of Master Funakoshi, which later became the karate practice developed by Master Egami.

Shu-Ha-Ri (守破離) : 守 "SHU" meaning "fit into the mold," 破 "HA" meaning "break the mold," and 離 "RI" meaning "develop your own expression." This model of progression is widely known in the martial arts and applies as much to the mastery of technique as it does to the personal development of the practitioner.

Shusho (主将) : Title designating the captain of a college group or club.

Sogo-budo Renmei (総合武道連盟) : From *sogo* (synthetic or holistic), *budo* (martial), and *renmei* (federation), i.e., Federation for a holistic martial art. It is the name of the autonomous organization that marked the transition from karate to shintaido. The term "sogo-budo" is used to refer to the martial art that emerged from the research of Rakutenkai. After a short period of use, this term was gradually replaced by the term shintaido.

Ten-no-kata (天の型) : See Chi-no-kata

Tenshingoso (天真五相): *Kata* synthesizing both the essence of martial movements and the phases of human life. Tenshingoso is considered to be Hiroyuki Aoki's masterpiece.

Tenso (天相): Extension of the sword or open hands, then the whole body, vertically to infinity. See also AH-UN.

Third-year (三年生): Refers to a student doing his or her third year in a university club. This is the year in which the efforts of the previous years are clearly visible in terms of progress in rank and leadership within the group or club. The third-years are therefore the models to follow. In addition to the practice, they take on various operational responsibilities (managing the *dojo*, organizing workshops, etc.)

Toate (遠当て): Control at a distance. Sometimes called "striking without touching."

Toitsu-kihon (統一基本): A set of basic movements.

Tokyo Taiiku-kan ((東京体育館)): Tokyo city sports facilities located near Sendagaya Station. The shintaido organization Sogo-budo Renmei rented sports halls and fields there for its weekly practices starting in 1970.

Tokyu Karate Dojo (東急空手道場): *Dojo* of Shotokai, owned by Tokyu Railways. That was where many members of Rakutenkai began their practice of karate.

Tsuki (突き): Direct attack with the fist.

Uchi (打ち): Various strikes with the fist, a stick, or a sword.

Uchi-deshi (内弟子): literally "in-house disciple." Most of the disciples of a weapons master were the *soto-deshi* (literally, "outside disciples"), who received weapons lessons from the master, for a fee, and also pursued their own activities. The *uchi-deshi* lived in and were a part of the master's house, and were thus permanently exposed to his influence.

The *uchi-deshi* often played the role of a servant, thus paying, as it were, his or her dues. There is much to be said about the different forms that the role of the *uchi-deshi* took in the martial arts, including many stories and legends of famous disciples of famous masters. The practice gradually fell out of use because of the resources it required - even if only in terms of space in a house - and also because of the dwindling number of candidates in a society where martial skills have lost their social utility.

Ueshiba-sensei (植芝先生): Founder of Aikido.

Uke (受け): Means "to receive". Designates different ways of receiving an attack. In partner practice, refers to the partner who plays the role of the receiver during a *kumite*. Finally, it refers to a person that an instructor takes as a partner during a demonstration or as a "guinea pig" for his research. With the master of a school, this privileged role allows learning of the highest order and is most often reserved for the first disciple.

Usagi-tobi (兎跳び): Rabbit jump, practiced by members of Shotokai karate, precursor of *kaikyaku-zenshin-sho* and *renzoku-soritobi*.

Wakame-taiso (ワカメ体操): An exercise in developing sensitivity that belongs to the *yoki-kei* style of shintaido practice.

Waza (技): Formal technique. A *kata* is usually composed of different *waza*. In some cases, a *waza* can be considered a *kata*, a canonical work or form of a single movement (i.e., Eiko); it is then capitalized.

Yoki-kei (養氣系): A flexible and relaxed mode of practice (belonging to the category of practices also called "internal arts"). See also *Kaiho-kei*.

Yoko-geri (横蹴り): Side kick.

Zenkutsu-dachi, zenkutsu (前屈立ち): Weight-forward stance.

Alphabetical Table of Member Biographies

Bibliography

Footnote references to online sites and materials in this bibliography freely available on the Internet will be collected at www.shakunetsu.net.

Ambaras R.D. (2005), *Bad youth, juvenile delinquency and the politics of everyday life in modern Japan*. Oakland CA: University of California Press.

Aoki H. (1992), *Shintaido –The body is a message of the universe*. San Francisco CA: Shintaido of America

Arrupe P. (1978), "Lettre sur l'inculturation" (14 mai 1978), in *Écrits pour évangéliser*, pp. 169-170. Paris: Editions Desclée de Brouwer.

Bouchez P. (2014), "Le chanoyu, cérémonie japonaise traditionnelle du thé, comme exemple d'éducation à la présence", in *Voix Plurielles / Iconicité et imaginaires collectifs*, Vol 11 N°1, pp. 31-38.

Bowring R. (2005), *The religious traditions of Japan 500-1600*. Cambridge: Cambridge University Press.

Breton H. & Gonzalez-Monteagudo J. (2019), "Engagement versus objectivité : 'Histoires de vie en formation' et recherche biographique en sociologie", in *Histoire de vie et recherche biographique : perspectives sociohistoriques*, A. Slowik, H. Breton & G. Pineau (eds.). Paris: Librarie L'Harmattan.

De Rosny É. (1981), *Les yeux de ma chèvre*. Paris: Editions Plon.

Egami S. (1975), *The heart of karate-do*. Tokyo: Kodansha International.

Foucault M. (1965), *Madness and civilization: A history of insanity in the age of reason*. New York: Vintage.

Ferrarotti F. (1990), Histoire et histoires de vie – La méthode biographique dans les sciences sociales. Paris: Editions Méridiens Klincksieck.

Hocart A.M. (1954), *Social origins.* London: Watts & Co.

Hokari K. (1989), *Origins: A history of shintaido.* San Francisco CA: Shintaido of America.

Ikeuchi Y. (2006), "Performances of masculinity in Angura Theatre: Suzuki Tadashi on the actress and Sato Makoto's Abe Sada's dogs", in *Performance paradigm - Japan after the 1960s: The ends of the avant-garde*, Peter Eckershall & Edward Sheer (eds.) n°2. Auckland, NZ.

Ishikawa K. (2004), "La France et la contre-culture du Japon dans la période de haute croissance économique (1960-1970)", in *La modernité française dans l'Asie littéraire (Chine, Corée, Japon)*, Haruhisa Kato (ed.). Paris: Presses universitaires de France.

Ito H.F (2016), *Ito Gaiden – Stories from the shintaido heritage.* San Francisco: Shintaido of America.

Iwahara C. (2007), "Les destins renouvelés d'un principe de mouvement : du shintaido à la création chorégraphique du buto," in *Japon pluriel 7 : Histoires d'amour, quelques modalités de relation à l'autre au Japon*, Arnaud Brotons & Christian Galan (eds.), Actes du septième colloque de la Société française des études japonaises. Paris : Éditions Philippe Picquier.

Jacquet B. (2011), "Dans les secrets du pavillon de thé, d'hier et d'aujourd'hui", in *Sigila / Architecture secrètes*, 28(2), 91-104. Paris: Editions Gris-France.

Juro K. (1977), *Tokkenteki nikutai ron (The theory of privileged Body)* (1968). Tokyo: Hakusui-sha.

Kroeber A.L., Kluckhohn C. (1952), *Culture: a critical review of concepts and definitions*, Papers of the Peabody Museum of American Archeology and Ethnology, Harvard University XLVII.

Lachaud F. (2010), "Matteo Ricci et les excentriques : épisodes curieux de la 'connaissance de l'Occident et de l'Orient'", in *Empires éloignés. L'Europe et le Japon, XVIe-XIXe siècles*. Dejanirah Couto & François Lachaud (eds.). Paris: Editions École française d'Extrême-Orient.

Lapassade G. (2002), "Observation participante", in *Vocabulaire de psychosociologie*, Jacqueline Barus-Michel (ed.). Ramonville-Saint-Agne: Editions Eres.

Le Grand J.L. (2000), "Repères théoriques et éthiques en histoires de vie collectives ", in *Histoires de vie collective et éducation populaire*, Marie-Jo Coulon et Jean-Louis Le Grand (eds.). Paris, Librarie L'Harmattan.

Lorentz K. (1974), *Evolution et modification du comportement : L'inné et l'acquis*. Paris : Petite Bibliothèque Payot.

Markiewicz-Lagneau J. (1976), "L'autobiographie en Pologne ou de l'usage social d'une technique sociologique", in *Revue française de sociologie*, 17-4. pp. 591-613.

Mercado, S.C. (2002), *The shadow warriors of Nakano – A history of the Imperial Japanese Army's elite intelligence school*. Lincoln NE, Potomac Book Inc.

Morin E. (2008) *California Journal*, Deborah Cowell (trans.). Chicago, Sussex Academic Press.

Morin E. (1970), "La mutation occidentale", in *Les États-Unis en révolution*, revue Esprit n°396, Octobre 1970.

Pineau G., Michelle M. (1983), *Produire sa vie: autoformation et autobiographie*, Paris: Editions Saint Martin.

Pranin A. S. (1991) *The Aiki News Encyclopedia of Aikido*. Irvine CA: Aiki News.

Pytlick D. (2015), *Chanoyu and Christianity in 16th-century Japan*, BA thesis, University of Adam Mickiewicz, Faculty of Neo-philology – Department of Japanistics, Album N°352807, Poznan Poland.

Quettier P. (1992), *Le corps, agent de formation*, Mémoire présenté en vue de l'obtention du Diplôme Professionnel de Formateur d'Adultes, INFAC.

Quettier P. (1995), *Ethnométhodes des instructeurs de shintaido*, Mémoire de DESS, Université Paris VIII.

Quettier P. (2000), *Communication des messages complexes par des séquences gestuelles - les kata dans les arts martiaux japonais - école shintaido*. Paris: Editions Arnt.

Quettier P. (2007), *Les dispositifs d'Ingénierie Socio-Cognitive*, mémoire d'Habilitation à Diriger les Recherches, Université de Bourgogne.

Quettier P. (2011), "Les deux temps de la conception japonaise d'inculturation – Sogo to Choetsu, Intégrer et transcender", in *La métamorphose des cultures*, P. Lardellier (ed.), pp. 113–25.

Roszak T. (1995), *The making of a Counter Culture*. Oakland CA: University of California Press.

Tokitsu K. (1995), *Histoire du karate-do*, Paris: Editions S.E.M.

Wada K. (2011), "The history and current state of drug abuse in Japan", *Annals of the New York Academy of Sciences: Addiction Reviews*, 1216(1), pp.62-72.

Wagda M. (2002), "La longue histoire de la cérémonie du thé au Japon", in *Hommes & Migrations / Flux et reflux*, n°1235, Jan-Feb 2002, pp. 126-129.

Watzlawick P. (1995), *Le langage du changement*. Paris, Editions du Seuil, 2014.

Wolfe T. (1968), *The Electric Kool-Aid Acid Test*. New York: Farrar Straus Giroux.

Yagyu M. (2003), *The life-giving sword: Secret teachings from the house of the Shogun*, William Scott Wilson (trans.). Tokyo, Kodansha.

Yoshida K. (2001), *Democracy Betrayed: Okinawa under U.S. occupation*, Eastern Asian Studies Press - 31. Bellingham WA, Western Washington University.

www.ingramcontent.com/pod-product-compliance
Lightning Source LLC
Chambersburg PA
CBHW062154270326
41930CB00009B/1526